LearningExpress's

GED LANGUAGE ARTS, READING

LearningExpress
NEW YORK

Copyright © 2008 LearningExpress, LLC.

All rights reserved under International and Pan-American Copyright Conventions. Published in the United States by LearningExpress, LLC, New York.

Permissions

Page 67: Scripture quotations are taken from the HOLY BIBLE: NEW INTERNATIONAL VERSION®. Copyright © 1973, 1978, 1984 by International Bible Society. Used by permission of Zondervan. All rights reserved.

Page 15: "From MY FAMILY AND OTHER ANIMALS by Gerald M. Durrell, copyright © 1957, renewed © 1985 by Gerald M. Durrell. Used by permission of Viking Penguin, a division of Penguin Group (USA) Inc."

Page 17–18: William Meredith, "Winter on the River," from Effort at Speech, Tri Quarterly Books, 1997, p. 142.

Page 18–19: Noel Coward, *Private Lives*, Samuel French, 1947, p. 25–26.

Page 72–73: From Bill Bryson, *The Life and Times of the Thunderbolt Kid*. NY: Broadway Books, 2006, p. 29.

Page 91: Excerpt from pp. 243–244 "I spent several days . . . in a suffering world" from "DEATH OF A PIG" FROM THE SECOND TREE FROM THE CORNER by E. B. White. Copyright © 1947 by E.B. White. Copyright Renewed. First Appearance in *Atlantic Monthly*. Reprinted by permission of Harper Collins Publishers.

Page 93: "From ESQUIRE, 1957–1962," from the PORTABLE DOROTHY PARKER by Dorothy Parker, edited by Marion Meade, copyright 1928, renewed © 1956 by Dorothy Parker. Used by permission of Viking Pengion, a division of Penguin Group (USA) Inc.

Page 104: Ogden Nash, "Good-By, Bugs," copyright © 1942 by Ogden Nash. Reprinted by Permission of Curtis Brown, Ltd.

Page 118: Robert Frost, "Closed for Good," *The Poetry of Robert Frost*, Holt, Rinehart, Winston, 1968, p. 415–416.

Page 132–134: From Frances Goodrich and Albert Hackett, *Diary of Anne Frank*, Houghton Mifflin, 1989, p. 89–91.

Page 135–136: From Neil Simon, *The Dinner Party*, Samuel French.

Page 147: From Robert Frost, "For John F. Kennedy," The Poetry of Robert Frost, Holt, Rinehart, Winston, 1968, p. 422–23.

Page 148: Malcolm Muggeridge, *The Infernal Grove (Chronicles of Wasted Time, Volume 2)*, NY: William Morrow and Company, 1974, p. 120.

Page 149–150: "From A RAISIN IN THE SUN by Lorraine Hansberry, copyright © 1958 by Nemiroff, as an unpublished work. Copyright © 1959, 1966, 1984 by Robert Nemiroff. Copyright renewed 1986, 1987 by Robert Nemiroff. Used by Permission of Random House, Inc."

Library of Congress Cataloging-in-Publication Data:
GED language arts, reading.
    p. cm.
  ISBN 978-1-57685-616-1
  1. General educational development tests—Study guides.   2. High school equivalency examinations—Study guides.   3. Language arts (Secondary)—Examinations.   I. LearningExpress (Organization)
LB3060.33.G45G38   2008
373.126'2—dc22
                                                                                                                                                      2008006533

Printed in the United States of America

9 8 7 6 5 4 3 2 1

First Edition

Regarding the Information in This Book

We attempt to verify the information presented in our books prior to publication. It is always a good idea, however, to double-check such important information as the test format, application and testing procedures, and deadlines, as such information can change from time to time.

For more information or to place an order, contact LearningExpress at:
  2 Rector Street
  26th Floor
  New York, NY 10006

Or visit us at:
  www.learnatest.com

About the Contributors

Gregory C. Benoit, MA, has written and edited several titles for LearningExpress. He is the author of numerous books on a wide variety of subjects, as well as a novel and a children's book. He taught college-level English, writing, and literature for 12 years.

A.C. Friss is a freelance writer living in New York City. She has had several poems published in literary journals and has helped develop standardized tests for public school systems. She is also the author of *Express Review Guides: Writing* and *Express Review Guides: Reading Comprehension*.

Contents

Introduction — 1
About *GED Language Arts, Reading* — 1
GED Test Overview — 3
What Is the GED? — 4
Alternate Languages — 4
Accommodations for Disabilities — 4
A Tough Exam — 5
GED Scoring — 5
The GED Language Arts, Reading Section — 5
Preparing for the GED Language Arts, Reading Test — 8

Pretest — 11

Chapter 1: Perfecting Your Study Skills — 25
Where Do I Start? — 26
I Need a Study Plan — 26
I Need a Study Place — 28
The Right Tools — 30
You Are Worth It: Motivational and Relaxation Techniques That Work — 32
Learning Strategies and Test-Taking Techniques — 34
Multiple-Choice Strategies — 40
The Endgame — 41
In a Nutshell — 43

Chapter 2: Reading Comprehension Strategies — 45
Determining Main Ideas and Themes — 46
Identifying Supporting Facts and Details — 54
The Difference between Fact and Opinion — 55
Making Inferences — 57

CONTENTS

Cause-and-Effect Relationships	60
Understanding Words from Context	62

Chapter 3: Reading Fiction — 65

What Is Fiction?	66
Types of Fiction	66
The Narrator	67
Important Characters	69
Setting	69
Atmosphere	70
Tone	70
Language and Style	72
Plot	75
Characterization	76
Theme	77
Practice Questions	78

Chapter 4: Reading Nonfiction — 85

Informational Nonfiction	86
Literary Nonfiction	88
Letters	91
Speeches	92
Critical Reviews	93
Analytical Techniques for Nonfiction	94
Practice Questions	95

Chapter 5: Reading Poetry — 103

Elements of Sound	104
Elements of Structure	108
Types of Poetry	109
Word Choice in Poetry	112
Practice Questions	114

Chapter 6: Reading Drama — 119

How Drama Compares to Fiction	120
The Structure of Drama	124
The Dramatic Stage	125
Types of Drama	129
Some Common Dramatic Terms	131
Practice Questions	132

Posttest — 143

GED Language Arts, Reading Answers and Explanations — 157

Appendix: Prefixes, Suffixes, and Word Roots — 177

Introduction

CONGRATULATIONS ON YOUR wise decision to take the General Educational Development examination—commonly known as the GED®. This decision shows that you have made some determination to advance yourself in life, to improve your education, and to widen your career choices. Perhaps you have decided to head to college to study some field that will open up new career opportunities. Or perhaps you want to advance in your present career, but need to establish your educational credentials first. These are the two most common reasons for taking the GED, but there are many others—setting a good example for your children, finding greater satisfaction in life, and so forth.

▶ About *GED Language Arts, Reading*

Whatever your reason for taking the GED, you have made the right first step: picking up this book to prepare for success. As you work through the following chapters, you will learn all that you need to know to master the Language Arts, Reading section of the GED. We will show you strategies for studying, explain techniques for greater reading comprehension, and explain in detail the various types of literature and questions that you will encounter on the test. Then, you can test yourself in advance with our practice tests to pinpoint the areas where you might need more work. But the book is only as good as the use you make of it, so familiarize yourself with what is inside this book and how it is organized.

INTRODUCTION

Contents at a Glance

Content	Chapter
Study Skills	1
Reading Comprehension	2
Fiction	3
Nonfiction	4
Poetry	5
Drama	6

Pretest

The pretest following this introduction is a sample GED Language Arts, Reading test. Be sure to take it before going on to Chapter 1.

Following the pretest is an answer and analysis section. Compare your answers with the correct choices given in that section, taking note of any that you got wrong. Then refer to the answer evaluation chart in that section to discern which areas are your weakest and which are your strongest. This will help you know where to concentrate as you go through the rest of this book.

Study Skills and Reading Comprehension

Chapters 1 and 2 will address some large general issues which are of vital importance: how to study most effectively and how to read with greater understanding. These chapters are important as you begin a routine of studying for the GED, but they will also prove immensely valuable as you go through life. The skills addressed in these chapters will apply again and again, whether you move on to college or begin a challenging professional career.

Much of this book also depends upon your basic understanding of reading skills and study habits, so don't skip these chapters. They lay the foundation for the rest of the book.

Reading Literature

Chapters 3 through 6 address the specific types of reading that you'll be questioned on in the GED. Even if you've never read poetry or drama before, these chapters will thoroughly prepare you to understand—and hopefully even enjoy—all types (or *genres*) of literature.

After reading through these chapters, review the results from your pretest. This will show you areas that could use some strengthening, and you will find it profitable to reread specific chapters that might have been unfamiliar.

Posttest

The posttest following Chapter 6 provides another example of what you'll find on the GED Language Arts, Reading test. This test should be taken after you have completed all the preceding chapters, and even after you have read through some chapters more than once. Remember, you will use the results from your pretest to determine which areas need the most work, and those areas will be worth studying in greater detail.

Once you have studied and strengthened your understanding of reading literature, block out an hour of time and take the posttest. Use the answer keys which follow to determine your results—which will be vastly improved over the pretest by this time—and see what areas might still be in need of strengthening. Then review the relevant chapters in this book.

Appendix

An appendix at the back of this book discusses how words are created—where they come from, how they

INTRODUCTION

build up with prefixes and suffixes, and how to recognize basic word roots. You will not be tested on vocabulary on the GED, but this information is still very valuable. When you encounter a word that you don't know in your reading, you'll be able to take it apart and figure out its meaning just by understanding these basic vocabulary principles.

By the time you're done with this book, you will be prepared to pass the Language Arts, Reading section of the GED. So grab a pencil and a notebook and read on!

▶ GED Test Overview

The General Educational Development (GED) exams are your key to unlocking a better future. A GED certification will open the doors to higher education, better jobs, higher pay, greater respect and prestige—it will open doors that may be locked against you at present. In fact, your decision to take the GED exam may prove to be one of the most significant decisions of your life.

And you're not alone in that decision: In 2005, more than 680,000 people took the test in the United States alone.

Reasons for Taking the GED

The American Council on Education (ACE), which oversees the GED exams, reports that the two most common reasons for taking the GED are to gain further education at the college level and to advance a career—either by improving a present job or getting something totally different.

In the United States, 61% of those taking the GED take it for educational reasons and 49% for employment reasons, while some take it for both reasons.

The fact that you are reading this book indicates that you are serious about your plans, and serious about taking—and passing—the GED examination. This book is the tool that you need to succeed on the Language Arts, Reading section of the GED. It will teach you the study skills needed to prepare for the exam, the specific information that you need to understand various types of literature, strategies that will help you immensely in both studying for the test and taking it, and several practice exams to test yourself in advance.

Gaining Respect

Nearly all U.S. colleges accept students with a GED, and most employers treat GED-holders the same as those with a traditional high school diploma.

You're in Good Company

More than 16 million people have taken the GED since it was first given in 1942!

INTRODUCTION

▶ What Is the GED?

The GED exams originated in 1942. They were designed to provide the equivalent of high school diplomas to soldiers who had left school in order to fight in World War II. Today they are used to assess whether a person has the basic knowledge and learning skills that one acquires through a standard American public education. Most colleges and employers in the United States readily recognize and accept the GED certificate as equal to a high school diploma.

GED Statistics

The American Council on Education oversees the GED exams, and reports the following:

- 680,874 people took the test in 2005 in the United States alone; 715,365 took it worldwide.
- 423,714 passed in the United States; 443,607 passed worldwide.
- 25% of GED test takers are between the ages of 20 and 24.

Born from War

The GED was created in 1942 in an effort to help U.S. soldiers who had fought in World War II, enabling them to pick up their education and careers where they'd left off prior to the war.

The GED exam consists of five separate tests: Mathematics; Language Arts, Reading; Language Arts, Writing (parts 1 and 2); Social Studies; and Science. The entire exam takes $7\frac{1}{2}$ hours! But don't let that frighten you away; you may retake any individual sections that you don't pass without retaking the entire exam.

▶ Alternate Languages

You may be able to take the GED in French or Spanish if English is not your primary language. Contact the GED test administrators for further information.

"Smarter Than the Average Bear"

The GED exam is deliberately designed to be more difficult than many high school courses. Passing the GED proves that you're in the upper percentiles!

▶ Accommodations for Disabilities

If you have special needs from a physical or learning disability, the test center will provide special accommodations. These disabilities include such concerns as blindness, deafness, and dyslexia. Contact the GED test administrators for further information.

INTRODUCTION

Contacting the GED Administrators

Here is how to obtain further information on disabilities, test times, locations, and so on.

1. Begin by contacting your local high school or adult education office.
2. Contact the American Council on Education, which oversees the GED:
   GED—General Educational Development
   American Council on Education
   One Dupont Circle NW, Suite 250
   Washington, D.C. 20036
   800-626-9433
3. Visit the ACE website at www.gedtest.org, or e-mail ACE at comments@ace.nehu.edu.

▶ A Tough Exam

In 2005, more than 423,000 people passed the GED—more than 60%. Yet these statistics also demonstrate an important fact you must not overlook: The GED is hard! In fact, the GED is designed so that only 60% of graduating high school seniors can pass. It is deliberately designed, in other words, to be difficult. You do not want to sail into the test center on exam morning and take the test cold, without any practice or preparation. People who do that end up taking the exam again, and they usually learn from their first experience that they need to prepare in advance.

▶ GED Scoring

Each section of the GED is scored separately on a 200- to 800-point basis—800 being the highest possible score. To pass the GED, you must reach a minimum score for each test section, *and* a minimum overall average score for the entire test. The minimum passing score is determined by each state or province, but most set the passing level at a minimum 410 on each section and a minimum 450 overall. This means that you can score as low as 410 on *some* sections, but the average score of all sections must be at least 450. Contact your GED test administrators to find out what is considered a passing score in your state or province.

A Tough Exam

According to the American Council on Education, only 60% of high school graduates pass the GED exam.

▶ The GED Language Arts, Reading Section

This book is not an overview of the entire GED exam, but a specific tool to help you prepare for the Language Arts, Reading section of the exam.

The Language Arts, Reading section of the exam consists of 40 questions and takes 65 minutes. Most of this section focuses on literature, while 25% of the questions are drawn from nonliterary texts. The literature includes fiction (45% of the questions), poetry, and drama (with 15% each). Nonliterary texts include informational text (such as news articles), reviews of the arts (such as movie reviews), business documents, and literary nonfiction.

GED at a Glance

Mathematics
50 items, 75 minutes

Content areas:

Numbers, Number Sense, and Operations	25%
Measurement and Geometry	25%
Data Analysis, Statistics, and Probability	25%
Algebra, Functions, and Patterns	25%

Language Arts, Reading
40 items, 65 minutes

Content areas:

Nonfiction Texts	25%
Literary Texts (Poetry, Prose, Drama)	75%

Language Arts, Writing, Part I
50 items, 75 minutes

Content areas:

Organization	15%
Sentence Structure	30%
Usage	30%
Mechanics	25%

Language Arts, Writing, Part II
Essay, about 250 words, 45 minutes

Social Studies
50 items, 80 minutes

Content areas:

U.S. History	25%
World History	15%
Civics and Government	25%
Geography	15%
Economics	20%

Science
50 items, 80 minutes

Content areas:

Life Science	45%
Earth and Space Science	20%
Physical Science	35%

The 40 multiple-choice questions in the Language Arts, Reading section are intended to test your ability to understand and apply written material. The types of writing will reflect what you would be expected to deal with in college as well as in a professional working environment. The questions themselves ask you to understand, apply, analyze, and draw inferences from the written passages.

INTRODUCTION

Passing Scores

Each state in the United States has its own standards on passing scores for the GED. Most states, however, require a minimum score of 410 on each section of the exam, and an average of 450 overall.

What You'll Be Reading

Most of the reading selections on the exam are drawn from literature, and each exam will include the following:

- poetry
- drama (plays, movie scripts, etc.)
- prose fiction written prior to 1920
- prose fiction written between 1920 and 1960
- prose fiction written after 1960

The remaining 25% of the test is based upon nonfiction writing. These written passages are drawn from:

- nonfiction prose
- critical reviews of the arts, such as movies
- professional and civic documents, such as legal documents, corporate mission statements, etc.

The reading passages in the exam are not long, running between 200 and 400 words for prose and 8 to 25 lines for poetry. Furthermore, before each passage of literature, the exam includes a purpose question designed to help you focus on some central idea as you read the passage. These purpose questions will give you a hint of the types of actual test questions which will follow the passage, and will assist you to pay particular attention to certain elements within the written passage.

What You'll Be Asked

Each written passage is followed by four to eight questions. These questions will test your abilities in the following areas:

- **Comprehension.** Comprehension questions simply test how well you understood the passage that you were asked to read. They will measure your ability to restate information, summarize ideas, and see relationships to other ideas.
- **Application.** Application questions test your ability to take information from a text and see how the ideas or principles apply in real-life situations.
- **Analysis.** Analysis questions require you to think more deeply about a passage, to go beyond merely understanding words and ideas. You will be asked to distinguish between facts and opinions, recognize an author's basic assumptions, identify cause-and-effect relationships, compare or contrast ideas, and draw conclusions.
- **Synthesis.** Synthesis questions are like analysis questions, except that they apply to the entire passage rather than to selected points within the passage. These questions will ask you to explain how a passage is organized, define the overall tone of a passage, identify the author's point of view, and so forth.

The Sections of the GED

The GED is composed of five separate tests in the following categories:

1. Mathematics
2. Language Arts, Reading
3. Language Arts, Writing, parts 1 and 2
4. Social Studies
5. Science

Literary Time Periods on the GED

As already stated, you will encounter a variety of literature on the GED, including poetry, drama, and fiction. These will be drawn from three groups: literature written prior to 1920, literature written between 1920 and 1960, and literature written since 1960.

The reasoning behind these categories is based upon the idea that literature went through drastic changes during the twentieth century. This notion is open to scholarly debate, but for our purposes it is helpful to understand, in brief, some elements that you will find in literature from each of those periods.

> **A Large Percentage**
>
> More than 39 million adults in the United States over the age of 16 (18% of the adult population) did not complete their high school education and are not enrolled in any education program.

Pre-1920. This time period is loosely referred to, for GED purposes, as Ancient and Classical writing. Obviously, it includes essentially everything ever written from ancient times into the twentieth century. This is quite a broad category to define in easy terms, but the writings that you will encounter from before 1920 will generally be dealing with broad themes: love, power, death, pride, and other universal concepts. You may encounter writing styles and vocabulary that seems strange, but don't allow yourself to be distracted by such things. Just read more carefully, and you will find that the central ideas of the passage will become apparent.

1920 to 1960. Literature from this period might be called Modern Literature. This is a period that saw many very significant worldwide events, including the aftermath of World War I, the trauma of World War II, and the worldwide Great Depression. Literature written during this period may seem easier to understand because vocabulary and writing styles have not changed significantly in the past 80 years. Yet you may also encounter different topics in this time period, including the conflict between Communism and Democracy; a distrust of those who hold power (such as government or industrial figures); and a new fascination with things such as psychoanalysis, the origins of mankind, nuclear power, and other modern controversies.

1960 to the Present. The literature of this period may be thought of as Contemporary Literature. It is typically written in a very informal style, using the sort of language and grammar that people use in everyday speech. In fact, it will often include specific dialects and use of slang, as it attempts to capture the thoughts and speech of certain groups of people. Contemporary Literature addresses ideas that should be quite familiar to you already, such as equal rights, feminism, the technological revolution (computers, the Internet, and so on), the environment, and so forth.

▶ Preparing for the GED Language Arts, Reading Test

By now, you may be tempted to panic. Perhaps you've never read much poetry, or maybe Shakespeare seems incomprehensible; you might feel some anxiety about having to read and answer questions on literature from time periods that you are unfamiliar with.

The most important rule for you to remember is this: *Don't panic!* Anxiety is your enemy, and the truth is that you have no reason to be anxious about these issues. This book is specifically designed to prepare you for all elements of the Language Arts, Reading section of the GED, and the fact that you are reading it proves that you are well on your way to gaining mastery.

> **Don't Panic!**
>
> Anxiety and fear can short-circuit both your test-taking skills *and* your preparation for the test. Anxiety makes you tense and redirects blood away from your brain—which is precisely where you need it! See Chapter 1 for techniques that will help you relax. Remember: Fear is your enemy, so don't allow yourself to become anxious about the exam.

Use the Book

The first step in preparing for the GED is to take advantage of all that this book has to offer. Take the pretest, and then spend some time reviewing your answers as well as the table provided after the test. The tables in the answer key at the back of the book for the pretest (and the posttest) will help pinpoint your strengths and weaknesses, thus helping you maximize your study time.

Study the chapters that deal with each specific type (or genre) of literature. Spend extra time on those chapters that address your areas of weakness, based upon the results of your pretest.

Familiarize yourself with the many reading strategies in Chapter 2, and develop the study skills taught in Chapter 1. Then *practice*! When you're not actively studying for the GED, spend time reading the newspaper or magazines, or pick up an interesting novel. This will give you the chance to practice the concepts of reading comprehension, and it will also become a lifelong habit. One nice side effect of the GED Language Arts, Reading test is that it will encourage you to become a habitual reader, if you aren't already.

Use the appendix in this book to familiarize yourself with vocabulary, prefixes and suffixes, and so forth. You will not be specifically tested on vocabulary in the GED, but an understanding of how words are built will strengthen your overall reading comprehension.

Finally, take the posttest at the end of the book, and then compare your results with the pretest. If you follow these steps, you will probably see a vast improvement in your scores.

Be Prepared—in Advance

Chapter 1 of this book gives you specific ways to prepare yourself in the time leading up to the GED exam. Follow these steps so that, when the day arrives, you will be fully confident that you have done everything possible to prepare yourself.

Have some sharp number two pencils ready before the day arrives, because that is what you'll be using on the test. Make sure that you have your admission ticket ready, if required, as well as some form of legal identification, such as a driver's license.

A day or two before the exam, gather together all the items that you'll need and have them together, ready to go. This may seem self-evident, but the knowledge that you are prepared and organized will actually give you a sense of confidence and relaxation. Remember: Panic is your enemy, and everything that you can do to prevent it is in your best interest.

Pretest

THE FOLLOWING PRETEST is similar in content and format to the official GED Language Arts, Reading test. Answer every question. If you are not sure of an answer, put a question mark by the question number to note that you are making a guess. On the official GED, an unanswered question is counted as incorrect, so making a good guess is an important skill to practice. We also suggest for this pretest that you ignore the time restraints of the official GED and take as much time as you need to complete each problem.

When you have completed the pretest, take a look at the detailed answer explanations and the review table at the back of the book. Be sure to use the answers and review table to help pinpoint your strengths and weaknesses and focus your studies.

Directions: Read each question carefully and determine the best answer. Record your answers by circling the answer letter choice. You may also use the answer sheet to bubble in your answer.

Note: On the GED, you are not permitted to write in the test booklet. For this pretest, practice by making any notes on a separate piece of paper.

▶ Pretest Answer Sheet

1. ⓐ ⓑ ⓒ ⓓ ⓔ
2. ⓐ ⓑ ⓒ ⓓ ⓔ
3. ⓐ ⓑ ⓒ ⓓ ⓔ
4. ⓐ ⓑ ⓒ ⓓ ⓔ
5. ⓐ ⓑ ⓒ ⓓ ⓔ
6. ⓐ ⓑ ⓒ ⓓ ⓔ
7. ⓐ ⓑ ⓒ ⓓ ⓔ
8. ⓐ ⓑ ⓒ ⓓ ⓔ
9. ⓐ ⓑ ⓒ ⓓ ⓔ
10. ⓐ ⓑ ⓒ ⓓ ⓔ
11. ⓐ ⓑ ⓒ ⓓ ⓔ
12. ⓐ ⓑ ⓒ ⓓ ⓔ
13. ⓐ ⓑ ⓒ ⓓ ⓔ
14. ⓐ ⓑ ⓒ ⓓ ⓔ
15. ⓐ ⓑ ⓒ ⓓ ⓔ
16. ⓐ ⓑ ⓒ ⓓ ⓔ
17. ⓐ ⓑ ⓒ ⓓ ⓔ
18. ⓐ ⓑ ⓒ ⓓ ⓔ
19. ⓐ ⓑ ⓒ ⓓ ⓔ
20. ⓐ ⓑ ⓒ ⓓ ⓔ
21. ⓐ ⓑ ⓒ ⓓ ⓔ
22. ⓐ ⓑ ⓒ ⓓ ⓔ
23. ⓐ ⓑ ⓒ ⓓ ⓔ
24. ⓐ ⓑ ⓒ ⓓ ⓔ
25. ⓐ ⓑ ⓒ ⓓ ⓔ
26. ⓐ ⓑ ⓒ ⓓ ⓔ
27. ⓐ ⓑ ⓒ ⓓ ⓔ
28. ⓐ ⓑ ⓒ ⓓ ⓔ
29. ⓐ ⓑ ⓒ ⓓ ⓔ
30. ⓐ ⓑ ⓒ ⓓ ⓔ
31. ⓐ ⓑ ⓒ ⓓ ⓔ
32. ⓐ ⓑ ⓒ ⓓ ⓔ
33. ⓐ ⓑ ⓒ ⓓ ⓔ
34. ⓐ ⓑ ⓒ ⓓ ⓔ
35. ⓐ ⓑ ⓒ ⓓ ⓔ
36. ⓐ ⓑ ⓒ ⓓ ⓔ
37. ⓐ ⓑ ⓒ ⓓ ⓔ
38. ⓐ ⓑ ⓒ ⓓ ⓔ
39. ⓐ ⓑ ⓒ ⓓ ⓔ
40. ⓐ ⓑ ⓒ ⓓ ⓔ

Questions 1 to 5 refer to the following excerpt from a memoir.

"I didn't know you were going to treat the arrival of a few friends as if it was a major catastrophe," Larry explained.

"But, dear, it's so silly to invite people when you know there's no room in the villa."

"I do wish you'd stop fussing," said Larry irritably; "there's quite a simple solution to the whole business."

"What," asked Mother suspiciously.

"Well, since the villa isn't big enough, let's move to one that is."

"Don't be ridiculous. Whoever heard of moving into a larger house because you've invited some friends to stay?"

"What's the matter with the idea? It seems a perfectly sensible solution to me; after all, if you say there's no room here, the obvious thing to do is to move."

"The obvious thing to do is not to invite people," said Mother severely.

"I don't think it's good for us to live like hermits," said Larry. "I only really invited them for you. They're a charming crowd. I thought you'd like to have them. Liven things up a bit for you."

"I'm quite lively enough, thank you," said Mother with dignity.

"Well, I don't know what we're going to do."

"I really don't see why they can't stay in the Pension Suisse, dear."

"You can't ask people out to stay with you and then make them live in a third-rate hotel."

"How many have you invited?" asked Mother. . . .

"Well, I can't remember now . . . if you budget for seven or eight people, I think that would cover it."

"You mean, including ourselves?"

"No, no, I mean seven or eight people as well as the family."

"But it's absurd, Larry. We can't possibly fit thirteen people into this villa, with all the good will in the world."

"Well, let's *move*, then. I've offered you a perfectly sensible solution. I don't know what you're arguing about."

"But don't be ridiculous, dear. Even if we did move into a villa large enough to house thirteen people, what are we going to do with the extra space when they've gone?"

"Invite some more people," said Larry, astonished that Mother should not have thought of this simple answer for herself.

—From *My Family and Other Animals*, by Gerald Durrell.

1. Which word best describes the tone of this passage?
   a. severe
   b. tense
   c. humorous
   d. angry
   e. neutral

2. What is the nature of the *conflict* between Larry and his mother?
   a. Larry is confused about how many people can fit in the house.
   b. Larry's mother is misunderstanding what Larry wants to do.
   c. Neither Larry nor his mother really wants any guests.
   d. Larry wants something that his mother thinks is unreasonable.
   e. The narrator has gotten confused.

3. What is the meaning of this sentence: "We can't possibly fit thirteen people into this villa, with all the good will in the world"?
   a. If we have enough good will, we can make it happen.
   b. No matter how much we want to, we can't do it.
   c. The 13 people might fit if they were nicer.
   d. Thirteen is an unlucky number.
   e. The villa is too small, and we should move to a larger one.

4. This passage is narrated in
   a. first person.
   b. second person.
   c. third person.
   d. fourth person.
   e. none of the above; there is no narrator.

5. From this passage, you might infer that Larry
   a. hates his family.
   b. is rather self-centered.
   c. has no sense of humor.
   d. has many friends.
   e. is wearing pajamas.

Questions 6 to 10 are based on the following passage.

I went to the woods because I wished to live deliberately, to front only the essential facts of life, and see if I could not learn what it had to teach, and not, when I came to die, discover that I had not lived. I did not wish to live what was not life, living is so dear; nor did I wish to practice resignation, unless it was quite necessary. I wanted to live deep and suck out all the marrow of life, to live so sturdily and Spartan-like as to put to rout all that was not life, to cut a broad swath and shave close, to drive life into a corner, and reduce it to its lowest terms, and, if it proved to be mean, why then to get the whole and genuine meanness of it, and publish its meanness to the world; or if it were sublime, to know it by experience, and be able to give a true account of it in my next excursion. For most men, it appears to me, are in a strange uncertainty about it, whether it is of the devil or of God, and have somewhat hastily concluded that it is the chief end of man here to "glorify God and enjoy him forever."

Still we live meanly, like ants; though the fable tells us that we were long ago changed into men; like pygmies we fight with cranes; it is error upon error, and clout upon clout, and our best virtue has for its occasion a superfluous and evitable wretchedness. Our life is frittered away by detail. An honest man has hardly need to count more than his ten fingers, or in extreme cases he may add his ten toes, and lump the rest. Simplicity, simplicity, simplicity! I say, let your affairs be as two or three, and not a hundred or a thousand; instead of a million count half a dozen, and keep your accounts on your thumb-nail. In the midst of this chopping sea of civilized life, such are the clouds and storms and quicksands and thousand-and-one items to be allowed for, that a man has to live, if he would not *founder* and go to the bottom and not make his port at all, by dead reckoning, and he must be a great calculator indeed who succeeds. Simplify, simplify. Instead of three meals a day, if it be necessary eat but one; instead of a hundred dishes, five; and reduce other things in proportion.

—From *Walden* by Henry David Thoreau.

6. What does the author mean when he says that he wanted "to live deliberately"?
   a. He wanted to avoid unnecessary distractions.
   b. He was trying to avoid disease.
   c. He had been depressed and was trying to get better.
   d. He wanted to know what it was like in the woods.
   e. He had no specific plan.

7. How does the author suggest that we "suck out all the marrow of life"?
   a. by partying every weekend
   b. by letting our neighbors do all our work
   c. by shirking our responsibilities
   d. by building a cabin in the woods
   e. by living as simply as possible

8. The word *founder* in the last paragraph probably means
   a. discover.
   b. establish.
   c. shipwreck.
   d. create.
   e. lose.

9. The author's purpose in this passage is to
   a. entertain.
   b. persuade.
   c. amuse.
   d. instruct.
   e. contradict.

10. This passage is an example of
   a. fable.
   b. essay.
   c. drama.
   d. poetry.
   e. melodrama.

Questions 11 to 15 are based upon the following poem.

Dawn
A long orange knife slits the darkness
from ear to ear. Flat sheets of Kansas
have been dropped where the water was.
A blue snake is lying perfectly still,
freezing to avoid detection—no, it is the
    barge-road.

Noon
It's six weeks past the *solstice*. What
is the sun thinking of? It skulks
above the southern woods at noon.
                  Two ducks descend
on the thin creek that snakes through the plain
    of ice.
They dream of a great flood coming
to devastate this plastic geography.
We can all remember other things than snow.

Dusk

At dusk the east bank glows a colder orange,
giving back heat reluctantly. (The sickle moon
gives it back quickly.) The snake is glacier-green
where an oil barge has lately churned it.
Tonight unlucky creatures will die, like so many
soldiers or parents, it is nobody's fault.

            —From "Winter on the River"
              by William Meredith.

11. What is the *long orange knife* referred to in line 1?
    a. a letter opener
    b. an orange peel
    c. the sunset
    d. the sunrise
    e. the moon

12. What is the *blue snake* mentioned in line 4?
    a. a blue snake
    b. a strip of rubber
    c. a piece of fruit
    d. a mirror
    e. a frozen river

13. What is the most likely meaning of *solstice* in line 7?
    a. the middle of winter
    b. a quiet place
    c. a bandage
    d. the previous month
    e. leap year

14. This poem is written in
    a. iambic pentameter.
    b. heroic couplets.
    c. rhyming dactyls.
    d. free verse.
    e. sonnet form.

15. This is an example of
    a. persuasive poetry.
    b. imagistic poetry.
    c. alliteration.
    d. personification.
    e. irony.

Questions 16 to 20 refer to the following excerpt.

AMANDA: [*delighted, like a child*] Do you realize that we're living in sin?
ELYOT: Not according to the Catholics, Catholics don't recognize divorce.
AMANDA: Yes, dear, but we're not Catholics.
ELYOT: Never mind, it's nice to think they'd sort of back us up. We were married in the eyes of Heaven, and we still are.
AMANDA: We may be all right in the eyes of Heaven, but we look like being in the hell of a mess socially.
ELYOT: Who cares?
AMANDA: Are we going to marry each other again, after Victor and Sibyl divorce us?
ELYOT: I suppose so. What do you think?
AMANDA: I feel rather scared of marriage really.
ELYOT: It is a frowsy business.
AMANDA: I believe it was just the fact of our being married, and clamped together publicly, that wrecked us before.
ELYOT: That, and not knowing how to manage each other . . .
AMANDA: [*crossing to RIGHT of table*] When we were together, did you really think I was unfaithful to you?
ELYOT: Yes, practically every day.

AMANDA: I thought you were, too; often I used to torture myself with visions of your bouncing about on divans with awful widows. [*she stands behind her chair*]

ELYOT: Why widows?

AMANDA: I was thinking of Claire Lavenham really.

ELYOT: Oh Claire.

AMANDA: [*pushing her chair into the table; sharply*] What did you say "Oh Claire" like that for? It sounded far too careless to me.

ELYOT: [*wistfully*] What a lovely creature she was.

AMANDA: [*sitting on the RIGHT arm of the settee*] Lovely, lovely, lovely!

ELYOT: [*blowing her a kiss*] Darling!

—From *Private Lives* by Noel Coward.

16. How would you describe Amanda and Elyot's attitude toward marriage?
    a. serious
    b. committed
    d. flippant
    d. angry
    e. celibate

17. This couple can best be described by which of the following sentences?
    a. An apple a day keeps the doctor away.
    b. Absence makes the heart grow fonder.
    c. Live and let live.
    d. Grab all the gusto you can.
    e. Every dog has its day.

18. Why did Elyot and Amanda probably get divorced?
    a. They got tired of one another.
    b. They met other people that they liked better.
    c. They were never married in the first place.
    d. They were incompatible.
    e. Each thought that the other was unfaithful.

19. This couple is most likely to
    a. be unhappy in any marriage.
    b. have many children.
    c. live happily ever after.
    d. become rich and famous.
    e. move to New Zealand.

20. This play most likely
    a. ends happily.
    b. ends sadly.
    c. has three acts.
    d. is in Shakespearean form.
    e. has no rising action.

Questions 21 to 28 refer to the following excerpt.

The door opened and Jim stepped in and closed it. He looked thin and very serious. Poor fellow, he was only twenty-two—and to be burdened with a family! He needed a new overcoat and he was without gloves . . .

Della wriggled off the table and went for him.

"Jim, darling," she cried, "don't look at me that way. I had my hair cut off and sold because I couldn't have lived through Christmas without giving you a present. It'll grow out again—you won't mind, will you? I just had to do it. My hair grows awfully fast. Say 'Merry Christmas!' Jim, and let's be happy. You don't know what a nice—what a beautiful, nice gift I've got for you."

"You've cut off your hair?" asked Jim, *laboriously*, as if he had not arrived at that patent fact yet even after the hardest mental labor . . .

"You needn't look for it," said Della. "It's sold, I tell you—sold and gone, too. It's Christmas Eve, boy. Be good to me, for it went for you. Maybe the hairs of my head were numbered," she went on with sudden serious sweetness, "but nobody could ever count my love for you. Shall I put the chops on, Jim?" . . .

Jim drew a package from his overcoat pocket and threw it upon the table.

"Don't make any mistake, Dell," he said, "about me. I don't think there's anything in the way of a haircut or a shave or a shampoo that could make me like my girl any less. But if you'll unwrap that package you may see why you had me going a while at first."

White fingers and nimble tore at the string and paper. And then an ecstatic scream of joy; and then, alas! a quick feminine change to hysterical tears and wails, necessitating the immediate employment of all the comforting powers of the lord of the flat.

For there lay The Combs—the set of combs, side and back, that Della had worshipped long in a Broadway window. Beautiful combs, pure tortoise shell, with jeweled rims—just the shade to wear in the beautiful vanished hair. They were expensive combs, she knew, and her heart had simply craved and yearned over them without the least hope of possession. And now, they were hers, but the tresses that should have adorned the coveted adornments were gone . . .

And then Della leaped up like a little singed cat and cried, "Oh, oh!"

Jim had not yet seen his beautiful present. She held it out to him eagerly upon her open palm. The dull precious metal seemed to flash with a reflection of her bright and *ardent* spirit.

"Isn't it a dandy, Jim? I hunted all over town to find it. You'll have to look at the time a hundred times a day now. Give me your watch. I want to see how it looks on it."

Instead of obeying, Jim tumbled down on the couch and put his hands under the back of his head and smiled.

"Dell," said he, "let's put our Christmas presents away and keep 'em a while. They're too nice to use just at present. I sold the watch to get the money to buy your combs. And now suppose you put the chops on."

—From "The Gift of the Magi," by O. Henry.

21. The couple described in this passage are probably
   a. members of royalty.
   b. ordinary working-class people.
   c. middle aged.
   d. overweight.
   e. not very religious.

22. The description that "Della wriggled off the table and went for him" suggests that
   a. Jim was frightening his wife.
   b. Jim was late for supper.
   c. Della was eagerly excited to see her husband.
   d. Della was furious with her husband.
   e. the couple were both embarrassed.

23. The word *laboriously* suggests that
   a. Jim was tired from a hard day at work.
   b. Della was making him work too hard.
   c. Jim was not very intelligent.
   d. Jim was struggling to understand.
   e. Della was pregnant.

24. Why does Della break into tears when she opens her Christmas present?
   a. She is disappointed in the gift.
   b. She cut her finger on the wrapping paper.
   c. Jim is glaring at her angrily, ruining the moment.
   d. She knows that she is about to divorce Jim.
   e. She is deeply touched by what Jim bought her.

25. The word *ardent* most likely means
   a. lovely.
   b. green.
   c. passionate.
   d. trees.
   e. late.

26. Della and Jim would most likely
   a. hate their jobs.
   b. have divorced parents.
   c. be politically active.
   d. give generous gifts to friends.
   e. not have many friends.

27. What has happened to Jim's watch?
   a. He lost it in a game of poker.
   b. He sold it to buy Della's combs.
   c. Someone stole it at work.
   d. Della took it to the repair shop.
   e. We are not told.

28. This passage is an example of
   a. personification.
   b. metaphor.
   c. climax.
   d. irony.
   e. dialogue.

Questions 29 to 35 refer to the following poem.

> Mark but this flea, and mark in this,
> How little that which thou denyest me is;
> Me it sucked first, and now sucks thee,
> And in this flea our two bloods mingled be;
> Confess it, this cannot be said
> A sin, or shame, or loss of maidenhead,
>   Yet this enjoys before it woo,
>   And pampered swells with one blood made of two,
>   And this, alas, is more than we would do.
>
> Oh stay, *three lives in one flea* spare,
> When we almost, nay more than married are.
> This flea is you and I, and this
> Our marriage bed, and marriage temple is;
> Though parents grudge, and you, we're met,
> And cloistered in *these living walls of Jet*.
>   Though use make thee apt to kill me,
>   Let not to this, self murder added be,
>   And sacrilege, three sins in killing three.
>
> Cruel and sudden, has thou since
> Purpled thy nail, in blood of innocence?
> In what could this flea guilty be,
> Except in that drop which it sucked from thee?
> Yet thou triumph'st, and saist that thou
> Find'st not thyself, nor me the weaker now;
>   'Tis true, then learn how false, fears be;
>   Just so much honor, when thou yield'st to me,
>   Will waste, as this flea's death took life from thee.
>
> —"The Flea," by John Donne.

29. What is the narrator suggesting in this poem?
  a. He is trying to seduce a woman.
  b. He is contemplating the life cycle of a flea.
  c. Life is full of sorrow.
  d. We should not kill living creatures.
  e. Yesterday is gone forever.

30. This poem is divided into
  a. rhyme pattern.
  b. couplets.
  c. stanzas.
  d. meter.
  e. pentameters.

31. What *three lives in one flea* is the narrator referring to?
  a. The flea has sucked blood from the couple, making three lives.
  b. The narrator is speaking of a former lover.
  c. The woman is pregnant.
  d. The narrator is referring to his in-laws.
  e. The meaning is unclear.

32. What are *these living walls of Jet* in the second stanza?
  a. a monastery
  b. an airplane
  c. the woman's hair
  d. the cat
  e. the flea

33. What is the rhyme scheme in the first stanza?
  a. *a, b, a, b, c, d, c, d*
  b. *a, a, b, b, c, c, d, d*
  c. *b, c, a, b, c, a, d, d*
  d. free verse
  e. no rhyme scheme

34. The narrator's attitude toward love is probably
  a. very serious.
  b. very casual.
  c. resentful.
  d. disengaged.
  e. descriptive.

35. What has happened in the third stanza?
  a. nothing
  b. The narrator has given up.
  c. Someone else has entered the room.
  d. The woman has left.
  e. The woman has killed the flea.

Questions 36 to 40 refer to the following passage.

The recent level of turnover in the company has been of some concern to management, and we are anxious to address the root causes.

  In the past 12 months, 17% of our total personnel have left the company for reasons other than retirement. This figure is up 3% from last year, and up nearly 5% from previous years.

  Exit interviews have revealed several recurring trends in these turnovers. Almost 15% of those leaving have cited labor union agitation as a key factor in their decision to leave. Of these, more than half specifically stated that they had been bullied and harassed by fellow workers who have been trying to force them to join the labor union.

  This trend must not be permitted to continue. Union agitators are certainly within their rights to lobby for increased dues and membership, but they are not permitted to use *coercion* on company grounds. Bullying is grounds for immediate termination, and instances should be reported to management immediately.

36. The purpose of this passage is to
   a. investigate employee turnover.
   b. put a stop to bullying.
   c. explain the statistics of recent events.
   d. gain information on employee turnover.
   e. avoid employee absences.

37. The word *coercion* in this passage most likely means
   a. to write a memo.
   b. a new job responsibility.
   c. to lose one's job.
   d. to gain cooperation by force.
   e. a promotion.

38. According to the passage, employee turnover rates are
   a. good for business.
   b. unrelated to anything else.
   c. decreasing each year.
   d. staying about the same.
   e. increasing each year.

39. The most important factor in employee turnover has been
   a. job dissatisfaction.
   b. union agitation.
   c. low pay.
   d. poor health benefits.
   e. It is not stated.

40. The tone of this passage is
   a. businesslike.
   b. humorous.
   c. flippant.
   d. angry.
   e. confrontational.

CHAPTER

1 ▶ Perfecting Your Study Skills

Thomas Edison said, "Genius is 1% inspiration, 99% perspiration." Here is our take on that: "GED exam success is 1% inspiration, 99% *preparation*." As with so many other things in life, the more prepared you are, the more you are likely to succeed. Whether that preparation involves practicing skills, researching information, memorizing lines, or developing a presentation, you make success possible by doing whatever you can to be ready for the situation.

PERFECTING YOUR STUDY SKILLS

▶ Where Do I Start?

Chances are that you already have a crowded to do list, and you may be wondering how you will fit in the time you need to prepare for the GED exam. You have a schedule that may include work and family obligations, so you don't have an unlimited amount of time to prepare. The key is to maximize the study time that you *do* have.

To study means "to give one's attention to learning a subject; to look at with careful attention." Notice that the word *attention* comes up twice in this definition. How you study is as important as how much time you spend studying. To study effectively, you need to focus all your attention on the material, so your preparation time must be quality time. This section of the book will help you determine the study strategies that are right for you. It also will provide you with techniques for overcoming the two most common roadblocks to successful studying: anxiety and distraction.

Visualize Your Future

If you are ready to prepare for the GED exam, you probably have a specific goal in mind—to improve your career, perhaps, or to get into a college or a technical school. It will be helpful to your studying and determination if you can keep your goal in mind at all times.

Let's say, for example, that you want to continue your education in college. Spend an afternoon on the campus of a nearby college and get a feel for student life there. Sit in on a class; attend a sporting event; chat with some students over coffee at the student union. This will help you visualize what it will be like when *you* get into a college program—which can only happen after you have passed your GED.

Perhaps you want to become qualified for a better job at your present place of employment. Spend time thinking what that job would be like on a daily basis; how a better salary will help you; where you'd like to travel on vacations. These desires will become a driving goal which will help you to stay focused and determined in studying for the GED.

Visualization is a powerful tool that motivates you to make your dreams a reality. Once you know where you want to be, spend a little time envisioning yourself there. What are you doing? Giving a presentation? Engaging in a conversation with an admired professor? Listening to an inspired lecture? Go over your vision, keep it in your mind, and use it to reinforce your resolution to study. Sticking to a study plan can be a real challenge. You would often rather be doing other things, and unforeseen obstacles may present themselves. You may be overwhelmed at times with the size of the task, or you may be anxious about your chances for success. These are all common problems. This book will show you how you can overcome them.

▶ I Need a Study Plan

The following pages will help you fine tune your study methods so that you can make the most efficient use of your time. The key to success in this endeavor, as in so many, is to take things one step at a time. Break this giant task down into manageable pieces. Your first step in successful studying is to create a study plan.

What Should I Study?

First, you must decide what you need to study. The pretest at the beginning of this book is designed to help you assess your strengths and weaknesses. If you haven't taken that test, do so now. Once you have completed it, review your answers, making a note of any that you answered incorrectly. Then refer to the chart which follows the pretest; this chart will show you what areas you need to concentrate on in your studies.

What kinds of questions did you miss? What patterns do you see? Do you need to work on understanding poetry? interpreting an author's message? Do nonfiction news articles leave you confused? Can you identify different types of figurative language that is used in literature? Once you are aware of what you know and what you still need to work on, you can effectively prioritize whatever study time you have available. Remember, no matter how you scored on the pretest and no matter what your weaknesses are, you will get better with practice. The more you study and the more effectively you work, the higher you will score on the actual exam.

How Do I Find the Time to Study?

Now is the time to create a realistic study schedule. You might be thinking that your life is too full without cramming in study time, too. But maybe you have more time available than you think. Consider your typical daily and weekly activities and determine when you have free time to devote to studying. Do not forget the short stretches—the 10 minutes here, the 15 minutes there. Sometimes you can do your best studying in short bursts. Make a special study calendar or mark up the calendar you use every day with specified study times to keep yourself on schedule. You might not feel like studying, but if you have it already written down as an obligation, you might be more likely to do it. If you cannot seem to find the time, ask yourself what is more important to you in the long run than achieving your goals. Your life may seem quite full, but you are bound to spend some time at less productive activities, such as watching television. You could use this time to help make your dreams a reality.

I Deserve a Reward

One excellent way to keep motivated is to set up a system of rewards. Write down a list of things that you enjoy; they will be the rewards to give yourself when you reach certain study goals. For example, if you keep your commitment to study for an hour in the evening, you can reward yourself by watching your favorite television show. If you stay on track all week, you can indulge in a Sunday afternoon banana split. Think carefully about what truly motivates you—only *you* know what will keep you on task—and use this strategy throughout your preparation time.

What's My Style?

Another way to make your study time more effective is to think about how you learn the best. We all have certain modes that we employ to make it easier to learn and remember information. Are you a *visual* learner, an *auditory* learner, a *kinesthetic* learner, or a combination of two or all three? Here are some questions to help you determine your dominant learning style(s):

1. If you have to remember an unusual word, you most likely
   a. picture the word in your mind.
   b. repeat the word aloud several times.
   c. trace out the letters with your finger.

2. When you meet new people, you remember them mostly by
   a. their actions and mannerisms.
   b. their names (faces are hard to remember).
   c. their faces (names are hard to remember).

3. In class, you like to
   a. take notes, even if you do not reread them.
   b. listen intently to every word.
   c. sit up close and watch the instructor.

A visual learner would answer **a**, **c**, and **c**. An auditory learner would answer **b**, **b**, and **b**. A kinesthetic learner would answer **c**, **a**, and **a**.

Visual learners like to read and are often good spellers. They may find it hard to follow oral instructions, or even to listen, unless there is something interesting to watch. When visual learners study, they often benefit from graphic organizers such as charts and graphs. Flash cards often appeal to them and help them learn, especially if they use colored markers, which will help them form images in their mind as they learn words or concepts.

Auditory learners, by contrast, like oral directions and may find written materials confusing or boring. They often talk to themselves and may even whisper aloud when they read. They like being read aloud to. Auditory learners will benefit by saying things aloud as they study and by making tapes for themselves and listening to them later. Oral repetition is also an important study tool. Making up rhymes or other oral mnemonic devices will also help them study, and they may like to listen to music as they work.

Kinesthetic learners like to stay on the move. They often find it difficult to sit still for a long time and will often tap their feet and gesticulate a lot while speaking. They tend to learn best by doing rather than observing. Kinesthetic learners may want to walk around as they practice what they are learning, because using their body helps them remember things. Taking notes and making flash cards are important ways of reinforcing knowledge for the kinesthetic learner.

It is important to note that most people learn using a mixture of styles, although they may have a distinct preference for one style over the others. Determine which is your dominant style, but be open to strategies for all types of learners.

▶ I Need a Study Place

So far, you have gathered information about the GED exam, taken a pretest to determine what you need to learn, and thought about techniques that will help you better absorb what you are learning. Now it is time to think about where you are going to work and what kinds of things will enhance your learning experience.

You know that in order to do your best work, especially when you are studying, you need to be focused, alert, and calm. Your undivided attention must be on the task at hand. That means that you have to use a lot of forethought when setting up your study time and environment.

Five Questions about Setting

Ask yourself the following questions to determine the study environment that will be most effective for you.

1. *Where do I like to work? Where do I feel comfortable and free from distractions?*

If you have a desk in your living space, you may be used to studying there, or maybe you usually work at the dining room table or the kitchen counter. If your usual spot is well lit and set up for your comfort and convenience, with all your study materials at hand, then it is an obvious choice for you. However, sometimes it can be hard to avoid distractions in shared living areas.

If you share a living space, you may find it best to study away from home, perhaps at the local library or coffee shop, or to schedule your study time when you know that your study area will be quiet. Remember that you are adding your GED exam preparation time to your usual daily schedule. Will this create any scheduling conflicts with your normal study space?

2. *What time of day is best for me to study? When am I most alert and focused? Are there potential conflicts with other duties or family members that need to be addressed?*

If you are a morning person, it might make sense for you to get up an hour or so earlier than normal while you are preparing for the GED exam. Early mornings are often a time of relative quiet, when you can work without interruptions.

If you do not think so well in the early morning, you can schedule another time of the day as your GED exam study time. Just be sure not to push yourself to stay up extra late in order to study. Studying is only productive if you are focused, and it is difficult to focus when you are tired. (Do not count on caffeine to keep you alert. Caffeine is only a temporary solution that can increase the problem.)

It is wise to establish a consistent time for study if possible (such as Monday through Friday from 7:00 A.M. to 7:30 A.M. and Saturday from 9:00 A.M. to 12:00 noon). Make sure that the people around you are aware that this is your study time. You can expect more support for your efforts if you let family members and friends know that you are working to achieve a goal and that you need to stay focused. Be sure to let them know that you appreciate their support when you receive it.

Set aside a time to study on the same day of the week and time of day that you have scheduled to take the exam. This is the very best time to prepare for the GED exam, especially in the weeks leading up to the test. If you practice taking the test and work on improving your skills on that day and at that time, your mind and your body will be ready to operate at peak efficiency when you really need them. For example, if you are scheduled to take the GED exam on Saturday morning, get into the habit of studying for the test during the actual testing hours.

3. *How do sounds affect my ability to concentrate? Do I prefer silence? Does music enhance my concentration?*

Some people need relative quiet in order to study because most noises distract them. If you are one of these people, you know it by now, and you have strategies that help you achieve the level of silence that you need. Earplugs can be a real blessing. Make sure that your study place and time can accommodate your need for quiet.

Maybe you do not mind a little noise; perhaps you even like music playing in the background while you study. Research has shown that the music of Mozart enhances math performance. Similar results have not been shown for other kinds of music, but if you have music that helps you relax and focus, then make sure that music is on hand when you study. If you have never tried studying to classical music, especially Mozart, now is a good time to try. If you do not think it enhances your concentration, then go back to techniques that work for you. The important thing is to be aware of the effect that sound has on your ability to concentrate. It does not do any good to sit in front of the books and sing along with your favorite CD.

4. *Is the light right? Does my study space have adequate lighting?*

Study lighting needs to be bright enough to read by comfortably. Lighting that is too dim can cause eyestrain and headaches, and can make you sleepy. Lighting that is too bright, though, can make you uncomfortable and make it difficult to relax and focus. You can't control the lighting in many situations, including the exam room itself, but you can create a lighting situation that's right for you when you study.

PERFECTING YOUR STUDY SKILLS

Experts say that the best light for reading comes from behind, falling over your shoulder onto your book. If that isn't a possibility for you, then at least make sure the light falls onto your books, not into your eyes.

5. *What about food? Should I snack while I study? If so, on what?*

Only you can answer these questions. Does food energize you, or does it slow you down while you digest? If you are not sure, pay attention to how your brain and body feel after eating. After a big meal, many people feel sluggish and sleepy as the blood from their brain and muscles goes to the stomach to aid in digestion. If the only time you have to study is right after dinner, you may want to pass on the second helpings and even on dessert so that you will be more alert.

On the other hand, it is also difficult to concentrate when you are hungry. If it has been a while since your last meal, you may want to snack before or as you study. Generally speaking, snacks are fine. However, you want to avoid two categories of foods: sugary snacks (candy, cookies, and ice cream) and caffeinated drinks (coffee, colas, and non-herbal teas).

Sugar surges into your bloodstream quickly, making you feel temporarily energized, but it leaves your bloodstream just as quickly and you experience a rebound effect of feeling more tired than ever. Try keeping track of this effect sometime. See if you can determine how long it takes you to crash after a dose of sugar.

Caffeine is another trickster. In moderation, it produces an effect of alertness, but it is easy to cross the line into being jittery, which makes it hard to focus and be productive. Also, consuming caffeine in the evening can interfere with a good night's sleep, leaving you feeling tired instead of well rested in the morning. It is best to stay away from caffeinated drinks after lunchtime.

▶ The Right Tools

You can spend hours trying to put a nail through a piece of wood with a rock, or you can get the job done in a few minutes with a hammer. The right tools can make all the difference, especially if your time is limited. Fortunately, you already have one of the most important tools for the GED exam: this book, which tells you all about the GED and the information and skills you need to be successful on the exam. You should also assemble some other important study tools and keep them in your GED exam study area:

- a good dictionary, such as *Merriam-Webster's Collegiate® Dictionary, Eleventh Edition*
- a notebook or legal pad dedicated to your GED exam notes
- pencils (and a pencil sharpener) or pens
- a highlighter, or several in different colors
- index or other note cards
- paper clips or sticky note pads for marking pages
- a calendar or PDA (personal digital assistant)

Take the time to choose tools that you will enjoy using; they can be a small daily reward for doing your work. Buy the type of pens that you like the most and select items in your favorite colors.

Information Gathering

As you gather your tangible tools, you also need to gather your intangible tools: the information that you need about the exam so that you can study the right material in the right way at the right time. If you have not already done so, read the Introduction of this book to learn about the GED exam and specifically about the Language Arts, Reading section of the test. The Introduction discusses what kind of test it is and what your scores mean, and where you need to go to get the most up-to-date information on what you need to do to register, when you can take the test, and what the testing center will be like.

Before you begin to work out a study schedule, spend some time going through this book and familiarize yourself with the specific types of literature and reading that you will find on the test. For example, Chapter 3 introduces you to fiction, while Chapter 5 deals with poetry. Perhaps you enjoy reading novels, but poetry has never been of much interest. You might, therefore, want to spend more time on Chapter 5, familiarizing yourself with the various literary techniques involved in poetry, while Chapter 3 would provide more of a brush-up on fiction.

The pretest at the beginning of this book is also a vital tool in this process, as it will show you what areas are your weakest. If you missed questions that deal with the theme of a piece of writing, for example, then Chapter 3 can help you strengthen that weakness.

The Study Plan

You have thought about how, when, and where you will study; you have collected your tools and gathered essential information about the GED exam. Now, you are ready to flesh out your study plan. Here are the steps:

1. *If you have not done so already, take a practice test.* You can use the pretest at the beginning of this book, or take one or more of the tests in LearningExpress's *GED Test Prep*. To create an effective study plan, you need to have a good sense of exactly what you need to study.
2. *Analyze your test results.* How did you do? What areas seem to be your strengths? Your weaknesses? Remember that these are just diagnostic tests, so if your results are not as good as you had hoped, do not be discouraged. You are committing to this study plan because you are going to improve your score. Fear and worry are your enemies here; let go of them. Just look at each question as you score it. Why did you answer that question correctly? Did you know the answer or were you guessing? Why did you miss that question? Was there something that you needed to know that you did not know? If so, what was it? Make a list of the things that you need to know and how many questions you missed because you didn't know them. Think of how your score will improve as you learn these things.
3. *Make a list of your strengths and weaknesses.* This will point you in the right direction. Use your analysis from Step 2 of why you missed questions. Now you know what specific reading skills you need to work on, and you know what test-taking skills you need to improve. Do not forget to congratulate yourself for the areas in which you did well.
4. *Determine your time frame.* Decide how much time you can devote each day and each week to your GED exam preparation. How many weeks are there until the exam? Be realistic about how much time you have available—life will go on, with all its other demands—but do not forget to note when you have a few extra minutes. You will learn how to make good use of small windows of opportunity.

Once you know how much time you have, estimate how long you need to work on each specific task. You may find it useful to break it down by question type (fiction, nonfiction, poetry, and so forth). You may have to prioritize your work in various areas, depending on how much time you have to prepare and in which areas you can most improve your score.

5. *Break it down.* Plan your studying week by week with specific interim goals. For example, "learn everything by April 1" is not a useful plan. But if you plot specific learning goals for each type of literature throughout the month, then your study plan will be a truly useful study guide.

   Let's say, for example, that you have eight weeks until your test date. One way to set up your study schedule is shown below.

   Week One: Learn about and practice reading comprehension skills.
   Week Two: Learn about and read fiction.
   Week Three: Continue with reading comprehension.
   Week Four: Learn about and read poetry.
   Week Five: Learn about and read nonfiction.
   Week Six: Learn about and read drama. Review all reading comprehension skills.
   Week Seven: Do two practice tests from LearningExpress's *GED Test Prep*.
   Week Eight: Review any question types that you do not understand. Get lots of rest!

   Naturally, if you have longer than eight weeks to prepare, your weekly schedule will be broken up differently. (And good for you for starting ahead of time!) You may want to work on all your skills each week, making progress simultaneously on all fronts. That is fine too. Adjust the schedule accordingly.

6. *Just Do It!* Stick to your plan. It is easy to say, but difficult to do. How can you stay motivated? How do you follow your schedule so that you do not fall behind? How do you keep from thinking about other things when you are supposed to be working? These are the really big questions, and there are no easy answers. The following sections discuss some tried-and-true techniques for maintaining self-motivation. Now you have to see what works for you.

▶ You Are Worth It: Motivational and Relaxation Techniques That Work

Whenever you find yourself tempted to give up your hard work for an hour or two of entertainment, remind yourself that many people never reach their goals because they seem so far away and difficult to achieve. It is important that you break down your preparation for the GED exam into small, manageable steps. It's also important to keep in mind why you are working so hard.

Remember your visualization about getting into college or landing a better job? The more often you practice that visualization, the more real it becomes to you. The more real it is, the more clearly you will see that your goal is within your grasp. Just stick to your plan, and take things one day at a time.

Sometimes your study plans are derailed for legitimate reasons. You get sick; a family member needs your help; your teacher or boss assigns a project that takes more time than you expected. Life happens, but don't let it discourage you; just pick up where you left off. Maybe you can squeeze in a little extra study time later. Keep working toward your goal.

One Step at a Time

Many people get discouraged when the task seems too big; they feel that they will never get to the end. That's why it's a good idea to break down all big undertakings, such as this one, into smaller, manageable tasks. Set small goals for yourself, such as "this week I will learn more about drama." "Learning more about drama" is a much more manageable task than "preparing for the GED exam"—even though it moves you in the same direction. Establish positive momentum and maintain it, one step at a time. That is how you get where you want to go.

Because You Deserve It
Don't forget to reward yourself for your progress. Your daily reward can be a small one, such as sending off a few chatty e-mails or paging through your favorite magazine. Your weekly reward might be something larger, such as buying a CD that you have wanted or renting a favorite film. Your biggest reward, of course, is being able to live out the dreams that you have visualized.

Reach Out
Another way to motivate yourself is to get other people to help you. Everybody likes being asked to help someone—it makes those around you feel important, especially when they are being approached for their expertise in a particular area. You will often be more motivated when studying means that you also get to be with people whose company you enjoy.

You may want to form a study group with one or more of your friends. Maybe reading informational literature, such as news magazines, just comes naturally to you, but you struggle with reading drama. Chances are that you have a friend who likes Shakespeare, but who may need help with reading comprehension skills. You could agree to get together once a week or so for a tutoring and drilling session. You take one subject to study and explain, while your friend explains a different subject to you. Now you are benefiting from your friend's expertise, reinforcing what you know by explaining it to someone else, having more fun than you would on your own, and helping yourself (and your friend) stay motivated to study.

Thought Police
Finally, as you struggle to stay motivated, it helps to check in periodically with your thoughts—the things that you sometimes find yourself thinking when you should be focusing on your work. If you sit down to study, thinking to yourself, "Oh boy, I'll have that last piece of chocolate when I finish this," you are in good shape. If you are thinking, "A TV show that I really like is on now," or "I could get in a few hoops before dark," you could be headed for trouble. It's not that there's anything wrong with television or basketball; it is just that you promised yourself that you would work right now. Often, just noticing such thoughts is enough to keep them in check. "Good try," you can tell yourself, "but you have other commitments, buster!"

If this doesn't work and you are still tempted to ignore your scheduled study time, sit down and think for a moment about why you are working so hard. Use your visualization. Promise yourself a bigger reward than usual when you finish your work. You can do it because you want to do it. This is the person that you want to be: disciplined, focused, and successful.

Another strategy is to trick yourself into a study mode. Start with something easy, such as a brief review of what you have already learned. Starting with a quick and easy task will often ease you into the work and motivate you to continue with your self-assigned task of the day. A review will also reinforce what you already know.

Take Care of Yourself
You may have noticed that the last thing on the sample study plan is "get lots of rest." During the last few days before the exam, you should ease up on your study schedule. The natural tendency for many people is to cram. Maybe that strategy has worked for you with other exams, but it is not a good idea with the GED exam. Cramming tends to raise your anxiety level, and your brain doesn't do its best work when

you are anxious. Anxiety produces a fight-or-flight response that sends blood away from the brain to the arms and legs, in case we need to defend ourselves or run away. Without a good supply of oxygen-carrying blood, your brain won't be able to think as well as it should, so it's important to reduce your anxiety about the GED exam by relaxing and changing your anxious attitude to one of calm self-assurance.

How to Relax

If you want to do productive work the night before the GED exam, spend the time working on your confidence ("I have worked hard and I will do well"). Visualize your goal—really see yourself there. Here are some other relaxation techniques that you can use if you find yourself feeling anxious at any time before or during the GED exam:

1. *Breathe.* When most people think about breathing, they think about inhaling. However, when you want to relax, it's more important to focus on breathing out. You want to be sure that you are exhaling completely. It's also important to breathe deeply and to use abdominal breathing rather than shallow chest breathing. Try this: Place one hand on your stomach and the other hand on your chest. Sit up straight. Now inhale deeply through your nose. Try to move your stomach as much as possible and your chest as little as possible. Exhale and feel your stomach deflate. Again, your chest should hardly move. Count slowly as you breathe to make sure that you spend at least as much time breathing out as you do breathing in. This kind of breathing relaxes you. It gets rid of carbon dioxide that can otherwise get trapped in the bottom of your lungs. You can practice this deep breathing anytime, anywhere you need to relax.

2. *Tense and relax your muscles.* As your anxiety mounts, your muscles tense, just in case they are going to be called on to fight or flee. Of course, in the case of the GED exam, you have to fight with your brain, and running away would result in a very low score. So the best thing you can do is to relax. It can be hard to know which muscles are tensed. Many people hold tension in their shoulders or their jaws and are never even aware that it's there. It's helpful to start with your toes and work your way up through all the muscle groups, first tensing (really tightly!) and then relaxing each muscle group. (Tense your toes, and relax. Tense your feet, and relax. Tense your calves, and relax . . .) Don't forget your facial muscles, especially your jaw.

3. *Visualize.* This is a different exercise from your goal visualization. This time, imagine yourself in a favorite place, a place you find especially soothing and pleasant. It could be a real place or one found only in your imagination. Focus on the sensations of your special place—what does it feel like, look like, or sound like? You want to feel as though you are really there. Take a few minutes just to relax in this place. It's there for you any time you need it, and it will always help you to be calm and focused.

▶ Learning Strategies and Test-Taking Techniques

Sometimes you just get lucky, and this is one of those times. Why? Because the following study techniques are also strategies that will help you when you take the GED exam. The more you practice them before the exam, the more natural they will be on test day.

Be an Active Reader

Being an active reader means *interacting* with what you read. Ask questions. Make notes. Mark up passages. Don't be a passive reader, just looking at words. Be a thinker and a doer. This is not only a study strategy; it's also an important technique for the GED exam's reading comprehension questions and an essential skill in life. Of course, for the GED, you won't be marking on the actual passage. Therefore, you may want to practice making notes on a separate piece of paper as you read. You should jot down key words, main ideas, and your own reactions to and questions about what you read. On test day, you will write on the scratch paper provided by the test center. You are allowed as much of this paper as you need, so use it.

Ask Questions

When you read a passage, such as the ones on the GED exam, ask yourself the following questions:

1. What is this passage about?
2. What is the main idea?
3. What is the author's point of view or purpose in writing this?
4. What is the meaning of this word in this sentence?
5. Is the author stating a fact or expressing an opinion?
6. Is this sentence part of the main idea, or is it a detail?
7. How does the author support the argument?
8. Why does the author draw this particular conclusion?
9. What does this passage suggest about the topic, the author, the future?

The more difficult the passage is, the more crucial it is that you ask these questions (and even more questions) about anything you don't understand. Think about a question as a clue to the answer. When you have asked the right questions, you are halfway to the right answer. These are the kinds of questions that you will need to ask in order to answer the exam questions correctly. In college and in many careers, you will use the same questioning technique to help you comprehend densely written material (of which you will see plenty). It's essential that you practice asking and answering these questions. Quickly— what is the main idea of this passage? Until you become very skilled at asking and answering questions about what you have read, it's a good idea to actually write questions out for yourself. For one thing, the act of writing helps you remember what questions to ask, especially for kinesthetic and visual learners. If you are an auditory learner, you will want to repeat them aloud as you write.

Mark It Up

Get in the habit of highlighting and underlining when you read. When you open your book, pick up your pen, pencil, or highlighter. When you see a main idea, mark it. If you come across an unfamiliar word or a word used in an unfamiliar context, mark it. However, the trick is to be selective. If you are marking too much of the passage, important information and key ideas will not stand out. You need to practice distinguishing between main and supporting details. (You will learn how in Chapter 2.)

You can practice asking questions and marking main ideas and supporting details by going through the sample test passages in this book and in LearningExpress's *GED Test Prep*. Check yourself by looking at the questions about those passages. How well do your ideas match up with the questions about the passages? Check your answers. Were they correct? If not, why not?

On the GED, you will write the key words and ideas on your scratch paper. You may want to prepare by practicing this technique as you study for the test. Of course, you will also want to practice it with any borrowed books that you use, such as library books.

Make Notes

Don't just *take* notes; *make* them. Making notes requires you to think about what you are reading. Asking questions, such as the ones mentioned previously, is one way to make notes. Another kind of note-making involves recording your reactions to what you are reading. For example, you may disagree with an author's opinion; if so, write down your reaction. Be sure to say why you disagree or agree, or why you are confused. When you read the kinds of challenging materials that you will find on the GED exam, it should be more like a conversation between you and the author than an author's monologue. So what if the author can't hear you? You can still hold up your end of the conversation. It will be more interesting for you, and you will get more out of what you read.

Make Connections

Another way of interacting with the material that you study is to relate it to what you already know. For example, if you are trying to learn the word *demographic*, you may know that *democracy* refers to government run by the *people*, while *graphic* refers to *information*, written or drawn. Then you can remember that *demographic* has to do with information about people.

Making connections differentiates *remembering* from *memorizing*. In the short run, it may seem easier just to memorize a word or a fact, but unless you understand what you are learning—unless you have connected it to what you already know—you are likely to forget it again. Then you will have wasted your study time and failed to improve your test score. Memorized information gets stored in your short-term memory, which means that it's forgotten within a few days or even a few hours. Your long-term memory has to file new information to fit in with your existing information. That means that you have to create connections to what you already know.

Break It Up

You do not train to run a marathon by waiting until the last minute and then running 20 miles a day for five days before the race. Similarly, you cannot effectively prepare for the GED exam by waiting until the last minute to study. Your brain works best when you give it a relatively small chunk of information, let it rest and process, and then give it another small chunk.

When you are studying the various elements of fiction, for example, don't try to memorize the whole list at once. The most efficient way to learn is to take two or three elements—such as characterization and symbolism—and make sure that you fully understand them before tackling the next. Making some kind of connection among the elements in each literary type will help you remember them. For example, you see the connection between plot development within fiction, and its use in drama.

Flash cards are a great study aid for the GED exam. The act of writing on the cards engages your kinesthetic learning ability. Seeing the cards uses your visual learning, and reading the cards aloud sets up auditory learning. Flash cards are also extremely portable and flexible in the ways they can be used and help you work on small chunks of material at a time. For example, you can pull them out while you wait for the bus, or look through a few while eating breakfast.

Remember, your brain works best when you give it small, frequent assignments and then give it time to process each one. Recent scientific studies show that sleep helps the brain process what it has learned. In other words, if you study before bed, when you wake up, you will know more than you did before you went to sleep. It's just one more reason for getting a good night's rest.

On the actual exam, it is important to give yourself permission to take a mini-break whenever you need it. If you need to stretch after every question, that's okay. A quick stretch or a deep breath and forceful exhalation can do wonders to keep you focused and relaxed.

Testing Psychology

As you already know, it's important to review reading comprehension techniques, improve your critical reasoning skills, and review the different types of literature (fiction, poetry, and so on) as you prepare for the GED exam—but it's not sufficient to do *only* these things. Like all standardized tests, the GED exam also measures your test-taking skills. In this section, you will learn some of the best test-taking strategies for success on the GED exam.

Get Familiar with the Exam to Combat Fear

In the previous sections, you learned that fear or anxiety is your enemy on the GED exam. What happens when you are feeling fearful or anxious? Your heart starts pounding, sending blood away from your brain to your limbs. Maybe you start feeling a little lightheaded, a little disconnected, or even a little woozy. Are you in good condition for test taking then? Of course not!

There is much truth in the saying that we fear what we don't understand. Therefore, the best way to overcome the anxiety that keeps you from doing your best on the GED exam is to learn as much as you can about the test. The more you know about what to expect, the more practice you have with the exam, the more relaxed you will be, and the better you will perform on test day.

Another way to eliminate a source of test-day anxiety is to familiarize yourself with the location of your official testing site. Take a drive there before test day, so you are familiar with the route.

Taking practice tests and working with the tips and strategies in this book will help you immensely. You will get used to the kinds of questions on the GED exam and learn how to maximize your chances of answering them correctly. You will build on what you already know and enhance the skill sets that you need for GED exam success. By the time you enter the testing center, you will be familiar with the format of the test and prepared for the length of the exam with strategies to help you succeed.

How to De-Stress

It is one thing to be told not to worry, and another thing to *actually* not worry. How can you stop yourself from worrying? You can start by replacing worried and anxious thoughts and actions with positive ones. The following sections examine some techniques.

Nip It in the Bud

What are you worried about? Maybe you are worried that you don't have enough time to prepare for the test, or perhaps you are afraid that you won't do well on the exam. That leads to anxiety about not getting into the right school or job. Pretty soon, you are convinced that your life is basically ruined, so why not just turn on the TV and resign yourself to a low-paying, dead-end job? Sounds silly when you put it that way, right? But fear has a way of escalating when you do not control it.

The best way to beat test anxiety is to *prevent* it. Don't let it get a grip on you. Whenever you catch yourself worrying or thinking anxious thoughts about the GED exam, firmly tell yourself that you have nothing to worry about because you are preparing for GED exam success. Of course, for that strategy to work, you have to establish and stick to your study plan. Therefore, beating test anxiety is made up of two components: *thinking* and *doing*.

Just Do It

Half the battle with test anxiety is how you *think* about the test and what kinds of messages you are giving yourself about the exam. The other half is what you *do* to prepare. These two halves are interrelated: If you are paralyzed by negative thoughts ("I'm not ready; I don't have enough time; I'm not smart enough; I don't want to think about the GED exam"), you are going to have a hard time getting yourself to do the work that you need to do.

On the other hand, if you can somehow get yourself to stop thinking those unproductive thoughts, you can start preparing. The very act of doing something makes you feel better and leads to more positive thoughts, which makes it easier to continue working.

Therefore, it makes sense to just begin work. Start by making a study plan based on the times you have available to study and on your assessment of your practice test results (see the section *The Study Plan* earlier in this chapter). Creating a study plan is easy. You have time to do it. Once you have it in place, you just follow it. You choose success. If you have not already made your study plan, what are you waiting for?

Once you have created a study plan, stick to it as though you had no choice. Of course, you do have a choice. You are choosing how you want your future to unfold. You are doing this for yourself.

Face Your Fears

Different people have different ways of manifesting test anxiety. You may deal with anxiety by working yourself into a frenzy, limiting yourself to six hours of sleep, and refusing to engage in leisure activities so that you can get more work done. Meanwhile, your anxiety level mounts. Or you may take the opposite approach and put off work because the task seems so large and the time available so short. Of course, the more you procrastinate, the shorter the time becomes. You end up feeling more anxious, so you avoid working and your anxiety level mounts. These two approaches are like two sides of the same coin, and the denomination of the coin is *fear*. Before you can get work done, you have to face your fears. Admitting that you are worried about the GED exam is the first step toward overcoming those fears.

It can be helpful to write about your anxiety. Start with the basic fear: You are worried that you don't have enough time to prepare. Once you have written that fear down, you can come up with a way to eliminate it. Prioritize what you want to study so that you work on the most important skills first. (Start by working your way through this book.) Look at your schedule again. Where can you squeeze in more study time? Remember that flash cards can be studied any time you have one free minute!

Maybe you've already allowed your anxieties to roam out of bounds by speculating about what would happen if you don't do well on the GED exam. Now you are seeing that this is a mistake, so go ahead and write down your fears of failure. What would happen? Would low scores keep you out of college? No. Perhaps you wouldn't get into your first choice program, but some things in life can't be predicted. If you think hard enough, you can surely remember a time when things didn't work out the way that you wanted them to, but they turned out for the best anyway. It's good to make plans and work to achieve your goals, but it's also important to put your goals and plans in perspective.

If you didn't get into your first choice school, would you be a less worthy person? No. Would your family stop loving you? No. Would the world come crashing down around you? Of course not.

Thinking about your fears in this way helps keep them in perspective. You know that the GED exam is serious business; that's why you are preparing for it. But if you can persuade yourself to think about it as a game that you want to play, you can control your fear and replace it with a simple, burning desire to win. You have nothing to be afraid of now. You just practice and prepare so that you will succeed on the test.

Stay Healthy

If you were preparing to run a marathon, you would be thinking about how to take care of your body. You would want to eat well, get enough rest, and condition your body for its endurance test. Taking the GED exam is much like running a marathon. You will need to perform at your mental maximum on test day. Your body and your mind both need to be ready. Here are the basics of caring for your marathon machine.

1. *Get enough rest.* Some people need more sleep than others. You know how much sleep you need to feel rested. Is it eight hours, or do you need more? Is six enough, or does that make you feel like a zombie the next day? Regardless of your individual need, make sure that you leave yourself enough time every day to get enough sleep. It's also important to remember that too much sleep can leave you feeling as groggy as too little sleep. Get the amount that you need to feel rested and no more. The best time of the week to study for the GED exam is Saturday morning, so do not sleep through that valuable time. If you regularly get up on Saturday morning and sit down to take a practice test, you will be ready to do your very best when exam day comes.

If you find yourself having trouble sleeping, first establish a bedtime routine. Maybe a warm bath or a glass of warm milk helps you relax. Whatever you do, do not get interested in a good book just before bed. Anxious thoughts can also keep you awake, so bedtime is a good time to practice a calming visualization or a series of visualizations using the techniques previously discussed.

Finally, if nothing seems to be helping you fall asleep, just get up and study. If you cannot sleep, you might as well be productive.

2. *Eat well.* Athletes have to pay attention to what they eat. A marathon runner, for example, maintains a healthy diet during training as well as just before the race. Your brain also needs good food to function at its peak.

A well-balanced diet based on the food pyramid will keep your body and brain in top form. You are better off avoiding fast food laden with grease, sugar, and empty calories. Rather than junk food snacks, try substituting the following:

INSTEAD OF	EAT/DRINK
doughnuts	low-sugar, multigrain cereal
chips	carrot sticks
cookies	natural granola bar
ice cream	lowfat yogurt
soda	fruit juice
coffee	herbal tea

PERFECTING YOUR STUDY SKILLS

Remember that caffeine interferes with sleep when consumed past midafternoon. It is also an addictive substance that tricks you into feeling more alert. If you feel that you need coffee, maybe what you need is more rest.

3. *Exercise.* Unless you have a daily workout routine, you may not be meeting your body's need for exercise. Our bodies appreciate a good aerobic workout every day. Exercise helps you sleep more soundly and feel more relaxed throughout the day. Vigorous exercise is a great way to combat anxiety because it releases endorphins, the body's natural feel-good chemical.

Light exercise, such as a walk, can also double as study time. You can study your flash cards during a walk around the neighborhood. You can record information to listen to as you run through the park. Get in the habit of identifying times when you can double up on studying and another activity to maximize your productivity.

If you take care of your body and brain by getting enough sleep, eating healthfully, and exercising adequately, your body and brain will take good care of you on the GED exam. You are in training now: Get with the program.

▶ Multiple-Choice Strategies

As we noted earlier, the GED exam, like all standardized tests, will measure your academic knowledge and skills, and it will also measure your test-taking skills. Fortunately, you can use specific strategies on standardized tests to help you determine the right answers to multiple-choice questions on the exam.

Avoid Distracters

All of the questions in the Language Arts, Reading part of the GED exam are multiple-choice questions. The good news about multiple-choice questions is that they provide you with the answer. The bad news is that the GED almost always provides *distracters* in addition to the correct answer. Distracters are wrong answers designed to look like possible right answers. Here is an overview of the technique for avoiding distracters:

1. *Read the question carefully.* Be sure that you know *exactly* what is being asked. Many test takers miss questions on the GED exam because they try to answer a question other than the one that is being asked. In particular, look for wording such as "All of the following conclusions can logically be drawn from the passage EXCEPT." Train yourself to notice any word in the question that is in all capital letters. Such a word will often completely change the meaning of the question. In the previous example, if you did not notice the word EXCEPT, you would look for answers that are logical conclusions drawn from the passage, when you should be looking for the one answer that is *not* a logical conclusion you can draw from the text.

2. *Write down the key words and phrases in the question.* These are words and phrases that help you pick the one correct answer. Think of them as clues, and think of yourself as a detective who must examine each question closely for clues to the correct answer. For example, you might have a reading comprehension passage about improvements in bicycle safety and then the question "The modern bicycle has all the following safety features EXCEPT . . ." The key words are *modern*, *safety features*, and *EXCEPT*. After you mark these words and phrases, look

in the passage for the safety features of the modern bicycle, then choose the answer that is *not* mentioned in the passage as a safety feature of the modern bicycle.

3. *Rule out incorrect answers.* In the previous example, as you identify safety features of the modern bicycle from the passage, you will mark them off as choices. Consider setting up your scratch paper with choices **a** through **e**. If you actually mark an answer as you eliminate it from your choices, you will know that it is not the answer and will not waste time mistakenly considering it again. You may only be able to eliminate one or two incorrect answers, but every wrong answer that you eliminate increases your chances of picking the correct answer.

4. *Watch out for absolutes.* One type of distracter question uses an absolute word such as *always*, *never*, *all*, or *none* within an answer. It is *possible* to find a correct answer that uses such an absolute, but if you are unsure, it is wise to avoid an answer that uses one of these words.

To Guess or Not to Guess?

If you do not know the answer to a question, skip it and come back to it later. Once you have completed all the answers that you *do* know, return to the ones that you left blank. It is important to know that there is no penalty for getting an answer wrong, so you should never leave any question blank. If you don't know, guess. You have a 20% chance of getting a right answer if you just randomly guess, and you increase those odds when you can eliminate some answers that you think are wrong. No matter what the question is, you should be able to eliminate one or two options. If you must guess between two or three possible answers instead of five, you dramatically increase your chances of answering correctly.

▶ The Endgame

If you are reading these words several weeks or more before you take the GED exam, you may want to bookmark this page and come back to it the week before the test. Your study routine during the last week before the exam should vary from your study routine of the preceding weeks.

The Final Week

Exactly one week before you take the GED exam is a good time for your final practice test. Then you can use the next few days to wrap up any loose ends. You should also read back over your notes on test-taking tips and techniques at this time.

During the final week, however, it is also a good idea to cut back on your study schedule. Cramming now will only make you feel less prepared and more anxious. As mentioned previously, anxiety is your enemy when it comes to test taking. It is also your enemy when it comes to restful sleep, and it's extremely important that you be well rested and relaxed on test day.

You want to substitute more visualization and relaxation for studying. Visualize yourself sitting in the testing center, working your way through the exam in a calm and focused manner, buoyed by the confidence that you have prepared for this exam. You remain confident even though you don't know all the answers. When you don't know an answer, you apply the techniques that you practiced as you worked your way through this book. Picture yourself smiling and stretching as you finish the exam, feeling good about the work that you have done. Then imagine the reward that you have waiting for yourself after the test. Don't forget to tell yourself out loud, especially if you are an auditory learner, how proud you are of your hard work and how confident you are of your success. If you sound unsure of yourself at first, repeat your words until you sound convincing—then you will believe yourself.

During that last week before the exam, make sure that you know where you are taking the test. If it is an unfamiliar place, take a test drive so that you will know how much time you need to get there, where you can park, and how far you will have to walk from the parking lot to the testing center. Do this in order to avoid a last-minute rush to the test, which would create additional anxiety.

Be sure to get adequate exercise during this last week. It will help you sleep soundly, and exercise also helps rid your body and mind of the effects of anxiety. However, don't tackle any new physical skills or overdo any old ones. You don't want to be sore and uncomfortable on test day.

Check to see that your test appointment confirmation and your forms of personal identification are in order and ready to go. You will not need anything else because you are not allowed to bring anything other than your pencils in with you to the testing area.

T-Minus One

It's the day before the GED exam. You have done your preparation, and you are as ready as you are going to be. Here are some dos and don'ts for this final part of the countdown:

Do

1. Relax!
2. Find something amusing to do the night before—watch a good movie, have dinner with a friend, or read a good book.
3. Get some light exercise. Walk, dance, swim, or stretch.
4. Get all of your test materials together: confirmation of your appointment and proper identification, and your sharpened number two pencils.
5. Practice your visualization of GED exam success.
6. Go to bed early. Get a good night's sleep.

Don't

1. Study. You have prepared. Now relax.
2. Party. Keep it low key.
3. Eat anything unusual or adventurous—save it!
4. Try any unusual or adventurous activity—save it!
5. Allow yourself to get into an emotional exchange with anyone—a sibling, a friend, a parent, or a spouse. If someone starts something, remind him that you have a GED exam to take tomorrow and you need to postpone the discussion so that you can focus on the test.

Test Day

On the day of the test, get up early enough to allow yourself extra time to get ready. If you have a morning appointment, set your alarm and ask a family member or friend to make sure that you are up. Even if your appointment is later, make sure that you don't sleep longer than you usually do. Too much sleep can actually make you feel tired all day.

Eat a light, healthy breakfast, even if you usually don't eat in the morning. If you do usually eat breakfast, eat whatever you normally eat. Remember that sugary foods are likely to let you down during the exam. Protein, which can be found in eggs and cheese, is more apt to keep on giving your brain fuel throughout the test. If you do not normally drink coffee, don't do it today. If you do normally have coffee, have one cup. More than that may make you jittery.

If you have scheduled an afternoon test, eat a light but satisfying lunch. Be sure not to stuff yourself before going in. Digestion drains blood from your brain, so it is best to eat at least an hour before exam time. Again, it's best to eat protein because that will give you sustained energy. Stay away from sugar—you can always promise yourself a sweet treat after the test.

Give yourself plenty of time to get to the testing center and avoid a last-minute rush. Plan to get there at least 15 minutes early.

Once you are settled at the test center, you will have as much time as you need to run through the testing procedures. They will be identical to the ones that you have practiced in this book. Just before you begin the actual test is a good time to visualize success one more time. Remember to breathe. Inhale fully into your abdomen and exhale at least as fully. If you feel your body tensing up, practice your relaxation exercises by tensing and releasing muscle groups to help them relax. Breathe.

Once the exam begins, quickly skim the directions. You will already know what to do, so a quick scan of the directions is all you need to make sure that nothing has changed.

If you find yourself getting anxious during the test, remember to breathe. If you need to, take a minute or two to slip into your relaxation visualization or your visualization of success. You have worked hard to prepare for this day. You are ready.

After the GED Exam
Celebrate! Reward yourself for a job well done.

▶ In a Nutshell

As you go through this review book, as you make your study plan, and as you prepare to take the GED exam, always remember why you are doing these things. You are doing them for your future and for your dreams, whatever they may be. Whenever you hit a snag, when you feel weary and unmotivated and are tempted to give up, remember why you committed yourself to this path. Call up the vision of yourself, with college degree in hand or doing the job of your dreams. Only you can make that vision a reality, but this book is here to help you take your first step. Read on.

CHAPTER 2
Reading Comprehension Strategies

Before considering the various types of literature that you'll find on the GED, you should start with some basic concepts on reading comprehension. The following chapters will address poetry and fiction and so forth, but those chapters will build on this chapter—you need the basic skills of reading comprehension before getting into the specifics of literary genres.

In this chapter, you will learn the six basic tools that are vital in understanding anything that you read:

1. determining main ideas and themes
2. identifying supporting facts and details of a main idea
3. distinguishing between facts and opinions
4. making inferences
5. identifying cause-and-effect relationships
6. understanding words in context

READING COMPREHENSION STRATEGIES

You will actually use these basic skills whenever you read virtually anything: fact, fiction, poetry, newspaper articles, and just about anything else. These form the basic toolbox of reading, so it will be important that you master these skills before proceeding to the next chapter.

▶ Determining Main Ideas and Themes

In order to understand the main idea of a passage, you must first understand the difference between the passage's *topic* and the point that it's making—or its main idea. Consider the following passage, and ask yourself these questions: What is this passage talking about? What point is the author trying to make?

> There are many different types of paint available today, from latex house paint to lacquer paints used on car bodies to the oil paints used by artists to paint great masterpieces on canvas. Selecting the right paint to use for your hobby can be a difficult matter if you don't know that different paints have different purposes for which they are designed. When painting miniature lead soldiers, for example, you would want to use paints that are specifically designed for use on metal. The selection is further complicated, however, by the fact that even metal paints are available in a variety of formats. You would need to choose between acrylic paints, which clean off with plain water, and enamel paints which require paint thinner to clean your brushes. Understanding the strengths and weaknesses of each type of paint will make your job much easier.

This passage is about paint, so paint is the topic of the selection. But paint is not the point that the author is making. The author is explaining that there are many different types of paint, and that each type has a specific application.

So the topic of this passage is what the author is talking about in general terms, while the main point is the idea that he is trying to get across—in this case, his main point is that it's important to select the right type of paint for your project.

One way to distinguish between topic and main idea is to ask yourself, What is the author trying to prove here? A main idea is generally an opinion or assertion that the writer is making, something that needs to be proven. In this passage, the writer is trying to prove that you must use the correct type of paint on your project, whether you're painting your house or working with miniature lead soldiers.

This concept of proving a point is important, and will lead into the next skill as you learn to identify the points of proof which an author provides in supporting the main idea—the supporting facts and details. These supporting details will often follow a main topic statement, so let's consider how to identify topic sentences.

Topic versus Main Idea

Topic: the general subject matter that a passage discusses

Main Idea: the point that an author tries to prove, something that is open to debate

Topic Sentences

The topic sentence of a paragraph or passage is frequently the very first sentence—frequently, but not always. So you cannot just assume that the first sentence in a paragraph is the topic sentence.

The topic sentence will lay out the general topic of a passage (which is why it's called the topic sentence), while other sentences will provide greater detail and proof of the topic sentence. Look again at the preceding passage about paints, and find the topic sentence in that paragraph.

> **Topic Sentences**
>
> A topic sentence identifies the topic of a paragraph. The topic sentence of a paragraph, however, may or may not be the topic of the passage as a whole—it might just be the topic of that particular paragraph.

Which of the following sentences is the topic sentence in the painting paragraph?

- a. "There are many different types of paint available today . . ."
- b. "Selecting the right paint to use for your hobby can be a difficult matter . . ."
- c. "When painting miniature lead soldiers, for example . . ."
- d. "You would need to choose between acrylic paints . . ."
- e. "Understanding the strengths and weaknesses of each type of paint will make your job much easier."

The first sentence, choice **a**, is introducing the topic of the passage, which is paint. Therefore, **a** is the correct choice. Notice that all the other sentences make statements of opinion—such as "selecting the right paint can be a difficult matter"—and therefore, they are too specific to be the topic. Such specific statements are the main idea, the point that the author is trying to prove, whereas the topic is whatever general thing the main idea is about—in this case, paint. The main idea is also often a general idea that needs details to support it. Both the main idea and the topic are general. The difference between the two is that while the topic is merely the subject of the passage, the main idea is the point that the author is making about that subject.

This leads us to the next type of sentence: the thesis statement.

Thesis Statements

A topic sentence introduces the general topic of a passage, while a thesis statement makes a point that must be proven. As we've already seen, the topic sentence of the passage about paint was the first sentence in the paragraph, which introduced the topic of paint.

But the thesis statement is the sentence in that paragraph which makes a claim that could be considered a matter of opinion, an idea that must be proven. In our paint passage, the thesis statement is actually the very last sentence: *Understanding the strengths and weaknesses of each type of paint will make your job much easier.*

A thesis is an idea, a proposition, a matter of opinion that can be debated. In the example under consideration, a person might conceivably argue that understanding the strengths and weaknesses of paint is actually not helpful to a hobbyist; it is a matter of opinion whether or not understanding paint will help you with any given project. This sentence, in other words, presents an opinion which is open to debate and requires support. This is what distinguishes a main idea (stated in the thesis statement) and a topic (introduced in the topic sentence).

As a general rule, the thesis statement is the main idea of a passage, so once you have identified the thesis statement, you've also identified the main idea.

> **Thesis Statements**
>
> The author's clear statement of a debatable point, a matter of opinion as opposed to a statement of fact, the thesis statement is something that the author needs to prove.

Practicing Main Ideas and Themes

Try your hand at identifying the topic and main idea for each of the following passages. Underline the topic and circle the main idea in each passage as you read it through; this will help you in answering the questions.

Passage 1

Reading is an important part of life. Critical reading, however, is a demanding process. To read critically, you must slow down your reading and perform specific operations on the text—with pencil in hand. Mark up the text with your reactions, conclusions, and questions. When you read, become an active participant.

1. The topic of this passage is
   a. how to pass reading tests.
   b. the hard work of critical reading.
   c. reading.
   d. a pencil is an important tool when reading.
   e. active participation is essential when reading.

2. This paragraph best supports the statement that
   a. critical reading is a slow, dull, but essential process.
   b. the best critical reading happens at critical times in a person's life.
   c. readers should get in the habit of questioning the truth of what they read.
   d. critical reading requires thoughtful and careful attention.
   e. critical reading should take place at the same time each day.

Passage 2

The Fourth Amendment to the Constitution protects citizens against unreasonable searches and seizures. No search of a person's home or personal effects may be conducted without a written search warrant issued on probable cause. This means that a neutral judge must approve the factual basis justifying a search before it can be conducted.

3. This paragraph best supports the statement that the police cannot search a person's home or private papers unless they have
   a. legal authorization.
   b. direct evidence of a crime.
   c. read the person his or her constitutional rights.
   d. a reasonable belief that a crime has occurred.
   e. requested that a judge be present.

4. The topic of this paragraph is
   a. the Constitution of the United States.
   b. the Fourth Amendment to the Constitution.
   c. a judge's role in search and seizure.
   d. the origin of search warrants.
   e. factual bases for search warrants.

Passage 3

Mathematics allows us to expand our consciousness. Mathematics tells us about economic trends, patterns of disease, and the growth of populations. Math is good at exposing the truth, but it can also perpetuate misunderstandings and untruths. Figures have the power to mislead people.

5. This paragraph best supports the statement that
   a. the study of mathematics is dangerous.
   b. words are more truthful than figures.
   c. the study of mathematics is more important than other disciplines.
   d. the power of numbers is that they cannot lie.
   e. figures are sometimes used to deceive people.

6. The topic of this paragraph is
   a. truth.
   b. expanded consciousness.
   c. using math to mislead.
   d. how math can help society.
   e. mathematics.

Finding the Main Idea in Nonfiction

Most works of nonfiction that you will encounter are intended to persuade the reader of some point or opinion. Some writing may seem purely objective—news articles, for example—but in reality, even newspapers and magazines are presenting information that could be debated. This type of writing is therefore called *persuasive writing*.

Persuasive writing often follows a simple pattern, in which the author presents his or her opinion and then supports that opinion with details that prove the opinion to be true. Later in this chapter we will discuss these supporting details more, but for now it's important to know how to use supporting details to find a passage's main idea.

The following diagram will help to illustrate the pattern that you will notice in most nonfiction writing.

READING COMPREHENSION STRATEGIES

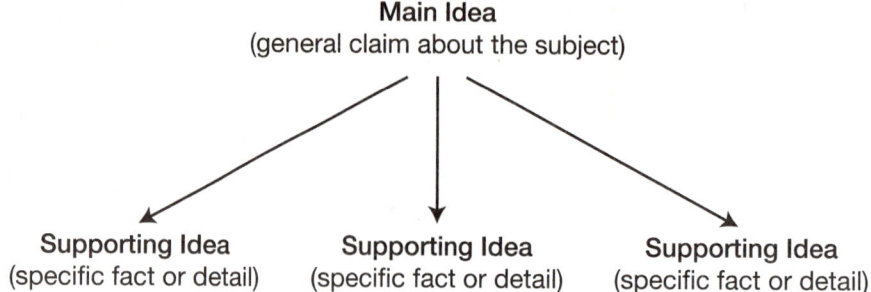

Most nonfiction passages that you'll encounter on the GED Language Arts, Reading exam will follow this basic pattern. The author will state a main idea, and then support that idea with evidence to prove that it's true. You must be on guard, however, because sometimes the main idea will be stated at the end or even in the middle of a paragraph—not necessarily at the very beginning. But as you learn to recognize supporting data, you will also gain the ability to quickly spot the main idea.

Read the following paragraph, underline supporting details, and circle the main idea.

> Automobile airbags have been known to knock passengers unconscious, and can even threaten the life of a child when they deploy. Airbags expand at such a rapid pace, with such tremendous velocity, that they can actually hit a person in the face with more force than he would sustain if he merely hit the dashboard. The intended purpose of airbags is to cushion any impact which the passenger might sustain in a collision, but in reality they merely create a dramatic collision of their own. There is no doubt that airbags should be an option, not a requirement in modern cars.

Which sentence in that paragraph presents the main idea, and which are supporting details that prove the main idea correct? This paragraph is tricky because the main idea is actually not the first sentence—it's the last sentence. That's why it is important to pay attention to the whole passage and not let your attention trail off, because the last sentence is often just as important as the first. The author is presenting his opinion that airbags should be optional rather than mandatory in modern cars, but he opens the paragraph with supporting evidence that proves his opinion. So the main idea in this paragraph is found in the last sentence, while all other sentences provide supporting information.

Supporting data will usually be statements of fact, things that are accepted as true and not open to debate. Notice that the first sentence in the sample paragraph states that airbags have knocked people unconscious. This is a fact, not an opinion. The second sentence states that airbags expand so fast that they can create a severe impact to a person's face—again, another fact and not an opinion. The only opinion statement in the above paragraph is the final sentence, which suggests that airbags should be an option on cars. You know that this is an opinion because there will be readers who disagree.

Of course, facts themselves can be debated, such as the author's claim that the airbag's force is greater than hitting the dashboard. But your job on the GED is not to determine whether the facts are accurate; your job is merely to distinguish between the main idea of a passage and the supporting details. In other words, remember that the author is presenting what he or she considers to be facts in order to support a main idea, and you can use those supporting facts to help point out the passage's main idea.

> ### Persuasive Writing
>
> Persuasive writing is any piece of writing that states an opinion. The writer is trying to persuade the reader that the opinion is valid. The most common method of persuasion is to state an opinion (see *Thesis Statements* earlier in this chapter), then support that opinion with proof—in the form of facts, statistics, examples, and so forth. This proof is known as supporting data.

Main Ideas versus Supporting Details

To determine quickly whether a sentence is a supporting detail or a main idea, just ask yourself this question: Does this sentence tell me specific information, such as facts and figures; or does this sentence make a statement that could easily be debated? If the sentence can easily be argued with, it's most likely the main idea. If the sentence provides facts and figures that are probably not open to much debate, then it's a supporting detail.

Let's look at another example. Again, underline supporting details (facts and figures) and circle the main idea (debatable opinion).

> Walnut trees are not a good selection for landscaping around private homes. Walnuts secrete a chemical into the soil that can kill other plants nearby. In fact, this chemical is not only secreted into the soil, but also carried to surrounding areas in the leaves, twigs, and nuts that the tree drops. This chemical will cause many plants to die—plants that are commonly used around homes. Studies have shown, for example, that more than 50% of homes in America have trees and shrubs in their yards that are susceptible to the walnut's secretions.

All the sentences in this paragraph provide facts and figures, things which are commonly accepted and not open to debate—all the sentences, that is, except for the first. In the first sentence, the author presents an opinion by stating that walnut trees are not good for landscaping. That is clearly a matter of opinion, while the other sentences present details that are *not* matters of opinion—such as the fact that walnut trees secrete a chemical into the soil.

Words That Signal Supporting Details

Another good way to spot supporting data is to look for certain words and phrases that are frequently used to introduce evidence. Here are some of these words:

- for example
- for instance
- in particular
- in addition
- furthermore
- some
- others
- specifically

A quick way to find the topic sentence in a paragraph is to begin by eliminating sentences that begin with these words. Sentences beginning with these signal words will usually be supporting data, and not the main idea. Don't eliminate them without reading the whole sentence, though. Just use the signal words as clues to which sentences are probably playing supporting roles.

READING COMPREHENSION STRATEGIES

Finding the Main Idea in Fiction

The main idea in literature is sometimes also called the theme. Don't be misled by such terminology, however; finding the theme in literature is the same as finding the main idea in nonfiction.

Remember also that the theme (or main idea) is different from the subject. The subject is the thing or idea that is being discussed, but the theme actually says something about the subject.

John Donne's poem "Death Be Not Proud" provides a good example. In this poem, the writer is discussing the topic of death, but his theme says something very specific about death as well: that people who worship God don't need to fear death. (As you read this poem, don't be confused by the strange spellings. Try reading it out loud and just pronounce words the way they're written.)

Sonnet 72

Death be not proud, though some have called thee
Mighty and dreadful, for, thou art not so,
For those whom thou think'st, thou dost overthrow,
Die not, poor death, nor yet canst thou kill me.
From rest and sleep, which but thy pictures bee,
Much pleasure, then from thee, much more must flow,
And soonest our best men with thee do go,
Rest of their bones, and soul's delivery.
Thou art slave to fate, chance, kings, and desperate men,
And dost with poison, war, and sickness dwell,
And poppy, or charms can make us sleep as well,
And better then thy stroke; why swell'st thou then?
One short sleep past, we wake eternally,
And death shall be no more; Death, thou shalt die.

The main idea of a text is the thought that holds everything together. Likewise, the theme of a work of literature is the thought that holds together the characters and action. It's the idea that guides every choice that the writer makes throughout the text.

Theme versus Subject

Theme: the *main idea* that a writer is putting forward in fiction, poetry, or drama

Subject: the general *topic* that a writer is addressing in fiction, poetry, or drama

For example, look at the poem "A Poison Tree," from William Blake's *Songs of Innocence and Experience*. The poem has four stanzas (groups of lines in a poem, just as a paragraph is a group of lines in an essay or story).

A Poison Tree

I was angry with my friend:
I told my wrath, my wrath did end.
I was angry with my foe;
I told it not, my wrath did grow.

And I water'd it in fears,
Night & morning with my tears;
And I sunned it with smiles,
And with soft deceitful wiles

And it grew both by day and night,
Till it bore an apple bright.
And my foe beheld it shine,
And he knew that it was mine.

And into my garden stole
When the night had veil'd the pole;
In the morning glad I see
My foe outstretchd beneath the tree.

READING COMPREHENSION STRATEGIES

To understand Blake's theme, you need to look carefully at what happened and then look at why it happened. In the first stanza, Blake sets up two situations. First, the speaker (the voice or narrator of the poem) is angry with his friend (line 1) and he tells his friend about it (line 2). As a result, the anger goes away (line 2—*my wrath did end*). But he acts differently with his enemy. He doesn't tell his foe about his anger (line 4), and as a result, the anger grows (line 4).

In the second stanza, the speaker *water'd* his wrath in fears and *sunned* his wrath with smiles and wiles. Blake isn't being literal here; rather, he's drawing a comparison between the speaker's anger and something that grows with water and sun, like some kind of plant. How do you know exactly what it is? Blake tells you in two key places: in the title and in the last line. The poem is called "A Poison Tree," and *tree* is mentioned again in the last line of the poem.

This kind of comparison is called a **metaphor**, and it is an important clue to the meaning of the poem. Blake could have compared the speaker's anger to anything, but he chose to compare it to a tree. Trees have deep, strong roots and often flower or bear fruit. (This tree bears an apple.) They need some nurturing (sun and water) to grow.

In the third stanza, the foe sees the speaker's apple. In the fourth, he sneaks into the speaker's garden at night. Finally, at the end of the poem, the foe is killed by the poisonous apple (the apple poisoned by the speaker's wrath).

That is what happens in the poem, but what does it all add up to? What does it mean? In other words, what is the theme?

Look again at the action. Cause and effect are central to the theme of this poem. What does the speaker do? He tells his friend about his anger and chooses *not* to tell his enemy. What happens to his anger, then? It grows and grows and it offers fruit that tempts his enemy. And what happens to his enemy? He steals the apple, but it is the fruit of anger. It is poisonous and it kills him. Thus, the idea that best summarizes the idea of the poem is this: If you don't talk about your anger, it can be deadly. This is the message or lesson of the poem.

In many poems, the theme is an idea, while in others, the theme is an emotion. That is, the poet wants readers to feel an emotion very strongly. Poets can accomplish this through language. The next poem, written by Stephen Crane in 1899, combines both action and language to convey theme. Read the poem out loud at least twice.

A Man Said to the Universe
A man said to the universe:
"Sir, I exist!"
"However," replied the universe,
"The fact has not created in me
A sense of obligation."

Look carefully at the language in the poem. What kinds of words has the poet chosen? Are they warm, friendly words, or are they cold, distancing

Words That Signal Supporting Details

- for example
- for instance
- in particular
- in addition
- furthermore
- some
- others
- specifically

Three Kinds of Point of View

When it comes to expressing point of view, writers can use three distinct approaches:

- **First-person point of view** is a highly individualized, personal point of view in which the writer or narrator speaks about his or her own feelings and experiences directly to the reader using these pronouns: *I, me, mine; we, us, ours*.
- **Second-person point of view** is another personal point of view in which the writer speaks directly to the reader, addressing the reader as *you*.
- **Third-person point of view** is an impersonal, objective point of view in which the perspective is that of an outsider (a "third person") who is not directly involved in the action. There is no direct reference to either the reader (second person) or the writer (first person). The writer chooses from these pronouns: *he, him, his; she, her, hers; it, its;* and *they, them, theirs*.

---

words? Do they make you feel comfortable and welcome, or uncomfortable and rejected? Are they specific or general? Do you feel like there's a personal relationship here, or are things formal and official?

Crane's word choice helps convey his theme. The words *sir*, *fact*, and *obligation* are cold and formal. There's no sense of personal relationship between the man and the universe. This is heightened by the general nature of the poem. It's just "a man"—not anyone specific, not anyone that you know—and not anyone that the universe knows, either. It's also written in third person; the poem would have a different effect if it began, "*I* said to the universe." The tone of the poem is cold and uncaring. That combined with action and word choice conveys Crane's theme: The universe is indifferent to humans.

▶ Identifying Supporting Facts and Details

We've already touched on the topic of supporting details, and we've seen how identifying supporting details can actually help us to identify the main idea of a passage.

But on the GED, it will also be important to identify supporting details for other reasons, such as to learn certain facts or statistics that are stated by the writer. You will need to demonstrate that you know how to find specific information in a written passage, information that will focus on some small detail of the passage. This is different from being asked what the main idea is, because you will need to show that you understood some of the smaller details given in the passage.

Here is an example of a question dealing with supporting details.

Passage 4

When you hear the word *potato*, you probably picture a rounded brownish vegetable with thick skin. But the truth is that there are thousands of different types of potatoes, and the differences between varieties can be quite striking. The United States alone produces an estimated 560 different types of potato! More than 2,400 varieties are grown in the Andes Mountains. One notable area of the Andes produces around 125 different varieties of potato, and many individual potato farmers specialize in 10 or 15 different types. The potato is much more than just the brown-skinned type that most Americans know.

7. Approximately how many types of potatoes are grown in the Andes Mountains?
   a. 560
   b. 2,400
   c. 125
   d. 10 to 15
   e. 2,525

▶ The Difference between Fact and Opinion

You'll remember that the main idea, or thesis statement, of a piece of writing is very often a matter of opinion—something that can be debated and needs to be proven. You've also seen how supporting details are frequently statements of fact that are used to support that thesis or opinion. By looking at those differences, we have already covered the first step to seeing the difference between a fact and an opinion.

Facts are those things that we know for certain: dates when events occurred; whether or not something exists; names of people; and so forth. Opinions, however, are those things that might or might not be true: whether something is nice or pleasant; whether an event is good or bad; and so forth.

In the passage about car airbags you read earlier, the author gave you both facts and opinion. He stated the fact that people have been knocked unconscious by airbags, and you can determine whether or not this is a fact simply by doing some research. He also stated his opinion that airbags should be optional on cars, but this is not a fact that can be proven true or false by research; it is the opinion of the writer.

Passage 5

8. Which of the following statements is an opinion?
   a. Abraham Lincoln was the sixteenth president of the United States.
   b. Abraham Lincoln was the greatest president of the United States.
   c. Lincoln was assassinated by John Wilkes Booth.
   d. Abraham Lincoln had a son named Robert Todd.
   e. President Lincoln was born in Kentucky.

Words That Signal Opinions

We have considered some words and phrases that are often used when a writer presents facts, such as *for example* and *specifically*. In the same way, we can often recognize when an author is about to state an opinion by recognizing certain words and phrases that often accompany opinions.

Some words and phrases suggest moral obligation, words such as *should* and *ought* and *must*. For example, a passage might state that *the government should not tax people for the necessities of life*. This states an opinion because it is suggesting that the government has a moral obligation of some sort.

Words That Signal Opinions

should	ought	had better
good	bad	great
excellent	terrible	interesting
fascinating	important	insignificant
boring	remarkable	disappointing

Other words express some form of personal judgment or evaluation. Such words include *good*, *bad*, *better*, *worse*, *always*, *never*, and many others.

Passage 6

Some cities have recently decided to outlaw burning wood in a home fireplace. This is an outrageous infringement upon traditional American liberties, and should be resisted at all costs. New Englanders once rose up and rebelled against laws that affected their right to drink tea, and this rebellion became famous as the Boston Tea Party. Those Americans were unwilling to support a government that passed laws restricting their basic human liberties. What America needs is a modern version of the Tea Party, in the form of a modern Fireplace Rebellion.

9. Which of the following statements from the text is a fact?
   a. "Some cities have recently decided to outlaw . . ."
   b. "This is an outrageous infringement . . ."
   c. ". . . should be resisted at all costs."
   d. "Those Americans were unwilling . . ."
   e. "What America needs . . ."

Passage 7

Read the following sentences, and then write *F* for *fact* or *O* for *opinion* in the blank.

10. ____ Hybrid cars use a combination of gasoline and electricity for power.

11. ____ Hybrid cars get better gas mileage than traditional gas-powered cars.

12. ____ Hybrid cars are safer than gas-powered vehicles.

13. ____ Hybrid cars are a better investment than traditional gas-powered cars.

14. ____ Hybrid cars cannot accelerate as quickly as comparable gas-powered cars.

You'll notice from these examples that some facts can easily be converted into opinions. For example, sentence 11 could easily be debated: One person might claim that hybrid cars get better gas mileage than gasoline-powered cars, while another person might argue that the gasoline savings is nullified by the hybrid's use of electricity.

This is where it becomes important to be a careful reader, learning to be on guard against opinions that are stated as if they were indisputable facts. It's actually very easy to write an opinion in words that suggest it's a proven fact. For example, a newspaper article might tell you that *the president's policy on taxes will cause an increase in poverty levels.* This is stated as though it is a proven fact, but you know that it's merely an opinion because it discusses something that might happen in the future. Nothing in the future can be considered a proven fact simply because the future hasn't happened yet.

Passage 8

Try taking a fact and converting it into an opinion. For example:

Fact:
A loaf of bread today costs about 10 times as much as it did 30 years ago.

Opinion:
A loaf of bread today isn't as healthy as it was 30 years ago.

Read the following statements of fact, and then convert each into an opinion.

15. **Fact:** The movie *Crash* won the Best Picture Academy Award in 2006.
    Opinion:

16. **Fact:** There are four distinct seasons: summer, fall, winter, and spring.
    Opinion:

17. **Fact:** Evergreen trees stay green year-round, while deciduous trees lose their leaves in winter.
    Opinion:

18. **Fact:** Coffee is a beverage made from beans, many of which are grown in Colombia.
    Opinion:

19. **Fact:** Most states and provinces in North America use Daylight Saving Time in the summer months.
    Opinion:

▶ **Making Inferences**

People often confuse the words *imply* and *infer*. You imply an idea by hinting at it without stating it directly. For example, you might tell a person that he's "on thin ice," by which you are implying that he's going to get into trouble if he doesn't change his behavior. The person who makes an implication is the person speaking or writing—not the person listening or reading.

When you infer an idea, on the other hand, you are the reader or listener—not the speaker or writer.

The concept works in a similar manner: you infer an idea by taking a hint. More specifically, you take different pieces of information from the written passage and draw a new conclusion. For example, a book might tell you that "there was a strong sense of tension in the air as Mary entered the room." From this statement, you could infer that something is about to happen as Mary enters the room—even though the writer does not directly make that statement.

Implications and inferences are part of the more subtle art of communication, something that one cannot define by strict rules or signal words—yet we all understand how to imply things, and we all know how to recognize another person's implied statements. In verbal communication, we often imply things using subtle gestures or tone of voice—raising an eyebrow, leaving a sentence deliberately unfinished while gesturing with our hands, and many other techniques. By using these subtleties, we communicate to other people without directly stating what we mean, and we also infer another person's unspoken meaning by reading body language or listening to a tone of voice.

Written communication uses clues to communicate implied meanings, and you can learn to detect those clues simply by being on the lookout for them. Read each of the following practice passages, looking for clues to the writer's implied meanings. In this way, you will get the feel of how to infer.

Passage 9

The following passage is from a memo written by the manager of a parking garage. Read through, asking yourself what information you might infer from what the writer says.

READING COMPREHENSION STRATEGIES

Radios have been stolen from four cars in our parking garage this month. Each time, the thieves have managed to get by the parking garage security with radios in hand, even though they do not have a parking garage identification card, which people must show as they enter and exit the garage. Yet each time, the security officers say they have seen nothing unusual.

20. Which of the following statements can be accurately inferred from this passage?
   a. The parking garage is very busy.
   b. Security guards at parking garages don't care about their jobs.
   c. The identification card system isn't working at the parking garage.
   d. There is a problem with the security at the parking garage.
   e. People should be more careful about locking their cars.

Imply versus Infer

Imply: to hint at or suggest something without actually stating it; a speaker or writer *implies*

Infer: to draw conclusions from a passage, even though those conclusions are not openly stated; a listener or reader *infers*

Passage 10

This passage is from a police report concerning a traffic accident. Again, see what you can infer from it.

John Smith was driving the car that collided with the telephone pole on Main Street on Thursday at 9 A.M. Witnesses said that they saw Smith's car drift from the left lane, through the right lane, and finally hit the pole. One witness also claims to have seen Smith at the traffic light two blocks earlier, and at that time the witness claims that Smith was "looking pretty sleepy." Smith admitted that he had worked a double shift the night before the accident. There were no injuries.

21. Which of the following might be inferred from this traffic report?
   a. Smith was drunk.
   b. Smith fell asleep at the wheel.
   c. The witnesses lied.
   d. Smith's car had a mechanical problem.
   e. Smith's job is wearing him out.

Passage 11

Sometimes you can make inferences based on the choice of words that a writer uses. Read the following, paying attention to the writer's descriptions and choice of words.

Coach Lerner, my basketball coach, is six feet ten inches tall with a voice that booms like a foghorn and the haircut of a drill sergeant. Every morning, he marches onto the basketball court at precisely 8:00 and dominates the gymnasium for the next three hours. He barks orders at us the entire time and expects that we will respond like troops on a battlefield. And if we fail to obey his commands, he makes us spend another 45 minutes under his rule.

22. Which of the following statements can be inferred from this passage?
    a. Coach Lerner is a bad basketball coach.
    b. Coach Lerner is a good basketball coach.
    c. It's hard work being a new member of a basketball team.
    d. Playing on Coach Lerner's team is like being a soldier in training.
    e. Basketball players need strict discipline if they are to play well.

This element of word choice is very important. If you pay attention to the words and phrases that a writer uses, you will very often get a good sense of what he or she is implying, even though the author may never directly state his or her true opinion. This is especially true of a newspaper or news magazine—periodicals that claim to be unbiased news reports, but that may actually be reflecting a writer's own bias.

Passage 12

The following passage is an excerpt from a newspaper article. It seems at first glance to be a straightforward account of a factual event, but read it carefully and notice the writer's use of words and phrases. See if you can detect what the author really thinks of President Bush.

President Bush visited his family's large estate in Kennebunkport, Maine, over the weekend. The huge compound is surrounded by high walls topped with barbed wire, and protected by armed guards at every corner, and once inside the Bushes enjoyed a relaxing weekend away from the pressing affairs of government. They played tennis, swam in the pool, and invited select friends for dinner. President Bush did not, however, answer questions concerning the war in Iraq.

23. Which of the following statements can be supported by this passage?
    a. The writer thinks that President Bush is a good leader.
    b. President Bush does not care about poor people.
    c. The president should always be protected by guards and barbed wire.
    d. It's good to get exercise, even if you're a world leader.
    e. The author feels that President Bush is avoiding his duties as president.

Passage 13

Literature will very often demand that a reader make inferences from a passage. This is especially true in poetry, but no less true in fiction and drama. Read the following passage from Mark Twain's *Tom Sawyer*, and see what you can infer. Young Tom has been commanded by his Aunt Polly to whitewash (paint) the fence, but he's been trying to bribe his friend Jim to do it instead. He has finally persuaded Jim by offering him a marble (alley) and a peek at Tom's sore toe.

Jim was only human—this attraction was too much for him. He put down his pail, took the white alley, and bent over the toe with absorbing interest while the bandage was being unwound. In another moment he was flying down the street with his pail and a tingling rear, Tom was whitewashing with vigor, and Aunt Polly was retiring from the field with a slipper in her hand and triumph in her eye.

24. Which of the following statements are supported by the passage?
   a. Aunt Polly hit Jim with her slipper.
   b. Tom was wrong to bribe Jim.
   c. Jim is a coward.
   d. Aunt Polly is abusive.
   e. The fence is hard to paint.

▶ Cause-and-Effect Relationships

Everything in life has both a cause and an effect. Rain is caused by water vapor in clouds that turns to liquid; rain has the effect of making things wet, watering plants, and so forth.

- **cause:** a person or thing that makes something happen or produces an effect
- **effect:** a change produced by an action or cause

You will be asked on the GED to identify certain causes or effects that are addressed in a piece of writing. These causes and effects may be either stated directly, or simply implied in the passage. If the passage clearly states, for example, that "World War I was caused by the assassination of Archduke Franz Ferdinand," then your job is fairly straightforward; you are merely being asked to look for supporting evidence which is clearly given in the passage.

On the other hand, you might be asked to find a cause or an effect—or both—from a passage that does not openly state them. In this case, you will need to bring in the inference skills you've just been developing. You will need to read what the author says directly, and then infer which thing caused something else, or what the effect was of some detail in the passage, or how one part of the passage has a cause-and-effect relationship with another part of the passage.

Sometimes you will be given a passage to read that does not directly discuss the causes or the effects of a given event, but merely discusses the event itself. You might then be asked to infer from the passage what caused the event, according to the author, or what effects the event produced.

Passages that discuss the cause of an event will generally be telling you why the event happened: Why did the cat climb the tree? For what reason did the chicken cross the road? Passages that discuss the effect of an event will generally be telling you what happened after the event: The fire department came (because the cat was in the tree). Traffic was tied up for an hour (because the chicken walked slowly).

This all may sound complicated, but it really isn't—it's a way of thinking and analyzing that we all do every day. Try a few for yourself and you'll quickly see that you already know how to look for causes and effects.

Words That Signal Cause

because	since
created by	caused by

Passage 14

Read the following sentences and then list the cause and effect in each.

Example: James overslept this morning, and was late for work.
Cause: James overslept
Effect: He was late for work.

25. We recently hired three new salespeople, and our income has doubled.
Cause:
Effect:

26. Since I met you, I've been very happy.
Cause:
Effect:

27. When Jim's car stalled, he immediately wished that he'd bought some gas.
Cause:
Effect:

28. Tom skipped breakfast, and found himself famished around noon.
Cause:
Effect:

29. Jane lost 35 pounds once she started on this new diet.
Cause:
Effect:

You will notice that cause and effect may not be directly stated, and also that they may not be given in any particular order. You may need to read carefully to detect that one event in the passage caused another event.

For example, question 27 does not state that Jim ran out of gas; it doesn't even state that Jim chose not to buy gasoline. The writer actually tells you that Jim wished that he'd bought some gas; you must infer from this that he *didn't* buy gas, and then infer that the lack of gasoline led to the car stalling.

You can make this sort of inference if the writer makes a deliberate connection between two events. Notice that the writer in question 27 makes a connection between Jim's failure to buy gas and the car stalling—without directly stating that there is a connection. He implies the connection; you must infer the connection, then draw a cause-and-effect relationship between them.

There are certain signal words and phrases that can also tip you off to cause-and-effect relationships. Some words that indicate cause include *because*, *since*, *created by*, *caused by*, and similar words and phrases. Some words that indicate effect include *since*, *therefore*, *consequently*, *hence*, *so*, and similar words and phrases.

Passage 15

. . . she thought about back home, about how she had been all alone most of the time then too, but this lonesomeness was different. Then she stopped staring at the green chairs, at the delivery truck; she went to the movies instead. There in the dark her memory was refreshed, and she succumbed to her earlier dreams. Along with the idea of romantic love, she was introduced to another—physical beauty. Probably the most destructive ideas in the history of human thought. Both originated in envy, thrived in insecurity, and ended in disillusion.

—From *The Bluest Eye*, by Toni Morrison.

30. What caused this character to go to the movies?
   a. loneliness
   b. a desire to see the movie
   c. curiosity
   d. a desire to become an actress
   e. romantic love

31. What effect did the movie have on the character?
   a. She decided to change careers.
   b. She stopped being bored.
   c. She learned a dangerous lesson about love.
   d. She became insecure.
   e. She remembered something that she'd forgotten to do.

Words That Signal Effect

| since | therefore | consequently |
| hence | so | |

▶ Understanding Words from Context

Everyone who reads will encounter words that are unfamiliar. The best way to learn a new word, of course, is to look it up in the dictionary. This will expand your vocabulary, and in time you will find that you rarely encounter words that you don't already know.

But even if you don't have a dictionary handy, you can still gain some idea of a word's meaning from the passage as a whole—which we call the *context*. Context refers to the meaning and ideas of a passage as a whole, as opposed to **diction**—the specific words and phrases used within the passage.

Read through the following passage and underline any unfamiliar words, or words that are used in unfamiliar ways. Don't use a dictionary just yet; see if you can determine the meanings just from the passage as a whole.

Television is a dangerous medium, because it shows the viewer artificialities and presents them as though they were real. An unsuspecting viewer can be so drawn into the television program that he forgets to remember that it is all make-believe. The images, sounds, actions; the characters, settings, plots—everything seems so very real that the average person gradually comes to believe that it *is* real. Other media, such as books and CDs, pose less of a threat to the average person, because one must engage one's mind to imagine what is described in writing or music. When we engage our imagination—indeed, when we engage our minds to any degree—we are less susceptible to the deceptions of fiction and drama. But television encourages the viewer to disengage his mind and just allow the actors to play out the story in front of him.

Look at the opening sentence: *Television is a dangerous medium*. The word *medium*, of course, is not unfamiliar; but perhaps you have never seen it used that way before. What exactly is a dangerous medium? But as you read on through the passage, you read the following: *Other media, such as books and CDs . . .* The context suggests that the author is comparing books with television, and he is calling them all "media." *Media*, of course, is another familiar word, and this time it is used in the way that we are all familiar with: to refer to television, radio, newspapers, and so forth. These are called media because they serve to provide something to consumers, just as

READING COMPREHENSION STRATEGIES

a waiter provides food to the diner in a restaurant. The waiter is the medium, the middleman if you will, who is bringing the food to your table. In the same way, television is the device which brings news and programs into your home.

Perhaps you underlined *susceptible*. Again, the context of the passage can give you a good hint on the word's meaning. The main idea of the passage is that television takes advantage of a viewer by encouraging him to *disengage his mind* and believe that fictional programs are actually real. So in this context, *susceptible* would mean that, in some way, books and music do not take advantage of human weakness, while viewers of television run the risk of being caught when they are weak—which is essentially the meaning of susceptible.

Sometimes you can get enough context to understand a word just from the way that it's used in a sentence; other times, you'll need to dig out the meaning from the context of the entire passage. The above exercise shows you how to define words in context of the entire passage. Now practice a few, picking up the definitions just from the way that each word is used in a sentence.

Context

Context refers to the words and phrases that surround a word; in larger terms, the entire passage as a whole. When we take an author's words out of context, we quote the literal words that were written but use them in a different way than they were originally used. Context determines subtle differences of meaning for words and phrases.

Passage 16

32. When Megan refused to lie to her parents about where she was spending the night, she was completely *ostracized* by her usually loyal friends, who had never shunned her before.
    a. excluded
    b. hurt
    c. cheered
    d. helped
    e. covered with feathers

33. Zachary is too inexperienced for the managerial position, but he is a willful young man and *obdurately* refuses to withdraw his application.
    a. foolishly
    b. reluctantly
    c. constantly
    d. stubbornly
    e. slowly

34. She read her supervisor's memo four or five times, but she still found his rambling message *ambiguous*.
    a. profound
    b. inspiring
    c. ridiculous
    d. unclear
    e. lizardlike

35. When people heard that timid Bob had taken up skydiving, they were *incredulous*.
    a. fearful
    b. outraged
    c. convinced
    d. disbelieving
    e. busy

36. The suspect gave a *plausible* explanation for his presence at the scene, so the police decided to look elsewhere for the person who committed the crime.
   a. unbelievable
   b. credible
   c. insufficient
   d. apologetic
   e. flexible

CHAPTER

3 ▶ Reading Fiction

THE NEXT FEW chapters address specific types of writing that you will encounter on the GED. This chapter considers general fiction; future chapters deal with nonfiction poetry, and drama.

READING FICTION

▶ What Is Fiction?

First, here are a few very general definitions to help you understand the different types or *genres* of literature. The word *fiction* refers to stories that are not literal accounts of factual incidents or people. History, for example, is different from fiction because a historical book describes real people and actual events—and does so as accurately and truthfully as possible.

Fiction, of course, might also be based upon actual events and real people. Mark Twain, for instance, wrote a novel about the life of Joan of Arc. She was a real person, and the major events in Twain's novel actually did take place. Yet the book is still a fictional account of Joan of Arc's life, because the author invented other characters and events and conversations that did not occur in real life.

Fiction is also generally written in prose. Prose refers to normal language; it is not poetry nor is it arranged the way that text is written in drama. We generally speak in prose; newspapers and magazines are written in prose; while poetry is written in lines and stanzas that may also rhyme and have meter. You will learn more about these things in a later chapter.

For now, it is enough to understand that fiction is an invented story that is written in prose—normal everyday language.

▶ Types of Fiction

There are many different types of fiction, but for the purpose of the GED, you need concern yourself only with the largest overall definitions, such as *novel* and *fable*. There are, of course, many different types of novels—detective stories, gothic romances, humor, and so forth—but again, you do not need to worry about these finer points for your GED preparation.

Novels and Short Stories

Novels are prose stories that are long enough to fill an entire book. Short stories, on the other hand, are just that: shorter stories that might be anywhere from a few pages to 35 or so pages in length, but not long enough to fill an entire book.

Length is essentially the major difference between short stories and novels. An author can create similar stories, dealing with similar issues and creating similar characters, in either a short story or a longer novel. The only real difference is that, in a novel, the author has more time and space to develop ideas and characters and so forth than would be possible in a short story.

You will find excerpts from both novels and short stories on the GED, but for the purposes of the test, it will make little difference.

Myths, Fables, and Parables

A *myth* is a fictional story that uses invented characters or settings to teach some abstract idea. The classical myths of the Greeks and Romans, for example, told stories of fanciful gods and their dealings with human beings, stories that tried to explain aspects of life on earth.

For example, one famous myth tells the story of Daedalus and his son Icarus. Daedelus was a master craftsman, a brilliant genius who could make almost anything. One day, he created a pair of wings from wax and fitted them onto his son, Icarus. Icarus took off and flew, but his pride got the better of him and he began to fly higher and higher—even though his father had expressly warned him not to. Eventually, Icarus flew too high, and the heat from the sun melted the wings—and Icarus fell to his death.

This great myth tells a fascinating story, but it also presents a warning: Do not become overconfident; do not "get above yourself" and try to fly higher than you ought.

A parable is very similar to a myth. It is a short story (some myths can be very long and can intertwine with other myths) that quickly teaches some specific principle or idea, and is often religious in nature. Parables are found in the writings of almost all major religions. For example, the Bible contains many parables that are very well known in our modern world, such as the parable of the Good Samaritan:

> But he . . . said to Jesus, "And who is my neighbor?" Then Jesus answered and said: "A certain man went down from Jerusalem to Jericho, and fell among thieves, who stripped him of his clothing, wounded him, and departed, leaving him half dead.
>
> "Now by chance a certain priest came down that road. And when he saw him, he passed by on the other side. Likewise a Levite, when he arrived at the place, came and looked, and passed by on the other side. But a certain Samaritan, as he journeyed, came where he was. And when he saw him, he had compassion.
>
> "So he went to him and bandaged his wounds, pouring on oil and wine; and he set him on his own animal, brought him to an inn, and took care of him. On the next day, when he departed, he took out two [coins], gave them to the innkeeper, and said to him, 'Take care of him; and whatever more you spend, when I come again, I will repay you.'
>
> "So which of these three do you think was neighbor to him who fell among the thieves?"
> —Luke 10:29–36, NKJV

The Bible relates that Jesus used a parable to answer a man's question. Jesus had been teaching his followers to "love your neighbor as yourself," and a man asked him, "Who is my neighbor?" Jesus answered him by telling this parable, a story which illustrated the idea that he wanted his listeners to understand. But notice that a parable expects the reader to figure out for himself what the lesson is; the writer of a parable may not come straight out and explain what it means.

A fable is very similar to a parable: It is a short story that illustrates some abstract principle or idea. Fables, however, frequently also explain the moral or lesson they are teaching. Also, parables generally involve people as characters, while fables often use talking animals and other nonhumans as characters.

You are probably familiar with some of the fables written in ancient Greece by a man named Aesop. One of the most famous and popular of Aesop's fables is "The Boy Who Cried Wolf." In this fable, a young boy gets bored while out tending sheep in the field all day, so he yells out, "Wolf!" Everyone from the village immediately rushes out to his aid, carrying pitchforks and other weapons to drive away the wolf—but there isn't any wolf. The boy, however, enjoyed the attention so much that he does the same thing the next day, crying out "Wolf!" at the top of his lungs when no wolf is there. He tries this once or twice more, each time with fewer people responding. Then one day a wolf really does come and attack his sheep; but when he yells out "Wolf!" nobody comes. This is where we get the expression *crying wolf*, meaning calling for help when no help is actually needed.

▶ The Narrator

All stories have a storyteller, or narrator. The narrator is the person who is telling the story—whether the storyteller is actually a character in the story or just the words of the author unfolding the story. It is important to understand that in fiction, however, the narrator is not the author. A narrator is a fictional character—whether that character is part of the story or not—and the things that a narrator says may or may not reflect what the author actually believes. We will discuss this further in a moment.

READING FICTION

There are many ways of telling fictional stories, and these methods are sometimes referred to as point of view. This simply means that a story is told from a particular viewpoint. It might be the viewpoint of the main character, who is retelling a story that happened to him. It might be the viewpoint of an unnamed narrator who is merely telling a story that he is not personally involved in.

The two major types of narrator are first-person narrator and third-person narrator. A story that is told in the first person is one where the narrator is actually a character in the story. Mark Twain's novel *Huckleberry Finn* is told by a character within the story: Huckleberry Finn himself. This is a first-person story. The first-person narrator often refers to himself within the story, using the pronoun *I*.

Here is an example of first-person narration, from the opening lines of *Huckleberry Finn*.

> You don't know about me without you have read a book by the name of *The Adventures of Tom Sawyer*; but that ain't no matter. That book was made by Mr. Mark Twain, and he told the truth, mainly. There was things which he stretched, but mainly he told the truth. That is nothing. I never seen anybody but lied one time or another, without it was Aunt Polly, or the widow, or maybe Mary. Aunt Polly—Tom's Aunt Polly, she is—and Mary, and the Widow Douglas is all told about in that book, which is mostly a true book, with some stretchers, as I said before.

The third-person narrator is not a character in the story, but someone who is simply telling the story without being part of it. "The Boy Who Cried Wolf" uses a third-person narrator. Here are the opening lines from that fable:

> A young boy was herding sheep in a field outside of his home town, and one day he became bored. He looked around for something to entertain him, and so he decided to yell out the alarm—"Wolf!"—at the top of his lungs to see what would happen.

Notice that the story is being told in the same way that we might tell a story about something that happened to a friend. The person telling the story is not actually taking part in the story. But if you rewrite this fable using a first-person narrator instead of a third-person narrator, this is what it might be like:

> One day, I was herding sheep outside of town, and man, was I bored! It was lonely work, too—I had nobody to talk to but a bunch of smelly sheep. Then I got a cool idea: what would happen if I yelled out "Wolf!" as loud as I could?

The third-person narrator might also be an omniscient (all-knowing) narrator, which means that the narrator knows what a character is thinking, and in fact knows everything about the characters within the story. Here is what this fable might be like with a third-person omniscient narrator:

> A young boy was herding sheep in a pasture outside of town, and he was very lonely and bored. He felt as though he had been abandoned by his family and friends, who never came to visit him. This made him feel very sad, but then his sadness turned into a bitter resentment. "I'll show *them*," he thought to himself. "I'll shake up their little world real good!" At that moment, he yelled "Wolf!" as loud as he could, then sat down in contentment to watch the fun.

Notice in this third example how the narrator knows what the boy is thinking and feeling, what his mind is preoccupied with, and so forth. As the story goes on, the narrator might also know what the townspeople are thinking, and what is motivating them to rush out to the field, and what they feel when they discover that it's a false alarm, and so forth. This is a deeper level of storytelling, in which the omniscient narrator is able to tell the reader a great deal more about the characters than merely what happened to them.

Technically, there is also another type of narrator: the second-person narrator. The second-person narrator would address the reader directly, speaking to the reader as *you*. This book, for example, is written using the second-person narrator. This form of narrator is rarely used in literature, however, and is found more frequently in nonfiction works, such as this book. You will learn more about this form of writing, also known as direct address, in Chapter 4.

▶ Important Characters

In addition to a plot and a setting, most fiction also contains characters—the people who are involved in the story itself. Some stories involve a great many characters, while other stories may be about just one or two characters. The novels of Charles Dickens, for example, generally involve a great many odd and amusing characters, while the novels of Thomas Hardy might involve just three or four.

We frequently speak about the main character in a story, by which we mean the most important character or characters within the story. But the more precise way of approaching characterization is to consider the protagonist and that antagonist.

The protagonist is the hero of the story. This is usually the character who is struggling to overcome the conflict of the plot. The antagonist, on the other hand, is the character who resists the protagonist, who struggles to do the opposite. The conflict of the plot may well be between these two characters, as they struggle in opposite directions.

This resistance can take just about any form, but the old-fashioned Western offers the clearest example. The protagonist in such a story might be Whisperin' Pete, the law-abiding citizen who comes into town and is reluctantly made sheriff. He is told that the dreaded Bozo Brothers gang is headed their way, and they intend to shoot up and wreck the dusty little town. The protagonist of such a plot would be struggling to resist evil and protect peace and justice. The antagonist, however, would be the characters—in this case, those ol' nasties the Bozo Brothers gang—who are trying to disrupt that peace and tranquility. They are the ones who are resisting the actions of the protagonist.

▶ Setting

The place where a story occurs and the time at which it occurs are called the *setting*. The parable of the Good Samaritan takes place on a road between Jericho and Jerusalem, so we would say that it is set on the road from Jerusalem to Jericho. We are not told when the story happened, so we must assume that the time period of the story was not important in the author's mind. In fact, Jesus deliberately made his settings very generic—just some farmer's field or some woman's house, at no particular time. He did this because he wanted his listeners to apply the morals of his stories to their own lives, effectively taking Jesus' ideas and applying them to their own settings—to their own place and time, rather than thinking only of some ancient time in some faraway land.

Mark Twain's *Huckleberry Finn*, by contrast, is set in Mississippi and Missouri in the early 1800s. This particular setting for Twain's novel is very important because the story includes situations that happened in that time period and place. For example, the novel includes a character named Jim, who is a runaway slave. Twain wrote *Huckleberry Finn* after the Civil War, when slavery was ended in the United

States, so he needed to set his novel in the past if he wanted to include runaway slaves.

▶ Atmosphere

A story's setting can also influence its atmosphere. The word *atmosphere* refers to the general feeling or mood that a reader detects in a story. You use these words in the same way when you speak of entering a room where there is an atmosphere of tension because people are having an argument, or when you speak about "the mood of the party" or "the feeling that I got in the job interview," and so forth.

Some stories deliberately try to bring out a specific atmosphere that is important to the story itself. For example, a ghost story will frequently strive for a spooky atmosphere. A good ghost story will use the setting to help bring out that atmosphere. This is why so many ghost stories are set in huge old mansions atop some lonely hill. These stories also frequently take place late at night—preferably on a dark and stormy night. All of these are part of the story's setting, and such a setting goes a long way to establishing an atmosphere that is perfect for a ghost story.

It is important to notice that the atmosphere of a story is related to the setting: The place and time where the story takes place create a certain mood or feeling as you read. This is quite different from another element of fiction—the tone of a story.

▶ Tone

The tone of a story is defined by the attitude of the author toward the subject matter. This is a very subtle concept, and it requires some practice to learn how to understand what an author is trying to convey to the reader—particularly because the author may not directly state his or her attitude. In fact, a piece of literature may actually say the opposite of what the author actually believes, and it is up to the reader to detect the author's true viewpoint by reading carefully.

First of all, it is important to understand that the narrator is not the author. Even when a story is told in the third person, the narrator is still a fictional character who is telling the story. The narrator, therefore, may not be speaking what the author actually believes.

Consider the following excerpt from *A Modest Proposal* by Jonathan Swift.

> I shall now therefore humbly propose my own thoughts, which I hope will not be liable to the least objection.
>
> I have been assured by a very knowing American of my acquaintance in London, that a young healthy child well nursed, is, at a year old, a most delicious nourishing and wholesome food, whether stewed, roasted, baked, or boiled. . . .
>
> A child will make two dishes at an entertainment for friends, and when the family dines alone, the fore or hind quarter will make a reasonable dish, and seasoned with a little pepper or salt, will be very good boiled on the fourth day, especially in winter.

Jonathan Swift is using tone to convey his true ideas to his readers—even though his narrator is actually saying the exact opposite. Swift wrote *A Modest Proposal* as a scathing attack on landlords and on the political economists in Ireland who seemed to be consumed by greed and indifference to the lower classes in the country. The tone in *A Modest Proposal* is ironic; it says the opposite of what it means.

READING FICTION

Irony is one major example of tone that you will frequently encounter in literature. An author is ironic when he or she says one thing but actually means something different. We all use irony from time to time in everyday speech—one form of irony is known as sarcasm. Let's say, for example, that you meet a friend who has made a drastic change to her appearance, dying her hair purple or something of that sort. You might say the following upon seeing the new hairdo:

"Wow, your new hairdo is . . . really nice."

Now, that statement can be interpreted in different ways. It could mean just what it says: that you truly like the new hairdo and think it's attractive. But it could also mean just the opposite: that you don't like the new hairdo, and that you think it's not attractive.

Try reading that sentence aloud twice. The first time, read it as if you really mean it; the second time, read it in a way that suggests you don't really mean it literally.

How did your two readings differ? What did you do differently the second time from the first? You probably conveyed your true meaning by your tone of voice. The words, taken literally, mean that you like the new hairdo; yet, by changing your tone, you are able to communicate to your friend that you don't like her new hairdo—even though your literal words are saying that you do.

This is an example of how authors use irony in writing, just as Jonathan Swift did in *A Modest Proposal*. An author establishes a certain tone by a careful use of words, settings, atmosphere, and other elements. One of the most important elements of tone is the author's word choice.

Word Choice

When reading that sample sentence earlier, you were able to convey two different meanings from the same words, and you did so by changing the tone of your voice, perhaps by winking or raising an eyebrow, perhaps with subtle hand gestures. But a writer cannot use hand gestures and voice intonations on the written page, so a specific tone must be established by other means if the reader is to understand the writer's meaning fully.

One of the most common methods of conveying subtleties of tone is to select words and phrases that will communicate that tone to the reader. Read the two following passages—both of which describe the same event. Pay attention to the wording of each passage, and consider how the choices of words and phrases convey two different opinions about the event.

A.
Drew had recently broken off his engagement to Lily, and Lily was feeling pretty sad about it. Just the other day, Lily walked into a restaurant for lunch—and found that Drew was there eating with his new girlfriend.

Lily didn't know what to do, and Drew was pretty embarrassed. He just sat there, looking at Lily and not saying anything. Lily finally turned and left the restaurant. Drew and his new friend just sat and finished their lunch.

B.
Drew went and backed out of his engagement to poor Lily, and it just utterly broke her heart. Then he has the nerve to go out for lunch with his new girlfriend—and to Kitchen Little, of all places, which he knew was Lily's favorite lunch spot.

So poor unsuspecting Lily walks into the restaurant the other day for lunch—and stops dead in her tracks! There's Drew and his latest "friend" plopped right in the middle of the joint, chowing down like nothing in the world was wrong!

Lily broke down and started sobbing—and Drew just sat there and glared at her! It was horrible. Finally Lily turned on her heel and rushed out, leaving selfish Drew to finish his guilty meal.

How does the author of passage B convey a clear sense of anger and resentment? Notice some of the words and phrases that are used in passage B that are different from A: *it just utterly broke her heart* versus *Lily was feeling pretty sad about it*; Drew is described as *chowing down* in passage B, while he is simply *eating* in passage A.

Notice also how the writer of passage B has used descriptive words to make the reader feel compassion for Lily, such as *poor Lily* and *unsuspecting Lily*. Then compare the descriptive words about Drew in passage B, such as *selfish* and *guilty*. In passage A, we are told that Drew *just sat there, looking at Lily*, but in passage B, we are told that he *glared at her*. The word *glared* suggests something very different from the word *looked*, and all these words and phrases subtly guide the reader to an understanding of the author's tone: that Drew is a selfish and uncaring person who broke innocent Lily's heart.

▶ Language and Style

Every writer has a unique style, a unique way of telling a story or expressing ideas, in the same way that every painter or sculptor or musician is said to have his or her own style. In the world of jazz, for example, the style of Louis Armstrong is very different from the style of Dizzy Gillespie—even though both musicians played the trumpet.

The same distinctions can be made in the world of fictional literature. Two writers may address the same topic, and yet their respective styles are very different. Consider, for example, these two excerpts from books about being a boy in the American Midwest. The first is from *Penrod* by Booth Tarkington; the second is from *The Life and Times of the Thunderbolt Kid* by Bill Bryson.

Penrod sat morosely upon the back fence and gazed with envy at Duke, his wistful dog.

A bitter soul dominated the various curved and angular surfaces known by a careless world as the face of Penrod Schofield. Except in solitude, that face was almost always cryptic and emotionless; for Penrod had come into his twelfth year wearing an expression carefully trained to be inscrutable. Since the world was sure to misunderstand everything, mere defensive instinct prompted him to give it as little as possible to lay hold upon. Nothing is more impenetrable than the face of a boy who has learned this, and Penrod's was habitually as fathomless as the depth of his hatred this morning for the literary activities of Mrs. Lora Rewbush—an almost universally respected fellow citizen, a lady of charitable and poetic inclinations, and one of his own mother's most intimate friends.

—From *Penrod*, by Booth Tarkington.

So this is a book about not very much: about being small and getting larger slowly. One of the great myths of life is that childhood passes quickly. In fact, because time moves more slowly in Kid World—five times more slowly in a classroom on a hot afternoon, eight times more slowly on any car journey of more than five miles (rising to eighty-six times more slowly when driving across Nebraska or Pennsylvania lengthwise), and so slowly during the last week before birthdays, Christmases, and summer vacations as to be functionally immeasurable—it goes on for decades when measured in adult terms. It is adult life that is over in a twinkling.

The slowest place of all in my corner of the youthful firmament was the large cracked-leather dental chair of Dr. D. K. Brewster, our spooky, cadaverous dentist, while waiting for him to assemble his instruments and get down to business. There time didn't move forward at all. It just hung.

—From *The Life and Times of the Thunderbolt Kid*, by Bill Bryson.

These two books deal with similar things, telling humorous stories about boyhood. But the two writers deal with the subject very differently, and their two styles are also very different. Tarkington, in the first passage, has a strong vocabulary and is able to use a wide array of words to describe his character; while Bryson uses very plain, everyday language. Tarkington's sentences are formal and carefully structured and punctuated; Bryson's sentences are very casual and almost careless in the use of punctuation.

You have already seen how word choice can affect the tone of a passage, but word choice can also be an important element of style. Words are frequently used metaphorically—that is, to mean something other than the literal definition found in a dictionary. This brings us to our next topic.

Figurative Language

Writers frequently use language to draw word pictures, to suggest ideas that may not be conveyed if one reads the words in a strictly literal sense. We all use language figuratively every day, whether we realize it or not. For example, you might speak about a person who got angry, saying that he *lost his temper.* The literal meanings of those words would suggest that a person had misplaced (lost) his hardened metal (*temper* refers to the strength of steel). But we understand that expression to mean that a person has gotten angry.

In this example, we used words to create a word picture, suggesting that a person who gets angry easily is like steel that is not properly tempered or hardened. Untempered steel breaks easily and does not bend and flex like a good sword blade, for instance. A person who quickly gets angry is like that steel: He cannot bend and flex with life's surprises, and he quickly snaps and gets angry.

There are many ways of using language figuratively, and we will consider some of the most common.

Simile

A simile is a comparison of two things that are not alike or related in which the writer uses the words like or as to suggest that the two unrelated things actually are related or comparable in some way. The word simile suggests that two things are similar—they are like each other. When you see a comparison using the words *like* or *as*, it is probably a simile.

Once again, we all use similes in ordinary conversation, whether we know it or not. A young man might tell a young woman that her eyes are "as blue as the sky." There is, on a literal level, no relationship or similarity between the sky and a pair of human eyes. Yet young lovers have compared the two since the beginning of time.

This is an example of a simile. The young man is telling his heartthrob that her eyes are blue—yet he is doing much more than that. Consider how the young woman might respond if the young man said, *Say, your eyes are blue!* Then consider how she might respond when he tells her, *Your eyes sparkle like the sun, and the sky itself envies their beautiful blue color!* Using similes helps the reader understand some idea or principle in a new way by drawing comparisons between things that we might not ordinarily consider to be related.

Metaphor

A metaphor is a simile which does not use the words *like* or *as*. A metaphor states that two things are identical, saying that Thing A is Thing B.

For example, the young man might tell his heartthrob, "Your eyes are sparkling gems." That is a metaphor, because he is saying that her eyes are sparkling gems—even though we know, on a literal level, that eyes are not gems. If he told her that her eyes were like sparkling gems, he would be using a simile.

We should also distinguish between *metaphors* and *definitions* or *descriptions*. A metaphor, like a simile, compares two or more things that are not directly related. A definition, on the other hand, describes the basic nature of something. If you say to someone, "Your plan is a bad idea," you are defining his plan, not using a metaphor. But you could use a metaphor by saying, "Your plan is a breath of fresh air." Fresh air and plans are not related; this figure of speech is a metaphor. "Your plan is as fresh as the morning dew" is a simile, because it uses the word *as* to make the comparison. Metaphor is a much stronger, more forceful way of making a comparison.

Personification

Another common writing technique is personification, which describes some abstract idea or principle as though it were a living being. A good writer will use personification to help the reader gain insight into some abstract principle.

Justice, for example, is an abstract idea, not a human being. Yet you have probably seen statues or pictures of Lady Justice many times. She is usually pictured as a woman wearing a blindfold, holding an old-fashioned set of scales in one hand and a sword in the other. This personification of the abstract idea of justice helps us understand several things about justice:

A. True justice is blind, not giving unfair favor to one person over another.
B. Justice discovers the truth by balancing one person's views against those of another person.
C. Justice must also have the power to enforce truth, punishing the guilty and protecting the innocent.

These concepts are pictured by the famous statue of the woman. Her blindfold represents principle A, showing that justice is blind. Her scales represent principle B, showing that justice weighs out the truth. Her sword represents principle C, showing that justice has power to defend the truth. Thus, the statue of justice is an example of personification.

Overstatement and Understatement

Writers will sometimes emphasize a point by deliberately overstating or understating some truth. Overstatement, sometimes called hyperbole (pronounced *high-PER-boh-lee*), is exaggerating the truth to the point that it is no longer true. You have probably heard overstatement used many times, in expressions such as "that person is older than dirt" or "he has more money than he knows what to do with" or "you missed it by a mile." These are examples of overstatement or exaggeration.

The opposite is understatement, in which a writer or speaker deliberately falls far short of the truth when describing something. You may have heard someone refer to the Atlantic Ocean as "the big pond," or describe someone who has been injured as "not amused." These are examples of understatement because they deliberately fall far short of the truth in their descriptions.

Writers use overstatement and understatement for many reasons. Mark Twain often used both to make his readers laugh; other writers use these elements of figurative language to emphasize a point. Describing the Atlantic as a pond, for example, causes a reader to stop and consider how very large the Atlantic really is.

Symbolism

We have been considering the ways that words and phrases can be used figuratively to mean something more than just a literal interpretation. Writers also use this technique on a larger scale, telling a story that makes sense in a literal interpretation but may also mean something more in a figurative interpretation. We call this technique symbolism.

Symbolism is the art of using a story to represent some abstract idea. Characters within the story might represent abstract principles, for example, and their actions within the story might be used to address some general, abstract ideas.

For example, Herman Melville's famous novel *Moby Dick* tells the story of Captain Ahab's lifelong struggle to catch a white whale. Ahab's ship is named *The Pequod*, which was also the name of an Indian tribe living in New England. The story of Ahab's pursuit of the whale is understandable on a literal level as a simple story about the life of a New England whaler in the 1800s. But it can also be read symbolically, to represent the pitfalls and consequences of maniacally chasing one's goals in life.

Another form of symbolism is called allegory. An allegory tells the story of very two-dimensional characters whose sole purpose is to represent some idea or principle, and whose actions represent that idea. (You will learn about two-dimensional characters later in this chapter.)

For example, John Bunyan wrote a famous allegory entitled *Pilgrim's Progress*. The characters in the story have names such as Faithful and Ignorance and Atheist and so forth. Each character represents some aspect of human nature, and each behaves in a way that illustrates that character trait. So a character named Mr. Greed, for example, would always be greedy, and everything that he would say would illustrate the concept of greed.

Allegory is a form of symbolism, but not all symbolic literature is allegory.

▶ Plot

Fictional literature generally tells a story, and stories always have a plot. The plot is simply what happens in the story, the sequence of events that the story describes. Most literature follows a very basic formula in developing a story's plot, and the most important element of that formula is conflict.

The conflict within a plot is generally some form of struggle between two parties. The struggle might be between two or more characters, such as in a war story that deals with soldiers from two armies. The conflict might be between a character and some outside force, such as nature or the law. The conflict within *Moby Dick*, for example, is a struggle for survival between the character of Captain Ahab and the whale he is hunting. The conflict might even be within a character's own nature, such as a hero or villain who is consumed with pride or greed or jealousy.

READING FICTION

The traditional plot is made up of five distinct parts: exposition, complication, climax, falling action, and resolution. We will discuss what these terms mean in a moment, but first it is helpful to visualize plot structure like a lopsided triangle, as in the following diagram.

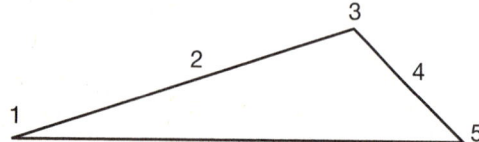

1. **Exposition:** The traditional plot begins with an exposition, which is the introduction of main characters, setting, and so forth. This is the opening of the story, in which the writer introduces some of the story's characters, and the place and time where the story takes place, and so on. Here is where the writer sets the stage for the story that will follow.
2. **Complication:** The complication occurs in a story when some element of conflict is introduced. This is the point where the reader discovers that something is wrong: There are two characters who are struggling against each other, or the main character is fighting against the forces of nature, or some such conflict.
3. **Climax:** The climax occurs in the plot when the conflict is brought to its greatest point of tension. This is the point where the two characters finally square off and confront one another, or where the main character is brought face to face with his own weakness, for example. At this point, the characters are frequently forced to make some major decision or take some drastic course of action. This is the point of reckoning.
4. **Falling Action:** This is the point in the plot where a reversal takes place, the point where the decision or action of the climax brings about some result. Perhaps the villain's power is broken, or the proud character is humbled, or the main character overcomes the forces of nature.
5. **Resolution:** The plot concludes with a resolution to the conflict. The warring characters might make peace, or one of them might be victorious over the other. The ending might be happy or it might be sad, but the conflict has been resolved in some way.

▶ Characterization

The characters in fiction are the people who take part in the story. Some stories include characters who act and think and speak like people that you meet in real life; other stories have characters who seem very predictable and unrealistic. We refer to the former as three-dimensional characters and to the latter as two-dimensional characters. For instance, *Pilgrim's Progress*, the allegory discussed earlier, presents very two-dimensional characters—people who don't act or speak like real-life people because their purpose is to represent specific character traits of human nature.

Most traditional plots have two major characters: a protagonist and an antagonist. The protagonist is frequently the main character, the person whose story we are most interested in. The antagonist is the person or thing that opposes the protagonist, the character that produces the conflict that is at the core of the plot. In fact, the antagonist may not be a person at all—it might be a force of nature, or even some aspect of the main character's own personality. But it is the antagonist who struggles against the protagonist, and their struggle is the conflict which drives the plot.

Some stories rely heavily upon the personality of its characters to move the story along. In such fiction, characterization is very important—that is, it is important that the reader gets to know the characters and understand what motivates them to do what they do.

There are many ways in which a writer enables a reader to get to know the characters. One of the most obvious methods is to have the narrator tell the reader what a character is thinking and feeling, explaining exactly why the character is about to say or do something. Here is an example:

> John was feeling trapped in his job, fed up with his boss's constant criticism and ever-changing priorities. He couldn't help wondering if she hated him just because he was a man—yet he was terribly afraid to say that out loud, lest *he* be accused of being "sexist." He struggled and seethed and wondered—quietly, always quietly—until the day he was passed over for promotion. On that day, something snapped. And John went haywire.

This story goes on to describe what John said and did when he *went haywire*, but the reader has no question as to why John went haywire. The narrator has clearly described what drove John to distraction.

Sometimes, however, a writer leaves it up to the reader to get to know the characters just by spending time with them within the story. This is more lifelike; after all, in real life we don't have a narrator explaining to us why another person behaves strangely—we only come to understand people by spending time with them.

A writer will frequently accomplish this through dialogue—the things that the characters say to one another. By paying attention to the dialogue in a story, we can gain deeper insight into a character's personality, background, motivations, and so forth. For example, a book might contain a character who speaks with a Southern accent and another who speaks with a New York accent. The narrator never tells the reader specifically where each character grew up, yet the reader can infer the characters' backgrounds without being told.

A character's actions also help to develop characterization. The notion that "actions speak louder than words" is just as true within fiction as it is in real life. An author can reveal a great deal about a character simply by describing what the character does in various situations. The narrator does not need to tell the reader explicitly what the character's motivations are, nor does the character come out and tell us within dialogue—yet we can still infer much information just based upon the character's actions or behavior in a given situation.

▶ Theme

Many pieces of fictional literature have some underlying idea or message that the author wants the reader to understand. This is called the theme of the story: the idea that the author is trying to convey to the reader.

A writer may address a theme from many different angles within a single novel. For example, one of the themes in *Huckleberry Finn* concerns the evils of slavery in America prior to the Civil War. Mark Twain developed this theme throughout the book by showing the bad treatment of slaves, the self-sacrificing goodness of the runaway slave character named Jim, the inconsistent ways that slaves were treated in the South, and so forth.

Understanding the theme of fictional literature will require you to use all of the things that we have discussed in this chapter: You look for repeated ideas that come out in action, dialogue, setting, atmosphere, characterization, and so forth. Sometimes it is tempting to read too much deeper meaning into a work of literature than the author intended. For example, reading Booth Tarkington's story about Penrod, you might think that the author's theme has to do with child abuse or some other controversial topic. Although this is not a theme of that novel, you might easily be misled into thinking that it is.

A theme is an idea that is addressed throughout the book or story, not just an idea that is addressed in passing. Themes are well developed, appearing and reappearing in the story through the dialogue that characters speak, actions that characters take, situations that characters find themselves in, and so forth.

Reading carefully and intelligently is important because it is easy to misunderstand what an author is trying to say if we are not careful. But when we understand how the elements of fiction work together—things such as characterization and dialogue and plot structure—we will be well equipped to interpret literature in the way that the author intended.

▶ Practice Questions

Read the following passages and their related questions.

Passage 1

Zeus, the highest of all gods, was angry with mankind because they had stolen fire from him and used it to burn sacrifices to other gods. So he created a new creature and named her Pandora. He also invited all the other gods to bring gifts to Pandora. One god gave her the gift of beauty, another gave her grace, another brought her charm—until finally Pandora was the most beautiful and delightful woman ever created.

But then Zeus gave her one last gift: a box that contained all the evils and sorrows that the world could ever imagine. He sealed the box tight and placed it in Pandora's hands; then he sent Pandora down to earth to be a gift for mankind.

The moment that humans saw her, they fell in love with the wonderful Pandora—for her beauty and charms were very great. As soon as mankind had gathered around her, they urged her to open her magical box, hoping to find yet more wonderful gifts from the gods. So Pandora opened the box that Zeus had given her—and out flew every form of evil and wickedness that the world could imagine. Death and disease and war and poverty all flew out of the box and engulfed the world of mankind. At the last moment, however, Pandora snapped shut the lid of the box, just before Hope could fly away. The only thing left inside her magical box was Hope itself.

1. Why did Zeus create Pandora?
   a. He loved people and wanted to make a nice gift.
   b. He didn't create Pandora; the other gods did.
   c. He was angry with humanity and wanted to punish them.
   d. He was lonely and created a partner for himself.
   e. Pandora created herself.

2. What is the meaning of the expression *you opened Pandora's box*?
   a. You have created all sorts of new problems.
   b. You have given someone a meaningful gift.
   c. You have invented a new and wonderful thing.
   d. You have done something of real merit.
   e. You have opened a path for communication.

READING FICTION

3. This passage is an example of
   a. paradox.
   b. personification.
   c. myth.
   d. allegory.
   e. free verse.

4. What type of narrator is telling this story?
   a. first person
   b. second person
   c. There is no narrator.
   d. third person
   e. direct address

Passage 2

Six blind men left the city of Calcutta one day to walk out and beg for money. But on the way they encountered an elephant.

Now none of these men, being blind, had ever seen an elephant before, but they had heard many people speak of the creature. So each decided that he would find out for himself what an elephant looked like.

The first man walked boldly up to the elephant—but tripped on a rock. He fell and hit his head against the animal's broad flank. "Why," he cried, "the elephant looks like a big wall!"

The second man reached out and felt a tusk. "No," he cried, "the elephant is like a spear!"

The third man took hold of the trunk. "You both are wrong! The elephant is just like a snake!"

The fourth man fumbled about until he found the elephant's leg. "No! No! No! This beast is just like a tree!"

The fifth man leaped up and happened to grasp an ear. "Tree? Snake? Never! The animal is just like a fan!"

The final man was at the rear, and he discovered the elephant's tail. "You all are wrong!" he proudly declared. "The beast is like a rope!"

And so, you see, do many of us, as we speak boldly about something that we have never seen.

5. What is the main idea in this passage?
   a. Don't speak conclusively about something that you've never seen.
   b. Don't become proud of your ignorance.
   c. Live and let live.
   d. People should treat animals better.
   e. Be nice to blind people.

6. How did the blind men find the elephant?
   a. The elephant had escaped from the zoo.
   b. Someone had sent them to find it.
   c. The elephant attacked them as they were walking.
   d. They were going outside of town to beg for money.
   e. They tripped and fell into it.

7. This passage is an example of
   a. irony.
   b. novella.
   c. allegory.
   d. fable.
   e. parable.

READING FICTION

8. What type of narrator does this story use?
   a. There is no narrator.
   b. third person
   c. first person
   d. indirect address
   e. personification

Passage 3

One hot summer's day, a fox went strolling through an orchard till he came to a bunch of grapes ripening on a vine. The vine was draped over a tree branch, well out of the fox's reach.

"Ah," thought the fox, "this is just what I need to quench my thirst." He jumped up and snapped at the grapes, but he could not reach them. He moved farther back, took a running start, and leaped as high as he could—and still missed the grapes. Again and again he jumped, leaping as high as he could go; but each time, his teeth snapped on thin air. He could not reach the juicy fruit no matter how hard he tried.

After a while, the fox gave up. He walked away with his nose in the air, despising what he could not reach. "I'm sure those grapes were sour anyway," he told himself.

9. Why did the fox not eat the grapes, even though he was thirsty?
   a. He didn't really like grapes.
   b. He could not reach them.
   c. The grapes were sour.
   d. A farmer had set a trap that stopped the fox.
   e. The grapes were an illusion; they weren't really there.

10. What is the main idea of this fable?
    a. Don't steal grapes.
    b. Foxes can't jump very high.
    c. It is easy to despise things that are beyond your reach.
    d. Grapes turn sour in the hot summer sun.
    e. Grape vines don't grow well on tree branches.

11. What is the topic of this fable?
    a. disappointment
    b. wild animals
    c. how to grow grapes
    d. summer weather
    e. thirst

12. What is the setting of this story?
    a. New York City
    b. No setting is defined.
    c. a Thursday
    d. another planet with talking animals
    e. an orchard

Passage 4

The solution to these tax problems is very simple and straightforward: America needs to reinstitute slavery. What we did wrong the first time was that we enslaved one particular group of people, based solely upon the color of their skin. This was clearly a mistake—we were far too narrow-minded.

We need to open up the grand tradition of servitude to all races and peoples, permitting every man, woman, and child in this great nation the true joy which comes from wearing the ball and chain. This will clearly remove the burden of taxes upon the common working class, since there will be no income to tax in the first place!

READING FICTION

Another problem with slavery was the multitude of masters. In this new scheme, we will all have the luxury of serving the same master—and that master is none other than our Uncle Sam! Imagine how good it will be to know that we are so closely related to the one who cracks the whip.

Besides, with taxes the way they are at present, we've nearly accomplished this anyway.

13. What is the narrator of this passage suggesting?
    a. that slavery is good
    b. that all Americans should be enslaved by the government
    c. that history has been misunderstood
    d. that Americans are the most free people on earth
    e. that wages should be higher

14. What clues does the author provide to let the reader know that he is not being serious?
    a. He comes out and states that he doesn't really mean what he is saying.
    b. The narrator makes statements that are absurd.
    c. Nobody would ever really suggest bringing back slavery.
    d. Uncle Sam isn't a real person, so it can't be serious.
    e. The narrator is in the third person.

15. This passage is an example of
    a. irony.
    b. fable.
    c. myth.
    d. parable.
    e. free verse.

16. What is the tone of this passage?
    a. happy
    b. hungry
    c. sarcastic
    d. sad
    e. angry

Passage 5

The suspect, James Robinson, was seen entering the store at approximately 3:15 on the afternoon of the robbery. He had no business to conduct in the store, and witnesses later testified that they were suspicious of his intentions from the moment he approached the cashier.

Robinson, of course, claims that he was merely lost and wanted to get directions, but the cashier said that Robinson's actions and appearance were threatening. Witnesses also have pointed out that Robinson's tone of voice was aggressive and threatening when he spoke to the cashier.

Robinson claims that he was only asking how to get to a certain address, and that he had to speak loudly because other people were making a lot of noise in the background. But the cashier said that other people in the store were only making noise because they were frightened by Robinson's presence in the store. They were not accustomed, the cashier maintained, to seeing men in clerical clothing in the neighborhood.

17. What is the tone of this passage?
    a. humorous
    b. ironic
    c. upbeat and energetic
    d. angry and spiteful
    e. factual

READING FICTION

18. What is the author's opinion of Robinson?
   a. He is misunderstood.
   b. He is probably guilty of some crime.
   c. He is the innocent victim in this situation.
   d. He is a handsome ladies' man.
   e. The author's real opinion is unclear.

19. What is the setting of this passage?
   a. a store in some unnamed location
   b. the setting is not defined
   c. a strange neighborhood in some city
   d. a dark, stormy afternoon
   e. a court of law

20. In the following paragraph, what do the words and phrases suggest about the author's opinions?

   Robinson, of course, claims that he was merely lost and wanted to get directions, but the cashier said that Robinson's actions and appearance were threatening. Witnesses also have pointed out that Robinson's tone of voice was aggressive and threatening when he spoke to the cashier.
   a. The author is completely neutral and has no opinion.
   b. The author believes that Robinson is guilty.
   c. The author believes that Robinson was framed.
   d. The author is trying to quote exactly what people said.
   e. There is no way to be sure of the author's opinions.

Passage 6

One tree, however, was different from all the others in the forest. This one grew at the very center of the woods, all alone in an open clearing. It gave off a sweet aroma, and anyone who passed by could not help wanting to sit beneath its shady boughs and rest a while.

It was a very tall tree—tall as the highest spire atop any church in the world. Its leaves shone and shimmered like reflections on a pond, and its fruit was as fragrant as sweet candy. Many people who passed by merely sat down for a rest in its shade, but a few more adventurous souls took the effort to climb its branches and taste of its fruit.

For those with courage to climb, the tree reserved its richest and greatest reward: wisdom. The rest and peace of its shade was sufficient for most people, but to gain real, lasting wisdom, a traveler needed to expend some effort and take some risk—effort of climbing and risk of falling—for the tree did not drop its fruit to be casually picked off the ground.

21. The tree in this story might be a symbol of
   a. caring for the environment.
   b. life after death.
   c. trees and forests.
   d. learning and knowledge.
   e. the dangers of pride.

22. The phrase *as fragrant as sweet candy* is an example of
   a. irony.
   b. metaphor.
   c. paradox
   d. word choice.
   e. simile.

23. What is the central idea of this passage?
    a. Trees are risky to climb.
    b. Knowledge and wisdom come only with risk and effort.
    c. Most people are lazy.
    d. Life's best treasures are found in the woods.
    e. Things that seem appealing on the surface might be dangerous.

Passage 7

The following extract, from *Roughing It*, by Mark Twain, describes a coyote.

He is always poor, out of luck and friendless. The meanest creatures despise him, and even the fleas would desert him for a [bicycle]. He is so spiritless and cowardly that even while his exposed teeth are pretending a threat, the rest of his face is apologizing for it. And he is so homely!—so scrawny, and ribby, and coarse-haired, and pitiful. When he sees you he lifts his lip and lets a flash of his teeth out, and then turns a little out of the course he was pursuing, depresses his head a bit, and strikes a long, soft-footed trot through the sage-brush, glancing over his shoulder at you, from time to time, till he is about out of easy pistol range, and then he stops and takes a deliberate survey of you; he will trot fifty yards and stop again—another fifty and stop again; and finally the gray of his gliding body blends with the gray of the sage-brush, and he disappears. All this is when you make no demonstration against him; but if you do, he develops a livelier interest in his journey, and instantly electrifies his heels and puts such a deal of real estate between himself and your weapon, that by the time you have raised the hammer you see that you need a minie rifle, and by the time you have got him in line you need a rifled cannon, and by the time you have "drawn a bead" on him you see well enough that nothing but an unusually long-winded streak of lightning could reach him where he is now.

24. What is the tone of this passage?
    a. serious
    b. angry
    c. informative
    d. humorous
    e. sad

25. Twain says that *nothing but an unusually long-winded streak of lightning* could catch a running coyote. This is an example of
    a. irony.
    b. personification.
    c. sarcasm.
    d. understatement.
    e. exaggeration.

26. Why does the author claim that *even fleas would desert* a coyote in exchange for a bicycle?
    a. He is being humorous.
    b. He hates coyotes.
    c. He hates fleas.
    d. The coyote doesn't have fleas.
    e. He is stating a scientific fact.

Passage 8

Time's cruel hand had ravaged the woman's fair face. Her eyes had been emerald gems that swam in a calm sea of alabaster; now the green fire had died, and the alabaster skin had become drawn and yellow.

But Time had been crueler still, not satisfied merely to wreck her former beauty. The grim reaper had also come, and stolen from her something far more sweet, more precious, more coveted than beauty and youth. He had stolen her heart.

27. *Her eyes had been emerald gems* is an example of
   a. tone.
   b. simile.
   c. metaphor.
   d. falling action.
   e. exposition.

28. The references to *Time* are examples of
   a. resolution.
   b. fable.
   c. parable.
   d. personification.
   e. irony.

29. What has happened to the woman in this passage?
   a. She has been robbed of her possessions.
   b. She has lost both beauty and love.
   c. She has overcome hardship.
   d. She has become a successful businesswoman.
   e. We are not told.

30. What is the author implying about the *grim reaper*?
   a. The woman has no sense of humor.
   b. The woman has been sexually assaulted.
   c. The story takes place on a farm.
   d. The woman is having a heart attack.
   e. Someone that the woman loved has died.

CHAPTER 4 ▶ Reading Nonfiction

READING NONFICTION WILL use many of the skills you developed in the last chapter on reading fiction—but there are two important differences between fiction and nonfiction. First, nonfiction is not fictional—that is, it purports to be a factual and accurate recounting of actual events involving real people and places. Note that we say it *purports* to be true—in other words, nonfiction writing claims to be true. This will be a very important distinction to understand in some areas of nonfiction. Nonfiction writing addresses real issues and people and events—but it may also be presenting a matter of opinion rather than simply stating a string of facts. We will discuss this more fully as we go along.

Second, nonfiction does not use a narrator in the way that fiction does. You'll remember that some fiction might be told by a first-person narrator referred to in the text as *I* and *me*. In nonfiction, however, the words are directly those of the author, not of some fictional narrator who is created for storytelling purposes.

This is an important distinction as you move from fiction into nonfiction. Keep in mind that in fiction, an author might use a narrator to say things that are directly contrary to what the author believes.

This is generally not the case in nonfiction, however. In this sense, reading nonfiction is more straightforward and less complicated than reading fiction. The exception to this, of course, is when an author uses irony to make a point, saying the opposite of what he or she means in order to underscore a point. We will discuss this further in this chapter.

There are countless types of nonfiction writing. Every time you send an e-mail or jot a note for someone, you are writing nonfiction. If you write a memo or fill out a report at your job, you are writing nonfiction. There are as many types and styles of nonfiction writing as there are people and careers in the world. But, for purposes of preparing for the GED, we will divide nonfiction literature into three broad categories: informational nonfiction, literary nonfiction, and visual communication.

▶ Informational Nonfiction

The term informational nonfiction refers to written pieces whose sole purpose is to inform the reader of something. This is probably the broadest of the three categories, as it includes almost anything that is written for the purpose of passing on information. If you leave a note for your spouse or roommate saying where you've gone, you are writing informational nonfiction—assuming, of course, that you are telling the truth!

Informational nonfiction can be divided into a variety of subsections covering the sorts of nonfiction writing that you will encounter on the GED. This list is by no means exhaustive, but it will give you a good overview of how to read and interpret informational nonfiction.

Business Documents

One of the most important areas of informational nonfiction that you will be called upon to understand is the type of document that you will encounter in the workplace. Understanding how to read and interpret such documents will do more than prepare you for the GED—it will also assist your career goals.

Business documents include memos, reports, proposals, employee handbooks, and many other forms of business writing. You will quickly notice that there is a key difference between most business documents and the fiction that we looked at in the last chapter: business documents come straight to the point and stick to it.

Good business writing is clear and easy to understand, and makes its point plainly and without any extra side issues. Most business documents include all the basic information that is needed right at the beginning—such as whom they are addressed to (the audience), what they're about (the subject), and what the major points include (the thesis). Consider the following memo as an example.

TO: J. Miranda
FROM: P. Aspensen
SUBJECT: Tomorrow's Meeting
DATE: January 12, 2008

Mr. Miranda:
The agenda for tomorrow's meeting does not include the topic of the storm drains, which we have discussed recently. Please add that to the list of things to discuss, as the problem is getting worse every day.

We hope the committee can find a quick solution to the drainage issues that are making life so difficult for our drivers.

Sincerely,

Paul Aspensen

Notice that the memo begins by stating basic information: who the recipient is (M. Miranda), who wrote it (P. Aspensen), and what it's about (tomorrow's meeting). Sometimes a memo uses *RE:* (which means *regarding*) instead of *SUBJECT:* at the top. This approach to writing leaves nothing to the reader to infer, as everything is clearly stated in a straightforward manner.

Journalism

The category of journalism includes newspaper stories, magazine articles, radio and television news, documentaries, and so forth. This is an area where it becomes very important to understand the difference between nonfiction and matters of opinion, though these two concepts are not mutually exclusive.

A newspaper article, for example, is considered nonfiction because it addresses contemporary, real-life events and issues, but it may also be stating the author's personal opinions on those issues and events. Journalists generally put their writing into different categories, such as hard news, feature stories, editorials, and such. A hard news story supposedly presents nothing but facts, telling the reader what happened to whom at what time and how. An editorial, on the other hand, openly presents the writer's opinions on those events.

It is also important to recognize that many hard news stories are actually presenting a reporter's opinion in very subtle ways. These articles claim to be completely factual and unbiased, but in reality they often are not. This is where the skills from Chapter 3 become especially valuable to a good reader. By paying attention to word choices, what facts are included and what facts are omitted, and other details, you can frequently detect what the reporter's bias is.

Read the following news story, looking for clues to the writer's opinion.

The Groton Town Council last night failed to resolve the question of what to do with the burned-out building on Main Street. This is the fourth Council meeting in a row which has reached a non-consensus position on the question.

Peter Treychor, Town Council Chairman, called the deadlock "a travesty," and warned that, if the Council does not proceed soon with some rebuilding project, there will be "dire repercussions."

"This issue has been before the Council for over five years," Treychor stated, "and there is no excuse for it to keep dragging on. This town will face dire repercussions if we don't resolve this soon."

Other Council members did not agree with Treychor's assessment, claiming that the issue is "more complicated" than Treychor implies. But one landowner who was present expressed his concern that the hesitant members of the Council are "stonewalling."

"These people are just stonewalling the whole process," said Miklos Ververis, who owns "Painted Tiger" on Main Street. "They have no excuse to be making this take so long. That burned-out building is an eyesore and a health hazard, and we need to get rid of it."

First of all, this news article is a hard news story, which means that it is nonfiction that deals strictly with facts. But a careful reader will still be able to detect the reporter's bias, and will recognize that the reporter may not be telling both sides of the story—even though the reporter claims to be doing just that.

READING NONFICTION

Notice, for example, the writer's word choices in the first paragraph. The Town Council has "failed to resolve the question" concerning the burned-out building. The writer might just as easily have said that the Town Council "did not reach a consensus" on the issue. But by using the words *failed* and *resolve the question*, the writer subtly suggests that the Town Council itself is a failure.

Consider also whom the author quotes, and whom he does not quote. Notice that he quotes two people who hold the same opinion—that the building should be torn down and rebuilt—but only summarizes the views of those with a different opinion.

These are just a few of the techniques used by journalists to present matters of opinion within nonfiction writing, and you will need to read carefully to recognize that you are being told the writer's opinion of the facts, rather than being given a purely objective presentation of all sides of an issue.

Research Reports

You may also be asked to address research writing on the GED. This is another area of nonfiction that can be either purely factual or a matter of opinion. In research writing, however, the author generally states quite openly whether he or she is presenting an opinion of an issue—and will use facts and figures from research to support that opinion.

A research report addresses some area of scientific study, providing many facts, figures, and statistics that were learned during the study. This type of writing can include almost any subject, from medical research to political opinion polls to a company's annual financial report. Research reports frequently also include charts and graphs that visually illustrate the study's findings—whether it's a simple chart showing a company's increased profits over a period of time, or more complex diagrams illustrating various trends in public opinion or chemical reactions under differing conditions.

Some research reports also present the author's opinions or conclusions that he or she has drawn from the facts in the study. These opinions, however, are generally clearly stated as opinions, rather than disguised as purely factual reporting, such as can be found in journalistic writing. The author may believe that a company needs to take certain steps to increase profits and decrease costs, and will use the facts from the study to demonstrate why this is so.

▶ Literary Nonfiction

Another form of nonfiction writing is called literary nonfiction because it uses many of the techniques and styles that we discussed in Chapter 3 on fiction. Informational nonfiction deals with facts and figures and statistics, while literary nonfiction deals with opinions, perceptions, and ideas that are held by the author. It is still nonfiction, because the subject matter is real and not make-believe, yet it is not strictly informational, because the author is not merely trying to educate but to persuade the reader, to present an opinion and convince the reader that it is the correct opinion.

Again, there are many types of literary nonfiction, but we will examine just a few of the major types that you may encounter on the GED. These types of literary nonfiction include biographies, essays, letters, and speeches.

Biographies

A biography is the story of a person's life. It is nonfiction because it deals with facts concerning a real person who really lived at some point in history. A biography is written by an author about someone else, which distinguishes it from memoirs or autobiographies (which we will discuss in a moment).

The word *biography* comes from the Greek words *bios*, meaning life, and *graph*, meaning writing. So a biography is literally a *life writing*, a story about someone's life. This could technically include the life story of a fictional character, but in general the term biography is used to refer to the story of a real person.

Once again, you will discover that biographies are factual and nonfictional—yet they may still present matters of opinion. There are many biographies written about Abraham Lincoln, for example, yet not all draw the same conclusions about his career as president of the United States. Two different writers might write biographies about the same person and address the same facts and historical events, yet the authors may use those facts and events to draw very different conclusions about the person.

Biographers (the people who write biographies) draw their information from many different sources. If the person they are writing about is still living, a biographer will base much of his or her information upon conversations with that person. Many biographies, however, are written about people who are no longer alive—and who have been dead long enough that there is nobody alive who actually knew that person. In this case, there is obviously no chance to talk with the subject or the subject's friends, and biographers must rely upon other sources of information to learn the accurate facts and dates and statistics of the person's life.

For example, an author might write a book about Julius Caesar, an emperor of Rome. Julius Caesar lived more than 2,000 years ago, so the biographer will be forced to draw information about him from other documents—books that have been written by other writers, historical documents, and similar sources.

This sort of biography is similar to research reports in one important detail: It provides the reader with many facts and dates, and it tells the readers where those facts came from. This is known as documenting one's sources-telling the reader where the author found a certain fact or figure so that the reader can verify the author's accuracy.

Autobiographies

The word *autobiography* is obviously based upon the word *biography*—meaning "life writing"—with the extra prefix *auto*, which means *self*. Thus, an autobiography is a life writing about self, or a person's own life story. Autobiographies, therefore, are about the life of the author.

Autobiographies are similar to biographies in that they are nonfictional, dealing with a real-life person and addressing factual events, people, and places. They are different from biographies, however, in that the person who is telling the story is actually the person who lived the story.

This means that there will not be an objective viewpoint on the subject's life, because the subject is also the author. A biography, on the other hand, might present a very unbiased account of a person's life as told by someone who was not immediately involved in the events.

One key advantage that an autobiography has over a biography is the fact that a reader can gain insight into the thinking and emotions of the person who actually had the experiences. For example, you might have an interest in Ulysses S. Grant, an American president who also served as a general in the Civil War.

You could read a biography about Grant, written by a modern-day scholar. This book would give you a good knowledge of the facts and dates and important events and people in Grant's life. But if you wanted to know what it was like to *be* Ulysses S. Grant, you would want to read his autobiography, in which he tells you his own story from his own perspective.

Memoirs

Memoirs differ slightly from autobiographies, and are often confused with each other. While autobiographies tend to center on the entire life of the writer, memoirs usually focus on a particular, often defining, period of the writer's life, feelings, and emotions.

Essays

The word *essay* literally means a *test* or *experiment*. In literary terms, an essay is a short prose (nonpoetic) piece of writing that presents the author's views on some subject. The term suggests that the essay is the author's experiment to put forward an idea and demonstrate that it is worthwhile in some way. Obviously, this is a fairly broad category that includes a wide variety of writing.

For our purposes, we can group essays into four basic categories:

- **descriptive:** an essay that describes a person or event or location
- **narrative:** an essay that tells a story—such as something that the author has experienced
- **expository:** an essay that explains something, such as how to make a pizza or why water freezes
- **persuasive:** an essay in which the author tries to persuade the reader that his or her opinion is correct on some subject

As you can see, these four types of essays are written for very different purposes. One author might write an essay describing a trip overseas; another might write one that argues against some political issue. These two essays would have very different subjects and very different purposes—yet they would have one thing in common: a thesis statement.

We discussed the thesis statement in Chapter 2 when we learned about topic sentences. As you'll remember, a *thesis* is an idea or a matter of opinion that can be debated—something that one person might agree with and another person might disagree with. *The sky is blue* is hardly a matter of opinion, and therefore would not be a thesis statement. But *blue skies are more pleasant than gray skies* is a matter of opinion; there might be someone who prefers overcast days to sunny days; therefore, this could be considered a thesis statement.

An essay generally presents a thesis—an opinion that might be disagreed with—and then sets out to prove the thesis. An author proves his or her thesis by providing supporting evidence to demonstrate that the thesis is true and correct.

For example, an author might write an essay about blue skies. His thesis would be that blue skies are more pleasant than gray skies. For evidence, he might go on to explain that 1) blue skies don't bring rain; 2) blue skies allow the warmth of the sun to shine through; 3) gray skies make people depressed; and so forth. Each of those numbered ideas is a bit of supporting evidence, which the author will explain more fully, using them to prove his thesis.

Which of the following sentences could be used as a thesis statement in an essay about chocolate?

1. Chocolate is high in calories.
2. Hershey is one of the most popular brands of chocolate.
3. Chocolate cures depression.
4. Chocolate comes in many different types.
5. The price of chocolate has gone up this year.

The answer is **3**, that chocolate cures depression. The other answers are simple statements of fact, but *chocolate cures depression* is a statement that might be open to debate—it needs to be proven.

Sometimes an essay will not come out and state the author's thesis clearly. In such cases, you will need to use the many tools of reading comprehension that you have been acquiring thus far. Read the following, which is the opening of "Death of a Pig," by E.B. White.

> I spent several days and nights in mid-September with an ailing pig and I feel driven to account for this stretch of time, more particularly since the pig died at last, and I lived, and things might easily have gone the other way round and none left to do the accounting. . . .
>
> The scheme of buying a spring pig in blossomtime, feeding it through summer and fall, and butchering it when the solid cold weather arrives, is a familiar scheme to me and follows an antique pattern. It is a tragedy enacted on most farms with perfect fidelity to the original script. The murder, being premeditated, is in the first degree but is quick and skillful, and the smoked bacon and ham provide a ceremonial ending whose fitness is seldom questioned.
>
> Once in a while, something slips—one of the actors goes up in his lines and the whole performance stumbles and halts. My pig simply failed to show up for a meal. The alarm spread rapidly. The classic outline of the tragedy was lost. I found myself cast suddenly in the role of pig's friend and physician—a farcical character with an enema bag for a prop. I had a presentiment, the very first afternoon, that the play would never regain its balance and that my sympathies were now wholly with the pig. . . . He had evidently become precious to me, not that he represented a distant nourishment in a hungry time, but that he had suffered in a suffering world.

White's thesis is not openly stated, but you can infer it from the context of the passage—a skill we have worked on in previous chapters. He is dealing with the irony of raising a pig with the specific intention of killing it for ham—only to find himself working long hours trying to keep it alive. His thesis is that people become instantly sympathetic towards creatures that are suffering, because we all live together in a world of suffering.

▶ Letters

You may be asked to read an excerpt from a letter on the GED. The letter may have been written by a famous writer or politician, and will be selected for its literary style and depth of content.

Here is a letter that Mark Twain sent to the Hartford, Connecticut, gas and electric company in 1886, concerning the lights on his street.

> Gentlemen,
>
> There are but two places in our whole street where lights could be of any value, by any accident, and you have measured and appointed your intervals so ingeniously as to leave each of those places in the center of a couple of hundred yards of solid darkness. When I noticed that you were setting one of your lights in such a way that I could almost see how to get into my gate at night, I suspected that it was a piece of carelessness on the part of the workmen, and would be corrected as soon as you should go around inspecting and find it out. My judgment was right; it is always right, when *you* are concerned. For fifteen years, in spite of my prayers and tears, you persistently kept a gas lamp exactly half way between my gates, so that I couldn't find either of them after dark; and then furnished such execrable gas that I had to hang a danger signal on the lamp

post to keep teams from running into it, nights. Now I suppose your present idea is, to leave us a little more in the dark.

  Don't mind us—out our way; we possess but one vote apiece, and no rights which you are in any way bound to respect. Please take your electric light and go to—but never mind, it is not for me to suggest; you will probably find the way; and anyway you can reasonably count on divine assistance if you lose your bearings.

This is an actual letter, yet it contains some fine examples of Twain's humor. Notice his use of exaggeration as he describes the poor placement of gas street lamps on his street. Notice also his humorous word choices, such as suggesting that the gas company intends to *leave us a little more in the dark*, and his indirect but clever way of telling the gas company "where to go."

▶ Speeches

You may be asked to read an excerpt from a speech on the GED. A speech is different from other nonfiction that we've been looking at because it is written text intended to be read aloud. In a sense, speeches are more like drama than written text (drama will be discussed in Chapter 6), but for our purposes in studying for the GED, they are treated as literary nonfiction.

Speeches will use many of the literary techniques which we discussed in Chapter 3. These elements might include irony, figures of speech (such as metaphor and simile), careful word choices that make a point more emphatic, and so forth.

Speech writing also reminds us of an important point about nonfiction writing: Nonfiction may still present a matter of opinion, not a matter of fact. You'll remember the earlier discussion of the different types of essays, ranging from descriptive to persuasive. Speeches have a similar range: they can be written for practically any occasion when people will gather together. Here are some types of speeches that you might encounter on the GED:

- **introductory:** a speech that introduces a person or event or location to the audience, such as introducing a celebrity or dedicating a new building
- **narrative:** a speech that tells a story—such as something that the speaker has experienced
- **congratulatory:** a speech that congratulates someone for an accomplishment, or that thanks the audience for an award or recognition; such speeches are often used, for example, at the Academy Awards ceremony, or by politicians who have just been elected into office
- **expository:** a speech that explains something, such as how to succeed in college or why taxes have gone up
- **persuasive:** a speech in which the speaker tries to persuade the audience that his or her opinion is correct on some subject

Reading speeches is very similar to reading essays. The chief difference between an essay and a speech is that the essay is intended to be read on paper, while a speech is intended to be spoken aloud to an audience. But speechwriters will use the same techniques and styles that essayists use, so understanding and analyzing the two forms of nonfiction uses the same set of tools you've been learning.

▶ Critical Reviews

The final area of nonfiction that the GED deals with is that of critical reviews of the arts. You have probably read such reviews yourself; for example, most people will read reviews of new movies to help them decide if they're worth seeing.

The GED may have selections from critical reviews of almost any art form, including movies, fine arts (such as paintings or sculptures), photography, computer art, and television programs. Sometimes the test may also include a picture or photograph of the art being discussed.

Your approach to understanding critical reviews will be the same regardless of what art form is being addressed, and you will find that the tools and techniques used in critical reviews to be the same tool-set that we have been learning thus far in this guide. For example, here is Dorothy Parker's review of Jack Kerouac's novel *The Subterraneans*.

> Mr. Kerouac, possibly the inventor and certainly the historian of the Beat Generation, calls his latest work *The Subterraneans*. The Subterraneans "are hip without being slick, they are intelligent without being corny, they are intellectual as hell and know all about Pound without being pretentious or talking too much about it, they are very quiet, they are very Christlike." So those are the Subterraneans. The only point in the summary with which I can agree is that they are hip . . .
>
> Doubtless my absence of excitement over Mr. Kerouac's characters is due to a gaping lack in me, for, and I regret the fact, I do not dig bop. I cannot come afire when I hear it, and I am even less ecstatic in reading about it.
>
> . . . The Beat Ones never have to be anywhere, never want to go anywhere except just to some other place. There is little laughter among them, and they speak mainly to tell one another how great they are . . .
>
> I think, as perhaps you have discerned, that if Mr. Kerouac and his followers did not think of themselves as so glorious, as intellectual as all hell and very Christlike, I should not be in such a bad humor.

You will quickly see that critical reviews are organized similarly to a persuasive essay. Dorothy Parker's review takes the thesis that Jack Kerouac's book is not very good, and she supports that thesis by providing the reader with supporting evidence—such as the many character flaws she detects in the so-called "Beat Generation" Kerouac wrote about.

Parker also uses many of the literary techniques we have been studying, such as the irony or sarcasm she employs when suggesting that her *absence of excitement* about the novel is *due to a gaping lack* in her own character—by which she expects us to understand that she means just the opposite.

▶ Analytical Techniques for Nonfiction

As you have already seen, many of the reading techniques that you learned for fiction will also apply when you are reading nonfiction. For example, you will want to determine the main idea of the passage, recognize the writer's tone, pay attention to context, and so forth. With nonfiction, however, there are some techniques you can also use that are helpful in reading comprehension.

Determine the Audience and the Purpose

Nonfiction is frequently written to a very specific audience (the person or people who will read the document or listen to the speech). This information is often stated directly within the passage. In a business memo, for example, the intended audience is listed in the *to* and *from* sections. A letter is addressed directly to the person or people that it is written to.

The next step in analyzing nonfiction is to determine the passage's purpose. Why is the author writing this in the first place? What is he or she trying to accomplish? This is frequently stated openly in business communications, often listed as "re:" at the document's opening. Other nonfiction may not state the purpose quite as openly—such as with speeches—but remember that the whole function of nonfiction literature is to communicate something to the audience. Once you have determined what that something is, you are prepared to address the questions on the exam.

Look for Clues

When reading fiction, you learned how to look for the clues that an author gives the reader, such as word choice and tone and atmosphere. In reading nonfiction, you do the same thing—except that the clues are often much easier to spot.

One obvious example is the use of headings within a document. Nonfiction passages are frequently divided into smaller sections, each section having a heading or subheading that describes what the passage is about. This book makes use of that technique. You can tell at a glance that this paragraph has something to do with looking for clues, because there is a heading stating that at the beginning.

Lists and tables and other supporting data will also provide a quick clue to the author's purpose. When you see a bulleted list, for example ("bullets" are the dots or squares that are placed at the beginning of each line), you can quickly scan the list and determine its purpose. What do all the items in the list have in common? Why is the author including this list? These questions will quickly help you narrow down the purpose of the passage.

Find the Supporting Evidence

Another important technique in reading nonfiction is to pinpoint any supporting evidence the author has included. In business documents, this will be found in the clues discussed earlier—lists, tables, and so forth.

In other types of nonfiction, however, the supporting evidence may not be listed in such tidy fashion. This will require that you use the reading comprehension tools that we have been developing in this book. Look for clue words that point to supporting details: *such as*, *for example*, and so forth.

If the author makes a statement of opinion—something that can be debated—ask yourself, "How do I know this is true? Why is this author's opinion right?" Then look through the passage to find the places where the author attempts to answer those questions. Those points will be the supporting data.

READING NONFICTION

▶ Practice Questions

Read the following passages and answer their related questions.

Passage 1

The following is the Gettysburg Address, delivered by Abraham Lincoln in 1863.

> Four score and seven years ago our fathers brought forth on this continent a new nation, conceived in Liberty, and dedicated to the proposition that all men are created equal.
>
> Now we are engaged in a great civil war, testing whether that nation, or any nation, so conceived and so dedicated, can long endure. We are met on a great battlefield of that war. We have come to dedicate a portion of that field, as a final resting place for those who here gave their lives that that nation might live. It is altogether fitting and proper that we should do this.
>
> But, in a larger sense, we can not dedicate—we can not consecrate—we can not hallow—this ground. The brave men, living and dead, who struggled here, have consecrated it, far above our poor power to add or detract. The world will little note, nor long remember what we say here, but it can never forget what they did here. It is for us the living, rather, to be dedicated here to the unfinished work which they who fought here have thus far so nobly advanced. It is rather for us to be here dedicated to the great task remaining before us—that from these honored dead we take increased devotion to that cause for which they gave the last full measure of devotion—that we here highly resolve that these dead shall not have died in vain—that this nation, under God, shall have a new birth of freedom—and that government of the people, by the people, for the people, shall not perish from the earth.

1. How many years prior to this speech had the United States become independent?
   a. 47
   b. 87
   c. 74
   d. 125
   e. 52

2. What is the occasion at which Lincoln gave this speech?
   a. the end of the Civil War
   b. the beginning of the Civil War
   c. to address the atrocities of war
   d. to dedicate a graveyard for those fallen in battle at Gettysburg
   e. The occasion is not stated.

3. What does the word *hallow* mean?
   a. to carve out the center of something
   b. to make something holy or sacred
   c. It was a form of greeting in the 1800s.
   d. It is a valley between mountains.
   e. It is a color.

4. Why does Lincoln say that "we cannot consecrate . . . this ground"?
   a. because the men who gave their lives have already done so
   b. because ground cannot be consecrated
   c. because the Civil War hasn't ended yet
   d. He doesn't say that; he says the opposite.
   e. He doesn't address this question.

READING NONFICTION

5. What is the *unfinished work* that Lincoln refers to in the third paragraph?
   a. finishing the work on the cemetery
   b. remembering their names in the future
   c. freeing the slaves
   d. finishing the Civil War
   e. ensuring the future of the United States

6. What is *the last full measure of devotion* mentioned in the third paragraph?
   a. living a good life
   b. being loyal to yourself
   c. giving one's life for one's country
   d. performing some act of service for charity
   e. It is not stated.

Passage 2

The following passage is from an employee handbook.

Dress Code

Employees are to be professional in their appearance at all times. Professional attire is a flexible term to some degree, but the final judgment shall be left to management in all areas. Some guidelines include the following:

Men
- Neckties are recommended for all salaried and exempt employees. Non-exempt and hourly employees may or may not be required to wear neckties, depending upon job duties and the discretion of management.
- Sweaters or sports jackets are not required, but may still be considered appropriate for certain situations, such as meetings with clients. Management retains the option to *mandate* such in certain circumstances.
- Bluejeans are never appropriate, except on certain specified days—such as casual Fridays or dress-down days, at the discretion of management.
- Sneakers and running shoes are not appropriate unless the employee's duties require excessive walking or stand-up work, or when required by medical or health issues. Management shall retain the right to make specific exceptions as necessary.

Women
- Pantsuits are acceptable, provided that they retain a professional appearance.
- Shorts, hot pants, culottes, and similar attire is never appropriate. This includes dress-down days and other times of casual attire.
- Skirts and dresses should be of at least moderate length, reaching the knees.
- Dresses and skirts above the knees are considered inappropriate at all times, including dress-down days and other times of casual attire.
- Bluejeans are never appropriate, except on certain specified days—such as casual Fridays or dress-down days, at the discretion of management.
- Sneakers and running shoes are not appropriate unless the employee's duties require excessive walking or stand-up work, or when required by medical or health issues. Management shall retain the right to make specific exceptions as necessary.

7. What is the main idea of this passage?
   a. Employees must follow orders.
   b. Management has the final say.
   c. Bluejeans are unacceptable in the work place.
   d. Employees must always appear professional.
   e. Fridays are dress-down days.

8. What does the word *mandate* mean in the second bulleted item under *Men*?
   a. to make something optional
   b. to make something a requirement
   c. to enjoy a social outing with friends
   d. It is an official logo of a company.
   e. It is a common form of office communication.

9. When might running shoes be considered appropriate attire?
   a. always
   b. never
   c. when an employee has back problems
   d. when the boss is on vacation
   e. It is not stated.

10. From this dress code, you could infer that T-shirts are
    a. always appropriate.
    b. never appropriate.
    c. left up to the discretion of the employee.
    d. acceptable if they have no writing or advertising.
    e. unacceptable unless worn with bluejeans.

11. How often does this company have casual days?
    a. every Friday
    b. every other Friday
    c. on Fridays and special holidays
    d. never
    e. It is not stated.

12. What is the tone of this memo?
    a. angry
    b. informative
    c. sad
    d. humorous
    e. confrontational

Passage 3

The following is a newspaper story.

Traffic Commission Debates Bus Restrictions
The West Harbor Traffic Commission last night debated the questions concerning the "no-bus" restrictions on certain roads, without reaching a final conclusion.

Certain streets in West Harbor are posted with "No Bus" signs, forbidding any motor vehicles larger than a typical SUV.

Martin Fillman, chairman of West Harbor Chamber of Commerce, has asked the Traffic Commission to remove some of those signs, arguing that the loss of bus traffic has hurt some local businesses.

"We are a tourist-based economy here," Fillman said last night while testifying before the Commission, "and we rely on bus traffic to bring customers to some of our restaurants and gift shops. Denying them access to places like Lighthouse End and Teaticket effectively puts some people out of business."

Many residents, however, have argued that the bus traffic endangers children and small animals, and causes traffic inconvenience.

"We live here, and we intend to have our children safe to play in the streets," stated Melanie Greenhouse in an impassioned plea. "Those buses pollute the environment with their smelly diesel fumes, and it's almost impossible to get to the mall during the summer when they're rolling in and out of Teaticket Take-Out." Greenhouse is chairwoman of the Teaticket Women in Transit Safety (TWiTS), a citizens' response group that monitors the West Harbor Traffic Commission.

The Traffic Commission listened to input from local residents and business owners, but shelved debate on the issue for the next meeting, scheduled for next Wednesday at 7 P.M.

13. What is the central issue that is causing confrontation in this article?
    a. tourist traffic in the summer
    b. streets that don't allow buses
    c. undisciplined children playing in the streets
    d. tourist buses polluting the environment
    e. the incompetence of the Traffic Commission

14. What is the central thesis of Martin Fillman's argument?
    a. The special restrictions are bad for tourist business.
    b. The special restrictions are unconstitutional.
    c. The Traffic Commission is part of the problem.
    d. Buses don't really pollute the environment.
    e. He has no central thesis.

15. What is the central thesis of Melanie Greenhouse's argument?
    a. Buses pollute the environment.
    b. Children should be allowed to play in the street.
    c. Her SUV gets blocked in her driveway in the summer.
    d. The mall is too far away.
    e. She has no central thesis.

16. Why didn't the Traffic Commission make a decision?
    a. They were divided 50/50 on the issue.
    b. They are not empowered to make such a decision.
    c. They wanted more information.
    d. They were hoping to be bribed.
    e. It is not stated.

Passage 4

I entered this world more than a half-century ago, which sounds like such a great length of time. Yet somehow it isn't; yet somehow it is. One might say, "it's an entire lifetime ago!" When that lifetime is someone else's, it is indeed a half-century. But when that lifetime is one's own, it is but yesterday.

I've known too many yesterdays, and too few tomorrows—yet all considered together they are both too many and too few. And somehow, for all men, it is always today. Today is never enough, and today can be far too long. Today is the first day of the rest of your life, according to a popular poster when I was young, and that philosophy sounded so wise to my teenage mind. But to my half-century mind, I recognize it for the silly *tripe* that it really is; for if today is the first day of the rest of my life, what will tomorrow be? And what was yesterday—the final day of my former life?

It is true, of course, that I can choose to make today be the starting point of a whole new lifestyle. But what will I do tomorrow? Will I revert tomorrow to the habits of yesterday, ignoring the resolution of today? If so, I have merely chosen to start a whole new lifestyle, not recognizing that it is the lifestyle which I have always known—and I have only deceived myself. Either way, I have redefined myself for the future; and either way, I can erase that redefinition tomorrow and start yet another whole new future which accomplishes no more than my past.

Such philosophies are pleasing to the shallow mind, but the deeper soul will be driven to insanity if one attempts to embrace them.

17. This passage is probably an excerpt from
   a. an essay.
   b. a biography.
   c. an autobiography.
   d. a memo.
   e. a hard news story.

18. What does the author mean by "I've known too many yesterdays, and too few tomorrows"?
   a. His memory is fading.
   b. Life is too short.
   c. He is disappointed with his life.
   d. He has great hopes for the future.
   e. He has already lived out most of his life.

19. What does *tripe* mean in the second paragraph?
   a. something of no value
   b. a type of fish
   c. three-part
   d. to stumble and fall
   e. a decoration

20. What is the central thesis of this passage?
   a. We can never hope to change.
   b. We deceive ourselves with shallow resolutions to change.
   c. There is no yesterday and no tomorrow, only today.
   d. Today is the first day of the rest of your life.
   e. Eat, drink, and be merry, for tomorrow we die.

21. What is the tone of this passage?
   a. angry
   b. defensive
   c. fearful
   d. thoughtful
   e. humorous

Passage 5

The following excerpt is from a speech given by Winston Churchill during World War II.

You cannot tell from appearances how things will go. Sometimes imagination makes things out far worse than they are; yet without imagination not much can be done. Those people who are imaginative see many more dangers than perhaps exist; certainly many more than will happen; but then they must also pray to be given that extra courage to carry this far-reaching imagination. But for everyone, surely, . . . this is the lesson: never give in, never give in, never, never, never, never—in nothing, great or small, large or petty—never give in except to convictions of honor and good sense. Never yield to force; never yield to the apparently overwhelming might of the enemy. We stood all alone a year ago, and to many countries it seemed that our account was closed, we were finished. All this tradition of ours, our songs, our School history, this part of the history of this country, were gone and finished and liquidated.

Very different is the mood today. Britain, other nations thought, had drawn a sponge across her slate. But instead our country stood in the gap. There was no flinching and no thought of giving in; and by what seemed almost a miracle to those outside these Islands, though we ourselves never doubted it, we now find ourselves in a position where I say that we can be sure that we have only to persevere to conquer.

Do not let us speak of darker days: let us speak rather of sterner days. These are not dark days; these are great days—the greatest days our country has ever lived; and we must all thank

God that we have been allowed, each of us according to our stations, to play a part in making these days memorable in the history of our race.

22. Why does Churchill repeat *never give in* so many times?
   a. It is a typographical error.
   b. He is speaking to people who are hard-of-hearing.
   c. to show that he is open to compromise
   d. to strongly emphasize his point
   e. It is a common technique in speech-writing.

23. What does it mean that Britain *had drawn a sponge across her slate*?
   a. Other nations thought that Britain was going to collapse.
   b. Tomorrow is a new day.
   c. The shortage of ammunition has created hardship in Britain.
   d. Germany's bombings have destroyed Britain's heritage.
   e. Britain has a shortage of pencils and paper.

24. What does it mean that *our country stood in the gap*?
   a. There is an economic shortage in Britain.
   b. Britain is located between Germany and France.
   c. The British were waiting for help from other countries.
   d. The Germans had created gaps in the streets with their bombs.
   e. British soldiers were willing to risk their lives to stop the enemy.

25. What is the tone of this passage?
   a. informative
   b. humorous
   c. inspirational
   d. angry
   e. flippant

26. What is the thesis of this passage?
   a. There is little hope of winning the war.
   b. Britain is going to win in the end, if they don't give up now.
   c. Compromise is better than fighting.
   d. War is evil.
   e. If people just tried harder, we could all get along.

Passage 6

The following is a review of the film *Lawrence of Arabia*.

The Pride of Man

The film *Lawrence of Arabia* may be somewhat dated by modern special-effects standards, but it remains a high-water mark in the annals of filmmaking. Since we're on the subject of CGI and other computer-generated special effects, *Lawrence* has practically none for the simple reason that it was actually filmed using real people who really performed the action. The long, slow scenes of camels walking in the desert may seem dull to the modern animation-jaded viewer, but those willing to pay attention to the underlying themes will be well rewarded by what the movie is saying.

And it is the theme of *Lawrence* that really stays with a viewer, even today, some 40 years after it was released. That theme is the age-old story of *hubris*—the pride of a man which raises him above his peers, only to dash him on the rocks of self-indulgence by the end.

READING NONFICTION

We see this tragic foible of mankind worked out fully in the character of Lawrence himself, who begins the film as a brilliant genius who is eager to get involved in the desert conflicts of World War I. His cocky attitude irritates his superiors and amuses the Arabs fighting alongside the British, but his genius for details and strategy soon overcome all obstacles. Lawrence's brilliant victory at the Suez Canal could only have been accomplished by Lawrence, and his own self-sacrifice and commitment to his followers display the best of his character.

Unfortunately, the baser elements of that character gradually take control as the film moves along, and Lawrence slowly declines into a dangerous blend of despair and self-assurance. The problem gradually becomes evident: Lawrence has grown to believe that he is equal to God, the one who both gives life and takes it away again.

27. This excerpt is an example of a
   a. fable.
   b. paradox.
   c. first-person narrator.
   d. memoir.
   e. critical review.

28. What is the central theme of *Lawrence of Arabia*, according to this passage?
   a. the importance of the Suez Canal
   b. Man's pride will bring about his destruction.
   c. The Arabian Desert is a hostile environment.
   d. It is a documentary on World War I.
   e. One man can make a difference.

29. What is the meaning of *hubris* in the second paragraph?
   a. hair
   b. pride
   c. a square shape
   d. a halo
   e. death

30. You might infer that the author of this passage
   a. admires the film *Lawrence of Arabia*.
   b. does not like the character of Lawrence.
   c. has traveled in the Middle East.
   d. is a World War I historian.
   e. knows nothing about the Suez Canal.

CHAPTER

5 ▶ Reading Poetry

UNTIL ABOUT a hundred years ago, poetry was fairly easy to define: A poem was a piece of literature that conveyed its meaning through rhyme scheme and meter. In the past century, however, the concepts of poetry have changed so drastically that it is difficult to give a short definition of poetry. In general, however, a poem still conveys its meaning to the reader by the use of a number of poetic elements that will be defined in this chapter.

The traditional poem had two unique traits that distinguished it from prose: rhyme scheme, by which we mean that it rhymed; and stanzaic structure, by which we mean that it was composed in stanzas, or groups of short lines. For our purposes in preparing for the GED, however, we will look at these two elements as *elements of sound* and *elements of structure*.

READING POETRY

▶ Elements of Sound

First of all, it is important to understand that poetry is intended to be read aloud, not just read silently from a book. When you read a poem out loud, you will discover that part of its power is drawn from the sound of the writing. The following humorous poem by Ogden Nash is entitled "Good-By, Bugs." Read it silently to yourself, then read it again out loud.

> Some insects feed on rosebuds,
> And others feed on carrion.
> Between them they devour the earth.
> Bugs are totalitarian.

In reading that poem silently, you probably got the humorous sense of what Nash was saying—that bugs are trying to take over the world. But in reading it out loud, you may have been surprised to hear yourself pronouncing *totalitarian* in an unusual way. The full sense of Nash's humor in this little poem only becomes clear when you read it aloud and find yourself rhyming *totalitarian* with *carrion*.

This is part of the power of poetry: It uses the sounds of words as well as the sense or meaning of words to convey its ideas to the reader.

Rhyme, Alliteration, and Onomatopoeia

The most common element of sound that poetry uses is rhyme. Two words that sound alike—such as *cat* and *bat*—are said to rhyme. Words can rhyme in various ways. The words *cat* and *bat*, for example, are called exact rhymes because they differ in only one sound—the initial consonants *c* and *b*. Technically an exact rhyme requires that the words rhyme completely, regardless of the number of syllables. For instance, *buffer* and *rougher* are exact rhymes. For our purposes, however, we will include any words whose final syllables rhyme. This would, therefore, include such word pairs as *suggest* and *behest*. Here is an example of exact, or perfect, rhyme, from Joyce Kilmer's poem "Trees":

> I think that I shall never see
> A poem lovely as a tree.

A half-rhyme occurs when two words share only the same final consonant. The words *hot* and *cat* would be considered half-rhymes because they share the final consonant *t*. Some other examples of half-rhyme include *trolley* and *bully*; *soul* and *oil*; *Firth* and *fourth*. Here is an example of half-rhyme:

> The coffee in the pot
> Is not quite ready yet.

Note that the above example is a half-rhyme because the final consonant is the same in *pot* and *yet*. These two lines would become exact rhymes, however, if they were changed to this:

> The coffee in the pot
> Is not very hot.

A less common type of rhyme is called eye-rhyme. Eye-rhymes actually don't rhyme—they just look as if they should rhyme. The words *cough* and *bough* and *rough* all look as if they'd rhyme, but they actually don't when spoken aloud. Here is an example of eye-rhyme:

> The man walked through
> even though
> the way was rough.

Alliteration occurs when a consonant sound is repeated throughout a line or stanza of poetry. Here

READING POETRY

is an example of alliteration, drawn from the ancient Anglo-Saxon poem *Beowulf*:

> Now Beowulf abode in the burg of the
>   Scyldings,
> Leader beloved, and long he ruled
> In fame with all folk, since his father had gone
> Away from the world, till awoke an heir,
> Haughty Healfdene, who held through life,
> Sage and sturdy, the Scyldings glad.

Read these lines aloud, and take note of the consonant sounds that repeat in each line. In line 1, the letter *b* is repeated frequently: *B*eowulf; *a*b*ode; *b*urg. Line 2 uses the letter *l* frequently: *L*eader; be*l*oved; *l*ong; ru*l*ed. Line 3 repeats the letter *f*, and so forth. This is known as **alliteration**.

Another element of sound is *onomatopoeia*, pronounced *on-oh-maht-ah-PEE-ah*, meaning *words that sound like what they describe*. You may not have heard of *onomatopoeia* before, but you've used it just the same—words such as *bang* and *pop* and *hiss* and *buzz* are all examples of onomatopoeia, words that describe something by imitating it.

Rhyme Scheme

Poems that rhyme will often follow a specific rhyming pattern, which is called the poem's *rhyme scheme*. There is no set formula for how a poem should rhyme—in fact, many poems don't rhyme at all—but let's look at a couple of examples. Here is some more of Joyce Kilmer's poem "Trees":

> I think that I shall never see
> A poem lovely as a tree.
>
> A tree whose hungry mouth is prest
> Against the sweet earth's flowing breast;
>
> A tree that looks at God all day,
> And lifts her leafy arms to pray;

Notice that the rhyming words are *see* and *tree*, followed by *prest* and *breast*, and so on. We would call the *see/tree* rhyme *a*, *prest/breast* would be *b*, *day/pray* is *c*, and so forth. Thus we would say that this poem has a rhyme scheme of *a, a, b, b, c, c*.

But suppose that Kilmer had repeated some of the rhymes—let's say that he added the line "This is what I love in thee" to each stanza. Perhaps it might read like this:

> I think that I shall never see
> A poem lovely as a tree.
>   That is what I love in thee.
>
> A tree whose hungry mouth is prest
> Against the sweet earth's flowing breast;
>   That is what I love in thee.
>
> A tree that looks at God all day,
> And lifts her leafy arms to pray;
>   That is what I love in thee.

In this imaginary rewriting, we have changed the rhyme scheme to *a, a, a, b, b, a, c, c, a*, and so on. In other words, each time that we end a line with a word rhyming with *tree*, we are returning to the *a* rhyme—the first rhyme. Read the following lines from John Milton's "On the Morning of Christ's Nativity," and see if you can determine the rhyme scheme:

> This is the Month, and this the happy morn
> Wherein the Son of Heav'n's eternal King,
> Of wedded Maid, and Virgin Mother born,
> Our great redemption from above did bring;
> For so the holy sages once did sing,
>   That he our deadly forfeit should release,
> And with his Father work us a perpetual peace.

The first line ends with *morn*, which we label *a*. The next line ends with *King*, which does not rhyme with *morn*, so it's labeled *b*. The third line, however, ends with *born*, which does rhyme with *morn*, so it's labeled *a* again because it rhymes with line *a*. Line 4 ends with *bring*, which rhymes with *King* and is therefore labeled *b*. Line 5 also rhymes with *King*, so it is also labeled *b*. Then the final two lines introduce a new rhyme of *release* and *peace*, so they are labeled *c*. So the rhyme scheme for these lines is *a, b, a, b, b, c, c*.

Here's one more example from John Milton, this time from his "Sonnet 19," which he wrote when he discovered that he was going blind (his *one Talent* refers to his ability to write poetry if he becomes blind):

> When I consider how my light is spent, [*a*]
> Ere half my days, in this dark world and wide, [*b*]
> And that one Talent which is death to hide, [*b*]
> Lodged with me useless, though my soul more bent . . . [*a*]

Finally, poetry that does not rhyme is called *blank verse*. Even if it does not rhyme, a poem may still be written in a specific meter, however, which brings us to the next element of poetic sound.

Meter

Another important aspect of sound in poetry is the poem's rhythm or meter. Meter is composed of stressed syllables and unstressed syllables within an individual line of poetry. A stressed syllable is the part of the word which we tend to accentuate when speaking.

For example, say the word *meticulous* out loud. (It is important to read poetry aloud if you want to hear the stressed and unstressed syllables correctly.) You probably spoke the word *meticulous* with a greater accent on the second syllable, like this: me-TIC-u-luss. Now try *thoroughbred*. With that word, you probably accented the first syllable. These are examples of stressed and unstressed syllables. The part of the word which you accent is the stressed syllable, and the other syllables are unstressed.

This same principle applies in poetry even when words are all one syllable. Read out loud the opening lines of Milton's "Sonnet 19," which you looked at earlier. Notice which words and syllables you instinctively stress, and which ones you don't stress.

Your out-loud reading may have sounded like this, where the stressed syllables are in **bold italics**:

> When ***I*** con***si***der ***how*** my ***light*** is ***spent***,
> Ere ***half*** my ***days***, in ***this*** dark ***world*** and ***wide***,
> And ***that*** one ***Tal***ent ***which*** is ***death*** to ***hide***,
> ***Lodged*** with me ***use***less, though my ***soul*** more ***bent*** . . .

What you have done in these lines is to take the first step toward identifying the meter that Milton used in this poem. A specific meter is determined by a pattern of stressed and unstressed syllables.

A useful way of recognizing which syllables are stressed and which are unstressed is to replace the words with a sort of metrical beat—saying *da-DUM da-DUM da-DUM* out loud as your eye reads through the poem. The *da* represents an unstressed syllable, and the *DUM* represents a stressed syllable. Try reading through those lines again, but this time, read the words silently while speaking the metrical rhythm out loud.

Your out-loud reading probably sounded like this: *da-DUM da-DUM da-DUM da-DUM da-DUM*. Now go back through and mark the lines with a pencil, marking a U over the unstressed syllables, and a slash (/) over the stressed syllables. Your markings will look something like this:

    U / U / U   /   U / U   /
When I consider how my light is spent,
  U   /   U   / U   /   U   /   U /
Ere half my days, in this dark world and wide,
   U   /   U   /   U   / U   /   U /
And that one Talent which is death to hide,
    /   U U   /   U   U   /
Lodged with me useless, though my soul
                U   /
            more bent...

Congratulations! You have now scanned a poem, which means that you have identified the stressed and unstressed syllables. You are now prepared to identify the metrical pattern that Milton is using in each of those lines.

There are a great many different types of meter, but here are some of the more common ones:

- **iambic:** one unstressed syllable followed by one stressed syllable. Iambic most closely resembles normal English speech, and is one of the most common meters used in poetry.
  Example:
  U /|U /|U /|U /|U /
  In every life a little rain must fall.

- **trochaic:** one stressed syllable followed by one unstressed syllable. This is the opposite of iambic.
  Example:
  / U|/   U|/   U|/ U
  You must work to earn your living.

- **anapestic:** two unstressed syllables followed by one stressed syllable.
  Example:
  U U /|U U   /|U U /
  If you look hard enough you will see
     U U   /
  that he's there.

- **dactylic:** one stressed syllable followed by two unstressed syllables.
  Example:
  / U U|/ U U
  Put her down tenderly.

Which type of meter is Milton's sonnet that we've been looking at? If you compare your scanned lines with the examples in each type, you will quickly see that Milton was using the iambic meter—one unstressed syllable followed by one unstressed syllable.

Now take another look at the examples provided for each of the metrical types. You will see that a new symbol, a vertical line (|) has been added to the U and / symbols. This line is used to separate the bits of meter from one another within each line.

Those bits of meter are called *feet*. A foot is one complete bit of iambic or trochaic or anapestic or dactylic meter. Now that you have identified Milton's sonnet as iambic, go back to your marked-up lines and add the vertical lines (|) between the iambic feet.

Your marked-up text should look something like this now:

U /|U   /|U   /|U   /|U /
When I consid er how my light is spent,
U   /|U   /|U   /|U   /|U /
Ere half my days, in this dark world and wide,
U   /|U   /|U   /|U /|U /
And that one Tal ent which is death to hide,
/   U U|/ U U|/ /
Lodged with me useless, though my soul
        U   /
    more bent...

The advantage to adding those vertical lines is that you can now count how many feet there are in each line. If you count the feet in the first line of Milton's sonnet, you'll see that there are five. This is the final piece of the puzzle in defining a poem's meter:

identifying how many feet are in a line. Here are the most commonly used patterns:

- **trimeter:** three feet per line
- **tetrameter:** four feet per line
- **pentameter:** five feet per line
- **hexameter:** six feet per line

Congratulations again! You have now fully identified that the opening lines of Milton's "Sonnet 19" are written in iambic pentameter—five feet per line (pentameter), each foot composed of one unstressed syllable followed by one stressed syllable (iambic).

Of course, you have probably already noticed that only the first three lines of Milton's sonnet are written in iambic pentameter; the fourth line is different. Can you identify what meter that fourth line is written in?*

▶ Elements of Structure

You have now learned one of the basic elements of poetical structure: that lines are broken down into metrical feet. The line is the basic structure of poetry, just as the sentence is the basic structure of prose.

But prose sentences are grouped together into a larger structure, called the *paragraph*. In the same way, lines of poetry are often grouped together into a larger unit called a *stanza*. Not all poems are constructed in stanzas, but when they are, they are known as *stanzaic* poems.

Another way to think of stanzas is to think of a popular song. Songs are frequently written in verses, each verse starting again at the beginning of the tune. The "Star Spangled Banner," for example, is a song with numerous verses (although most of us only know the first verse). In the same way, a poem that is constructed of stanzas will follow the same pattern for each stanza. The stanzas may also be set apart from one another visually on the page, although that is not always the case.

Rhymed and Metered Poetry

We have already considered both rhyme scheme and meter in the preceding section, so we don't need to reiterate it here. It is important, however, to understand that not all poetry rhymes, and not all poetry follows any specific meter. We looked at Milton's "Sonnet 19," which is both rhyming and metered; now let's look at some poems that are not. Here, for example, are the opening lines from another poem by John Milton, "Paradise Lost."

> Of Man's First Disobedience, and the Fruit
> Of that Forbidden Tree, whose mortal taste
> Brought Death into the World, and all our woe,
> With loss of Eden, till one greater Man
> Restore us, and regain the blissful Seat . . .

Take a moment now and scan those lines, using the techniques you learned in the previous section. Mark each line using the U and / symbols, separating each line into feet. What do you find?

You will discover that Milton is using iambic pentameter in this poem—but there are no rhymes. This is an example of blank verse, poetry that is written in a specific meter but does not rhyme. (Traditionally, blank verse was always written in iambic pentameter, but nowadays that is no longer the case.)

There is also a type of poetry that uses neither rhyme nor meter, called *free verse*, which is very popular in modern poetry circles. Here is a sample from Walt Whitman's "Song of Myself":

> I celebrate myself, and sing myself,
> And what I assume you shall assume,
> For every atom belonging to me as good
>   belongs to you.

---

*The fourth line of Milton's "Sonnet 19" is *dactylic tetrameter*.

Types of Poetry

As you can see by now, the world of poetry is very flexible and broad. A writer can create a poem using almost any rhyme scheme and meter—or none at all. In spite of this, however, there are many classifications within poetry: specific types of poems that follow a strict set of rules, and more general classifications of poetry that address a poem's purpose while leaving the actual structure undefined. We will start by looking at a few of the more specific types of poetry, then address some of the more generic categories.

Sonnets

The sonnet was a very popular form of poetry for hundreds of years, and even today it is still found in contemporary poetry. The sonnet form is very strict concerning the structure and rhyme scheme, although many poets still take some liberty in deviating somewhat from some of these structural rules.

In general, a sonnet is 14 lines in length, is written in iambic pentameter, and has a rhyme scheme (usually) of *a, b, a, b, c, d, c, d, e, f, e, f, g, g*. Obviously, this is a very strict set of rules, but the structure actually lends itself to some of the greatest poetry in the English language. Shakespeare, for example, used this structure for almost all of his poetry—and he wrote a great deal of it. So much so, in fact, that this structure is sometimes called the *Shakespearean Sonnet* form. Here is an example.

Sonnet 100
Some glory in their birth, some in their skill,
Some in their wealth, some in their body's force,
Some in their garments though new-fangled ill;
Some in their hawks and hounds, some in their horse;
And every humor hath his adjunct pleasure,
Wherein it finds a joy above the rest:
But these particulars are not my measure,
All these I better in one general best.
Thy love is better than high birth to me,
Richer than wealth, prouder than garments' costs,
Of more delight than hawks and horses be;
And having thee, of all men's pride I boast:
    Wretched in this alone, that thou mayst take
    All this away, and me most wretched make.

Practice your scanning skills on this sonnet, marking up the feet with the U and / symbols, separating each foot with a vertical line (|). Then mark the rhyme scheme for each line, beginning with the first line as *a*. You will find that it is written in iambic pentameter (five feet per line of one unstressed syllable followed by one stressed syllable), rhyming *a, b, a, b, c, d, c, d, e, f, e, f, g, g*.

Elegies

An elegy is literally a song for the dead, and as a poetical form is a poem that praises the virtues and laments the death of a person. The elegy can also be used to treat abstract subjects, such as death, war, or even love. Like the sonnet, the elegy was a very popular poetical form for hundreds of years, and is still used in contemporary poetry.

Elegies in general do not follow any specific rules for structure or rhyme. The subject of the poem does not even have to be a dead person; it can address abstract ideas, as we've already said, or even a person who is still alive. In general, however, an elegy is a serious poem that offers the reader some deeper insight into the subject.

Elegies are frequently rather long poems. Here is an excerpt from Thomas Gray's "Elegy Written in a Country Churchyard."

> For them no more the blazing hearth shall burn,
>   Or busy housewife ply her evening care:
> No children run to lisp their sire's return,
>   Or climb his knees the envied kiss to share.
>
> Oft did the harvest to their sickle yield,
>   Their furrow oft the stubborn glebe has broke:
> How jocund did they drive their team afield!
>   How bow'd the woods beneath their sturdy stroke!
>
> Let not Ambition mock their useful toil,
>   Their homely joys, and destiny obscure;
> Nor Grandeur hear with a disdainful smile
>   The short and simple annals of the poor.

Odes

The ode is another rather formal and lengthy poetical style, and it, too, generally deals with some weighty subject matter—death or war or the loss of someone important. Public odes are written for some important event or occasion, such as a funeral or an important national occasion. Private odes are written in response to the poet's own experiences, such as the loss of love or his own impending death. In general, odes of any kind are thoughtful and reflective, encouraging the reader to consider how the subject matter touches him or her.

Here is the opening stanza of "Ode to a Nightingale" by John Keats. The poem as a whole is addressed to a bird noted for its beautiful song, yet Keats is actually addressing much deeper subjects. In this first stanza, you can get a glimpse of the poem's sadness and struggle against despair.

> My heart aches, and a drowsy numbness pains
>   My sense, as though of hemlock I had drunk,
> Or emptied some dull opiate to the drains
>   One minute past, and Lethe-wards had sunk:
> 'Tis not through envy of thy happy lot,
>   But being too happy in thy happiness,
>   That thou, light-winged Dryad of the trees,
>   In some melodious plot
>   Of beechen green, and shadows numberless,
>   Singest of summer in full-throated ease.

There are many other specific types of poetry, but the sonnet, the elegy, and the ode are the most common types that you will find on the GED. Now let's move on to more generic classifications of poetry.

Emotive Poetry

An emotive poem is designed to arouse some emotional response in the reader. Some poems, such as elegies, try to lead the reader to a deeper understanding of some topic; this is not what emotive poems do.

Emotive poems attempt to describe something that is hard to describe—something that is essentially emotional. Consider this untitled poem by Alexander Pushkin.

> I have loved you; even now I may confess,
> Some embers of my love their fire retain
> but do not let it cause you more distress,
> I do not want to sadden you again.
> Hopeless and tonguetied, yet, I loved you dearly
> With pangs the jealous and the timid know;
> So tenderly I loved you—so sincerely;
> I pray God grant another love you so.

Pushkin is attempting to describe the mixed feelings of having loved someone who no longer loves you in return. He is not trying to persuade his lover to come back, nor is he trying to analyze and understand the causes of why their love has ended. His poem is concerned only with the emotions he is experiencing, and he is trying to convey those through this emotive poem.

Imagistic Poetry

Imagistic poetry attempts to describe an event or setting, helping you to visualize the subject matter as though you were actually experiencing it yourself. One well-known imagistic poet is T.E. Hulme; here is his poem "Above the Dock."

> Above the quiet dock in midnight,
> Tangled in the tall mast's corded height,
> Hangs the moon. What seemed so far away
> Is but a child's balloon, forgotten after play.

In this poem, Hulme is describing a scene, something that he sees: The moon rising in the sky, behind the masts of a sailing ship. As he stands watching the moon, he notices that it looks like a balloon that has floated upward and gotten tangled in the rigging of the ship's mast. This image is unusual, and in fact ironic: The moon is so far away and so huge, yet here it looks both small and close. This is the image the poet is trying to convey to the reader.

Narrative and Argumentative Poetry

A narrative poem tells a story, while an argumentative poem addresses some theme or idea, such as love or courage. Many of the poems we have looked at already are argumentative, because they address some deep subject. Gray's "Elegy," for example, addresses the danger of forgetting about those who have died.

Other poems tell a story. Ballads, for example, frequently recount some event or person. Such poems have been popular down through the ages because they tell interesting stories written in everyday language. This poetic form is still used today in much popular music.

Some poems do both together, telling a story in narrative style while also addressing some deep issues in argumentative style. Here is one by Robert Frost.

The Road Not Taken
Two roads diverged in a yellow wood,
And sorry I could not travel both
And be one traveller, long I stood
And looked down one as far as I could
To where it bent in the undergrowth;
Then took the other, just as fair,
And having perhaps the better claim,
Because it was grassy and wanted wear;
Though as for that the passing there
Had worn them really about the same,
And both that morning equally lay
In leaves no step had trodden black.
Oh, I kept the first for another day!
Yet knowing how way leads on to way,
I doubted if I should ever come back.
I shall be telling this with a sigh
Somewhere ages and ages hence:
Two roads diverged in a wood, and I—I took
    the one less traveled by,
And that has made all the difference.

This poem is first of all a narrative, because it is telling a story. Frost is describing the time that he was walking through the woods and came to a fork in the path. He had to decide whether to go left or right, and he noticed that one path appeared to be more frequently used than the other. He decided to continue down the path that was less frequently traveled.

But the poem is also argumentative, because Frost is using his walk in the woods both on a literal level (he had taken a real walk in a real forest) and also on a metaphorical level: The path in the woods can mean more than simply a path in the woods. He is using this experience to suggest that there are times when people should deliberately not follow the example of what everyone else does; sometimes we should take the path that is *less traveled by*, making a decision that might seem unusual to people around us. He also warns, however, that there can be consequences to making such a choice: It might be irreversible. He tells us, *I doubted if I should ever come back*, implying that his choice to take one path meant that he might never learn what lay at the end of the other path. These are deep subjects that Frost is tackling, and this is the argumentative aspect of the poem.

▶ Word Choice in Poetry

Poetry uses many of the elements of fiction addressed in Chapter 3, such as irony, metaphor, personification, symbolism, and so forth. Poems are different from most fiction, however, in the fact that they are relatively short pieces of writing (far shorter than a novel, for example) and must therefore compress a great deal of meaning and thought into a short space.

For this reason, word choice becomes critically important in poetry. In fact, one might say that word choice is the very essence of poetry—the ability to use words powerfully and succinctly, conveying a mood or idea in a very small space.

Poetry frequently takes advantage of the many-layered aspect of language. We all know how to use words and phrases that can be interpreted in more ways than one. One common form of this is called double entendre, a form of humor that describes something from everyday life but that also carries some other connotation—usually of a sexual nature.

Another example of such layered meaning is the common pun, a form of wording that takes advantage of a word's different uses to produce humor or to deepen the reader's understanding—although puns are usually used humorously. A pun can also be created by taking advantage of homophones, words that sound alike but have different meanings. The words *son* and *sun*, for example, are homophones because they sound the same but have very different meanings.

Here is an example of a poem that uses a pun to be humorous, playing on the double meaning of the word *maroon*, which can refer either to a color (a dark, bluish red) or to being stuck on a deserted island in the middle of the ocean. (*Festooned* means to be decorated.)

> Two ships collided with much ado:
> One ship was red, the other blue.
> With colors these ships had been festooned,
> But now their crews were all marooned.

The pun here lies in the idea that the colors of the ships were mingled to create the color maroon, while the sailors found themselves stuck in the ocean without a ship—they were marooned.

Limericks provide a classic example of this sort of word play. Most limericks are, shall we say, indelicate—they use double entendre and other forms of layered meaning to create a poem that can be interpreted either literally or metaphorically. As we've noted, these double entendres are very frequently of a sexual nature. Here is a limerick that avoids sexual innuendo but still plays with words.

READING POETRY

There once was a woman from Riga
Who smiled as she rode on a tiger.
    She came back from her ride
    With the lady inside
And the smile on the face of the tiger.

▶ Practice Questions

Read the following passages and answer the related questions.

Passage 1

The following poem is by Emily Dickinson.

The Chariot
Because I could not stop for Death,
He kindly stopped for me;
The carriage held but just ourselves
And Immortality.

We slowly drove, he knew no haste,
And I had put away
My labor, and my leisure too,
For his civility.

We passed the school where children played,
Their lessons scarcely done;
We passed the fields of gazing grain,
We passed the setting sun.

We paused before a house that seemed
A swelling of the ground;
The roof was scarcely visible,
The cornice but a mound.

Since then 'tis centuries; but each
Feels shorter than the day
I first surmised the horses' heads
Were toward eternity.

1. The image of death presented in stanza 1 is that of
   a. an indifferent driver.
   b. a kindly gentleman.
   c. an immortal god disguised as a human.
   d. a demon.
   e. none of the above

2. The main idea of the poem is that
   a. death kidnaps its victims and drives away emotionlessly.
   b. death is dull; its chief torment is boredom.
   c. death is a gentle timeless journey, simply leaving life's cares behind.
   d. death is an eternity.
   e. death is a horrific journey.

3. In stanza 2, the word *haste* can be defined as
   a. sorrow.
   b. hurry.
   c. guilt.
   d. happiness.
   e. hate.

4. The image described in stanza 4 most closely represents
   a. a blurring of life and death.
   b. an inability of the dead to focus on the world of the living.
   c. a description of the grave.
   d. a last image of security one sees before one dies.
   e. a description of a child's playground.

5. One can infer from the tone of the poem that the speaker
   a. views Death as a pleasant companion.
   b. views Death as an intruder.
   c. views Death as a figure of authority.
   d. views Death as an intimate friend.
   e. views Death as a bitter enemy.

Passage 2

The following poem is by Alfred, Lord Tennyson.

The Eagle
He clasps the crag with crooked hands;
Close to the sun in lonely lands,
Ring'd with the azure world, he stands.

The wrinkled sea beneath him crawls;
He watches from his mountain walls,
And like a thunderbolt he falls.

6. Given the tone of the poem, and noting especially the last line, what is the eagle most likely doing in the poem?
   a. dying of old age
   b. hunting prey
   c. learning joyfully to fly
   d. sleeping peacefully
   e. keeping watch over a nest of young eagles

7. To which of the following do the words *azure world* most likely refer?
   a. a forest
   b. the sky
   c. the cliff
   d. a grassy field
   e. nature

8. In line 1 of stanza 2, to which of the following does the verb *crawls* refer?
   a. waves
   b. sunlight on the water
   c. the eagle's prey
   d. the eagle
   e. an eaglet

9. The first line of this poem is an example of
   a. rhyme scheme.
   b. irony.
   c. alliteration.
   d. stanza.
   e. symbolism.

10. The last line of the poem is an example of
    a. personification.
    b. metaphor.
    c. paradox.
    d. falling action.
    e. simile.

Passage 3

The following poem is by Sir Walter Scott.

Patriotism

Breathes there the man with soul so dead,
Who never to himself hath said,
   "This is my own, my native land!"
Whose heart hath ne'er within him burned
As home his footsteps he hath turned
   From wandering on a foreign strand?
If such there breathe, go, mark him well;
For him no Minstrel raptures swell;
High though his titles, proud his name,
Boundless his wealth as wish can claim;
Despite those titles, power, and *pelf*,
The wretch, *concentred* all in self,
Living, shall forfeit fair renown,
And, doubly dying, shall go down
To the vile dust from whence he sprung,
Unwept, unhonored, and unsung.

11. What is the thesis of this poem?
    a. Those who do not love their country will not be honored.
    b. The poorest citizens are the truest patriots.
    c. Those who become rich must hate their country.
    d. Wandering around the world helps us love home.
    e. Patriotism is the last refuge for scoundrels.

12. What is the most likely meaning of the word *pelf* in line 11?
    a. stealth
    b. animal skins
    c. wealth
    d. to steal
    e. poverty

13. What does the poem mean when it states that such people will be *doubly dying*?
    a. They will not die alone.
    b. They will die, then rise again.
    c. Their death will be painful.
    d. Their death will be painless.
    e. They will die physically and also be forgotten.

14. One can infer from this poem that Sir Walter Scott
    a. hated America.
    b. loved his homeland.
    c. was from Great Britain.
    d. spoke many languages.
    e. was a traitor to his homeland.

15. What does the word *concentred* in line 12 most likely mean?
    a. swirling, curved
    b. arrogant, proud
    c. focused, centered
    d. loathsome, wayward
    e. none of the above

Passage 4

The following poem is by William Shakespeare.

> Shall I compare thee to a summer's day?
> Thou art more lovely and more temperate:
> Rough winds do shake the darling buds of May,
> And summer's lease hath all too short a date:
> Sometime too hot the eye of heaven shines,
> And often is his gold complexion dimm'd,
> And every fair from fair sometime declines,
> By chance, or nature's changing course
>   untrimm'd:
> But thy eternal summer shall not fade,
> Nor lose possession of that fair thou owest,
> Nor shall death brag thou wanderest in his
>   shade,
> When in eternal lines to time thou growest,
>   So long as men can breathe, or eyes can see,
>   So long lives this, and this gives life to thee.

16. This poem is an example of
  a. a limerick.
  b. a sonnet.
  c. an anapest.
  d. an ode.
  e. free verse.

17. What does it mean that *summer's lease hath all too short a date*?
  a. The warm weather of summer doesn't last long.
  b. People who rent houses for the summer don't stay long.
  c. Summer is just around the corner.
  d. Enjoy your youth while you're young.
  e. The warm weather of summer is overbearing.

18. What is *the eye of heaven*?
  a. a god
  b. birds
  c. the moon
  d. the sun
  e. a constellation

19. This poem is probably written to
  a. someone that owes the poet money.
  b. someone who wishes for immortality.
  c. the poet's mother.
  d. the reader.
  e. someone whom the poet loves romantically.

20. What do the last two lines refer to?
  a. death
  b. resurrection
  c. the fact that all men die
  d. the poem itself, which will live forever
  e. birth

READING POETRY

Passage 5

The following excerpt is from "Charge of the Light Brigade," by Alfred, Lord Tennyson.

"Forward, the Light Brigade!"
Was there a man dismayed?
Not though the soldier knew
Some one had *blundered*:
Theirs not to make reply,
Theirs not to reason why,
Theirs but to do and die:
Into the valley of Death
Rode the six hundred.

Cannon to right of them,
Cannon to left of them,
Cannon in front of them
Volleyed and thundered;
Stormed at with shot and shell,
Boldly they rode and well,
Into the jaws of Death,
Into the mouth of Hell
Rode the six hundred.

21. This poem is describing
   a. soldiers charging into war.
   b. old-fashioned weapons.
   c. a hot desert area.
   d. a veterinarian healing an animal.
   e. soldiers shying away from a battle.

22. The word *blundered* in line 4 most likely means
   a. a poetical form.
   b. the entrance to something.
   c. a mistake.
   d. an old-fashioned gun.
   e. wondered.

23. What does it mean that it was *theirs not to reason why*?
   a. The soldiers don't know how to fight.
   b. The horses are dangerous.
   c. Obedience is foolish.
   d. The men obeyed, even though it meant certain death.
   e. The men disobeyed orders.

24. The phrases *jaws of Death* and *mouth of Hell* are examples of
   a. cadence.
   b. personification.
   c. alliteration.
   d. iambic pentameter.
   e. simile.

25. What is the author's purpose in this poem?
   a. to describe the stupidity of war
   b. to honor soldiers who died
   c. to tell a story
   d. to make fun of Napoleon Bonaparte
   e. to describe a battle

Passage 6

The following poem is by Robert Frost.

Closed for Good

Much as I own I owe
The passers of the past
Because their to and fro
Has cut this road to last,
I owe them more today
Because they've gone away

And come not back with steed
And chariot to chide
My slowness with their speed
And scare me to one side.
They have found other scenes
For haste and other means.

They leave the road to me
To walk in saying naught
Perhaps but to a tree
Inaudibly in thought,
"From you the road receives
A priming coat of leaves.

"And soon for lack of sun,
The prospects are in white
It will be further done,
But with a coat so light
The shape of leaves will show
Beneath the brush of snow."

And so on into winter
Till even I have ceased
To come as a foot printer,
And only some slight beast
So mousy or so foxy
Shall print there as my proxy.

26. Why does the speaker in this poem say, *I owe them more today / Because they've gone away*?
  a. The people who made the road have left it to him to walk on.
  b. The people of the past were unpleasant company.
  c. He is in debt and can't pay it back.
  d. The people of the past don't owe him anything.
  e. He paid people to leave him alone.

27. What is the rhyme scheme of the second stanza?
  a. *a, a, b, b, a, b*
  b. *a, b, c, a, b, c*
  c. *a, b, a, b, c, c*
  d. *a, b, b, b, b, c*
  e. There is no rhyme scheme.

28. What does the word *proxy* mean in the last line?
  a. walking in the poet's footsteps
  b. doing something on behalf of the speaker
  c. gluing something to the tree
  d. standing next to the tree
  e. a will

29. What meter is this line written in: *They leave the road to me*?
  a. dactylic pentameter
  b. anapestic trimeter
  c. iambic trimeter
  d. iambic pentameter
  e. anapestic pentameter

30. This poem is an example of
  a. imagistic poetry.
  b. argumentative poetry.
  c. sonnet.
  d. elegy.
  e. acrostic poetry.

CHAPTER

6 ▶ Reading Drama

THE WORD *DRAMA* refers to a story that is specifically intended to be performed, whether on a stage in a Broadway playhouse or on a screen in a movie theater or on the television in your living room. By *performed* we mean that the story is acted out by real people—actors—who portray characters within the story and speak the words that are written by the playwright or author of the play.

Drama shares many of the same elements that were discussed in Chapter 3 on fiction, as does poetry. You will remember that one large difference between fiction and poetry is that fiction is intended to be read off the printed page, while poetry is intended to be spoken aloud. In the same way, drama is not intended to be read off the printed page but to be acted out in front of an audience. That audience might consist of living people who are sitting in a playhouse, watching live actors perform the story, or it might consist of the people who will watch the movie or television show at a later date.

In the case of film or television, we tend to think of the camera as taking the place of the audience, while the actors perform their roles in front of the camera so that real people can watch the performance at home or in the theater. Before the prevalence of television, the same approach was used in radio, where live actors treated the microphone as their audience—whether the real people were listening in front of radios at the same time, or the show was recorded for later broadcast.

▶ How Drama Compares to Fiction

Before we delve into the unique elements of drama, let's take a moment to review what elements drama has in common with fiction and poetry.

Plot Structure

One of the primary things that drama and fiction have in common is **plot structure**. We discussed this fully in Chapter 3, so we will only summarize it here. Refer back to Chapter 3 for a fuller treatment of these elements.

You will remember that a vital aspect of plot is conflict—there needs to be some element of conflict within the story, whether it's between several characters or within a specific character. The same holds true in drama: There needs to be some sort of conflict, some struggle taking place as the story unfolds.

The structure of plots in drama is essentially the same as in fiction, involving the elements of (1) exposition, (2) complication, (3) climax, (4) falling action, and (5) resolution. Here is the diagram again to refresh your memory. The numbers refer to the elements of exposition and so forth.

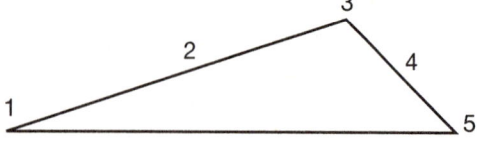

Setting and the Set

Drama, like fiction, takes place in a setting—the time and place where the story occurs. In fiction, the setting must be described by the narrator or by things that the characters say or do. In drama, however, the setting can be explained to the audience simply by the visual elements of the story, such as scenery and costumes.

In drama, we refer to the setting as the *set*, the visual space where the drama is performed. Stage plays are performed on a stage (obviously) in a playhouse, and the set consists of many elements. There might be a painted backdrop at the rear of the stage, perhaps a picture of distant mountains or a sandy beach. There might be props (short for *properties*) on stage, such as the front of a building with stairs leading up to a balcony. Placing that balcony prop in front of a painted backdrop of distant mountains will help the audience recognize that the story takes place at some mountaintop castle.

The time period in which the story takes place can be explained to the audience in many ways, as well. Costumes and props can convey the time period instantly, for example. An audience watching a man leap onstage with a drawn rapier, wearing a long cape and a broad-brimmed hat with a feather, will immediately surmise that the play takes place during the time of the Musketeers.

Speech patterns can also give clues to the time setting. Arthur Miller's play *The Crucible* has the characters speaking in a sort of 1600s style of English, referring to one another as *thee* and *thou,* and this alerts the audience to the fact that the play is set in Colonial America.

Atmosphere

Because it is a very visual medium, drama has the advantage in creating atmosphere that fiction and poetry do not have. When you read a novel, you must picture what is happening in your mind, visualizing for yourself the setting and the characters' appearance and so forth. But drama is performed right in front of your eyes, so you have no doubt what things look like.

This enables the dramatist to create very realistic atmospheres that will convey to the audience a particular mood in the drama. This can be easily accomplished with the many physical elements involved in drama, such as the lights that are used to illuminate the stage. For instance, if the playwright wants to evoke an atmosphere of anticipation, that something dreadful is about to happen, the lighting can be adjusted to create a dark, forbidding set.

Costumes and props can also convey a strong atmosphere. The drama *Les Miserables*, for example, takes place in slums and in wealthy homes. This contrast is strengthened by the costumes that the actors wear and the props and sets that they act with. The wealthy characters have beautiful clothes and live in rich homes, while the poor man and his family wear ragged clothes and live in squalor. These things are accomplished visually for the audience, and help a great deal in conveying the atmosphere that the playwright is striving for.

Of course, when you are reading a play, you cannot actually see the actors and the costumes and the set and so forth. But those details are frequently explained in the text that you will be reading in the form of stage directions. The author frequently describes what the set looks like or what the characters are wearing or what mood the lighting should convey. (We will discuss this more fully later in this chapter.)

Tone

The tone of a drama is essentially the same as what we discussed in Chapter 3 on fiction. Like fiction, drama conveys the author's desired tone through the actions and words of the characters within the drama. Here again, however, the dramatist has the added luxury of many visual elements to work with, and the tone of a drama can be accentuated through lighting, costumes, sets, and props.

Figurative Language

The elements of figurative language, such as metaphor and simile, which were discussed in Chapter 3, are also found in drama. There is one interesting difference, however, in the area of irony.

You'll remember that irony in fiction consists of a character or narrator saying something that is the opposite to what he or she really means—similar to sarcasm. Drama, however, can employ something called **dramatic irony**. (This is also used in written fiction, but its real strength is found in drama.)

Dramatic irony occurs when the audience knows something that the characters in the story don't know, or when a character knows something that the audience doesn't know. We encounter this technique frequently in movies. For example, the audience may be shown a scene where the villain is setting a trap for the hero, then another scene where the hero is walking toward the trap. The hero does not know about the trap, but the audience does. The hero might even make some comment to the effect that he has beaten the villain, but the audience knows that he has not.

The reverse can also happen. For example, the audience might be horrified when the villain grabs a gun and stops the hero in his tracks. The tension builds as the villain gloats over the fact that he's about to shoot the hero, and the audience is convinced that there's no escape for the character that they have been rooting for. But the hero remains calm, and finally the villain pulls the trigger—only to hear a harmless click. The hero knew that he had already taken the bullets out of the gun, but the audience did *not* know it (unless we guessed because we've seen this trick a hundred times in other movies). This is another example of dramatic irony.

You will notice that dramatic irony is not really an element of figurative language, because it is not spoken but acted out. This accentuates the chief difference between written fiction and drama: Drama is meant to be acted out, while fiction is meant to be read.

Personification

You will remember that *personification* refers to taking an abstract concept and turning it into a living being—such as the statue of justice, which we considered in Chapter 3.

This is used occasionally in drama as it is in fiction, although modern drama rarely uses it. For example, a character might find himself alone on stage, wrestling with some major decision. One classic way of handling this situation is through monologue, which will be discussed later in this chapter. But another way of showing the audience that the character is struggling with internal conflict is to use personification.

In this case, two other actors might come onto the stage, one on each side of the main character. The actor to the left tells the character, "You must do what you have planned! It is essential to your future!" The other actor disagrees: "No! Such a thing would be wrong! You must do what is right, even if it costs you your life!" In this example, the two actors are personifications of the character's struggle between doing what is right and doing what is expedient.

The Narrator

Generally speaking, drama does not use a narrator. You will remember that the narrator in fiction is the character who is telling the story—whether that character is part of the story or not.

This technique was actually used extensively in ancient drama, such as the drama of ancient Greece. In some Greek drama, a person would walk on stage to introduce the play and the setting and the characters, and might also appear from time to time between scenes to explain to the audience what has happened behind the scenes, in order to advance the plot. Other plays used a chorus of several people who actually sang or recited poetry, explaining to the audience things that were not acted out on stage.

In most modern drama, however, there is no narrator who explains things to the audience. The important parts of the drama are acted out onstage or onscreen. Things that are not acted out are quickly explained to the audience through the dialogue that the characters speak.

This technique is frequently seen in film. In a war movie, for example, two characters might be onscreen discussing strategy for the next day's battle. They might mention the fact that the enemy has just taken a strategic bridge that has complicated the soldiers' task. The audience does not see the battle for that bridge; it is just summarized by the characters on screen. This is an example of how the narrator fits into modern drama.

The Characters

Drama makes use of characters just as fiction does, and this includes the use of a protagonist and an antagonist. The protagonist is generally also called the **main character**, and is frequently (though not always) the hero of the story.

The antagonist, on the other hand, is the character that resists the protagonist. This is usually an actual character in the drama, but not always. In some dramas, the antagonist and the protagonist might actually be the same person.

The Greek tragedy *Oedipus Rex*, for example, concerns a man who is destined to marry his mother

READING DRAMA

and murder his father. The main character is Oedipus; he is the protagonist who is determined to escape this dreadful fate. Unfortunately, he also serves as the antagonist as he unwittingly sets about to commit these very crimes.

In this play, one might also consider the abstract concept of fate to be the antagonist, working against Oedipus to bring about the prophecy despite the protagonist's efforts to avoid it. Either way, we find that there are occasionally pieces of drama that include an unorthodox protagonist/antagonist relationship. Generally, however, these roles are filled by two different characters in the drama.

An Example of Dramatized Fiction

Let's take a look at a story that was written in two forms, both as a novel and as a drama. You are probably familiar with the story of *Peter Pan*, but you might not know that author J.M. Barrie wrote the story both as a novel and as a play. Here is an excerpt from Barrie's novel *Peter and Wendy*.

Chapter 14: The Pirate Ship

One green light squinting over Kidd's Creek, which is near the mouth of the pirate river, marked where the brig, the *Jolly Roger*, lay, low in the water; a rakish-looking craft foul to the hull, every beam in her detestable, like ground strewn with mangled feathers. She was the cannibal of the seas, and scarce needed that watchful eye, for she floated immune in the horror of her name . . .

"Quiet, you scugs," he cried, "or I'll cast anchor in you"; and at once the din was hushed. "Are all the children chained, so that they cannot fly away?"

"Ay, ay."

"Then hoist them up."

The wretched prisoners were dragged from the hold, all except Wendy, and ranged in line in front of him. For a time he seemed unconscious of their presence. He lolled at his ease, humming, not unmelodiously, snatches of a rude song, and fingering a pack of cards. Ever and anon the light from his cigar gave a touch of color to his face.

"Now then, bullies," he said briskly, "six of you walk the plank tonight, but I have room for two cabin-boys. Which of you is it to be?"

Now, here is the same scene written for performance on stage, from Barrie's drama *Peter Pan, or the Boy Who Wouldn't Grow Up*. (Incidentally, Barrie actually wrote the play first, then adapted it into the novel.)

Act 5, Scene 1: The Pirate Ship

The stage directions for the opening of this scene are as follows: —1 Circuit Amber checked to 80. Battens, all Amber checked, 3 ship's lanterns alight, Arcs: prompt perch 1. Open dark Amber flooding back, O.P. perch open dark Amber flooding upper deck. Arc on tall steps at back of cabin to flood back cloth. Open dark Amber. Warning for slide. Plank ready. Call Hook.

In the strange light thus described, we see what is happening on the deck of the *Jolly Roger*, which is flying the skull and crossbones and lies low in the water. There is no need to call Hook, for he is here already, and indeed there is **not a pirate aboard** who would dare to call him. Most of them are at present carousing in the bowels of the vessel, but on the poop [a deck of the ship] Mullins is visible, in the only great-coat on the ship, raking with his glass [telescope] the monstrous rocks within which the lagoon is cooped. Such a look-out is [unnecessary], for the pirate craft floats immune in the horror of her name . . .

HOOK: Quiet, you dogs, or I'll cast anchor in you! [*He descends to a barrel in which there are playing-cards, and his crew stand waiting, as ever, like whipped curs.*] Are all the prisoners chained, so that they can't fly away?

JUKES: Ay, ay, Captain.

HOOK: Then hoist them up.

STARKEY: [*raising the door of the hold*] Tumble up, you ungentlemanly lubbers.

[*The terrified boys are prodded up and tossed about the deck. HOOK seems to have forgotten them; he is sitting by the barrel with his cards.*]

HOOK: [*suddenly*] So! Now then, you bullies, six of you walk the plank tonight, but I have room for two cabin-boys. Which of you is it to be? [*He returns to his cards*]

These two passages depict the same scene in the story of Peter Pan, but they are written very differently. In the first passage, the narrator describes the setting of Captain Hook's ship floating in the bay. The narrator also describes what the characters are thinking and feeling, such as the "wretched boys" who are dragged into Hook's presence.

In the second passage, however, the author knows that the actors on stage will convey those thoughts and feelings to the audience visually. So Barrie provides stage directions for the actors, telling them what emotions to act out and where to stand and what to do—such as Hook's playing with a deck of cards.

The second passage also begins with lighting directions, those cryptic notes about the *Amber* and *Arc* lights. The author has instructed the performers on how to light the stage, and how to construct the various props—such as Captain Hook's ship, the *Jolly Roger*—and other elements which will set the proper atmosphere for the performance.

▶ The Structure of Drama

Drama does share many things in common with fiction and poetry, as we've been discussing, but there are other elements which are unique to drama. One area of uniqueness is in the way that drama is structured or put together.

Acts, Scenes, and Lines

Novels are written in chapters, and some novels even have separate sections that include multiple chapters. You may be familiar with J.R.R. Tolkien's *Lord of the Rings* story, which has been adapted into dramatic form for film. Each book that Tolkien wrote is divided into two sections, and each of those two sections contains numerous chapters.

This same technique is used in drama, except that a drama is divided into acts and scenes. Most dramas have numerous acts (although there are one-act dramas as well), and each act may be subdivided into several scenes.

Within each scene are the actors' lines. The actors who portray the characters within a drama are given lines to speak, which simply refers to the words that they are to say.

Look back at the two versions of *Peter Pan*. You will notice that the first passage, from the novel, is from Chapter 14. The second passage, from the dramatized version, is from Act 5, Scene 1. The lines from that scene are simply the words that the actors speak. Each set of lines begins with the name of the character who is to speak those lines, such as

"**JUKES:** Ay, ay, Captain" and "**HOOK:** Then hoist them up."

The lines within some plays are also numbered, making it easier to refer to a specific quotation within a drama. You are probably familiar with the famous line, "O Romeo, Romeo, wherefore art thou Romeo?" This is from Shakespeare's drama *Romeo and Juliet*, and it can be found in Act 2, Scene 2, line 33.

Dramatic Tension

Dramatic tension is sometimes called **suspense**. This refers to the sense of uncertainty that the audience feels during the course of a drama.

Remember that every plot will have some form of conflict, whether between two characters or some other form. The outcome of this conflict is uncertain in the audience's mind—will the hero marry his sweetheart, or will the villain get to her first?

Dramatic tension is used very heavily in modern film—so much so that we have a modern genre, or type, of film known as suspense films. The usual plot line of such movies is that a powerful villain is threatening some innocent people, and a very unlikely hero is forced (generally against his will) to intervene and save the day.

This technique, however, is not new. It has been a staple of drama for centuries. The dramatic tension in *Hamlet*, for example, is the fact that the audience is not sure whether Hamlet will overcome his doubts and uncertainties and avenge the murder of his father. It is this very uncertainty, this tension and suspense, which keeps the plot and its conflict interesting to the audience.

▶ The Dramatic Stage

Drama as we know it today had its origins in ancient Greece and Rome. The art form died away for many years, and was then revived during the Middle Ages in Great Britain. What we consider drama today was largely defined in the sixteenth and seventeenth centuries by playwrights such as William Shakespeare, Christopher Marlowe, and others.

Most drama was written to be performed on a stage by live actors in front of a live audience. The advent of radio, television, and film is relatively modern, yet many dramas today are written specifically for those media and not for live performance in a playhouse. Nevertheless, the structure and terminology of screenplays (scripts for movies) is still very close to the traditional structure and terminology of stage plays.

This structure consists of three rather general categories: the auditory element of drama, the physical element, and the audience.

Dialogue, Monologue, and Soliloquy

Drama is primarily concerned with what the characters have to say, which we refer to as the auditory element of drama. By auditory, we simply mean what the audience will hear. (The word *audience* itself refers to the people who are listening or hearing.)

As we have already seen, the actors who perform the roles of various characters are given words to speak, which we call lines. But there are many different types of lines that a drama can use.

The most common type of speech in drama is called **dialogue**. The word *dialogue*, which literally means *two speaking*, captures the essence of what dialogue is in drama: two or more characters who are speaking to one another. Here is a passage of dialogue from *The Importance of Being Earnest* by Oscar Wilde.

ALGERNON: How are you, my dear Earnest? What brings you up to town?

JACK: Oh, pleasure, pleasure! What else should bring one anywhere? Eating as usual, I see, Algy!

ALGERNON: [*Stiffly.*] I believe it is customary in good society to take some slight refreshment at five o'clock. Where have you been since last Thursday?

JACK: [*Sitting down on the sofa.*] In the country.

ALGERNON: What on earth do you do there?

JACK: [*Pulling off his gloves.*] When one is in town one amuses oneself. When one is in the country one amuses other people. It is excessively boring.

ALGERNON: And who are the people you amuse?

JACK: [*Airily*] Oh, neighbors, neighbors.

ALGERNON: Got nice neighbors in your part of Shropshire?

JACK: Perfectly horrid! Never speak to one of them.

ALGERNON: How immensely you must amuse them!

Note that dialogue is not necessarily between two characters only; there is no limit to how many characters might be speaking together.

When one character is speaking alone, it can be either monologue or soliloquy. **Monologue** generally refers to a character talking to himself or to the audience, perhaps thinking out loud. In Shakespeare's play *Othello*, for example, the villain turns to the audience and explains his plans to bring about the destruction of Othello and Desdemona. The character who is speaking the monologue might be the only character on stage, or there might be other characters in the background.

Soliloquy is a refined sort of monologue, in which a character speaks aloud as if to himself, and wrestles with some deep question as he makes a decision. The most famous soliloquy is probably that of Hamlet, where he asks himself, *To be or not to be, that is the question*. In this soliloquy, Hamlet is standing alone on stage, speaking to himself as he wrestles with the question of whether or not to commit suicide.

HAMLET: To be, or not to be,—that is the question:—
Whether 'tis nobler in the mind to suffer
The slings and arrows of outrageous fortune
Or to take arms against a sea of troubles,
And by opposing end them?—To die,—to sleep,—
No more; and by a sleep to say we end
The heartache, and the thousand natural shocks
That flesh is heir to,—'tis a consummation
Devoutly to be wish'd. To die,—to sleep;—
To sleep! perchance to dream:—ay, there's the rub;
For in that sleep of death what dreams may come,
When we have shuffled off this mortal coil,
Must give us pause: there's the respect
That makes calamity of so long life;
For who would bear the whips and scorns of time,
The oppressor's wrong, the proud man's contumely,
The pangs of despis'd love, the law's delay,
The insolence of office, and the spurns
That patient merit of the unworthy takes,
When he himself might his quietus [death] make
With a bare bodkin [dagger]? who would these fardels [burdens] bear,

To grunt and sweat under a weary life,
But that the dread of something after death,—
The undiscover'd country, from whose bourn
No traveller returns,—puzzles the will,
And makes us rather bear those ills we have
Than fly to others that we know not of?
Thus conscience does make cowards of us all;
And thus the native hue of resolution
Is sicklied o'er with the pale cast of thought;
And enterprises of great pith and moment,
With this regard, their currents turn awry,
And lose the name of action.—Soft you now!
The fair Ophelia! . . .

In this famous passage, Hamlet is standing alone on stage, talking out loud to himself. He is weighing the question of committing suicide, wondering whether it is more noble to endure suffering or to fight against it—by taking his own life. Why bear all of life's burdens, he asks himself, when a man can so easily take his own life with a "bare bodkin" or naked dagger? What keeps him from killing himself is the realization that he does not know what will come to him after death. In the last few lines of his soliloquy, Hamlet notices that Ophelia has come on stage, walking slowly toward him, and he moves out of soliloquy and back into dialogue as she approaches center stage.

A character who speaks a soliloquy is generally the only character on stage. A soliloquy is also generally longer than a monologue, and generally addresses some deep and weighty issue that the character is struggling with. This inner wrestling match is frequently also the turning point in a drama, as one of the main characters comes to a decision as to how he will act. In *Hamlet*, the main character finally decides not to kill himself but rather to confront his stepfather about his real father's murder.

Another form of speech in drama is an **aside**. This might be a character speaking directly (and briefly) to the audience, letting us in on a secret that none of the other characters knows. There may well be other characters on stage during an aside, but none of them hears what is being said—it's just a little comment between a character and the audience, or perhaps between two characters as a whispered comment.

In comedy, asides are sometimes used as one-liners, short quips that are funny but do not advance the plot of the drama. If you've ever seen any old Marx Brothers movies, you have seen many such asides and one-liners. This was a staple of their brand of humor, which is still used in modern film comedies.

Stage Directions

The next component of drama concerns the physical element: what the actors do while they are on stage, what props are on stage, how the set is lighted, and so forth.

Stage directions are instructions from the author on how to conduct the drama. These instructions might state what an actor should do, how the actor should deliver his or her lines, what the set should look like, what sort of music might be playing, what the lighting should be, and many other details.

The passages from *Peter Pan* that we looked at earlier included some stage directions. The playwright opens the scene with specific instructions on how to light the set. He includes details within characters' lines that instruct the actor what to do physically—such as his instruction that the actor portraying Captain Hook should be fiddling with a deck of cards while speaking his lines. Playwrights even instruct the actors on how to deliver their lines—*suddenly* in *Peter Pan*, *airily* and *stiffly* in *The Importance of Being Earnest*.

READING DRAMA

When you are reading a dramatic script, such as a play by Shakespeare, the stage directions can help you to picture in your mind what is happening visually during the performance. But keep in mind that Shakespeare wrote his plays for performance, not to be read from a book in a college classroom. This is, as we've noted already, the chief difference between drama and other forms of fiction: Drama is intended to be performed. Stage directions, therefore, are intended to assist the actors, directors, stagehands, and others in producing the drama as the author envisioned it.

These stage directions are a very important tool when you are reading a play, rather than seeing it acted out on stage. They tell you what the set looks like, what the actors are wearing, what the lighting is like—the atmosphere that is being evoked on stage. All of these details will be important as you are reading dramatic passages and answering the questions that you will encounter on the GED exam. Remember to watch for the stage directions!

Specific directions are also written to help the actors on stage and the many other people involved in creating a stage (or screen) production. You may encounter directions such as *stage right* or *down left*. These directions specify where exactly on the stage to stand or perform some action. Left and right, however, refer to the actor's left and right, which is the opposite of the audience. So *stage right* actually refers to the left side of the stage from the audience's perspective. The stage itself is divided into center, right, left, as well as front and rear. The *wings* are the sections to the sides of the stage (right and left) that the audience cannot see. This is where actors wait until their *cue* to come on stage.

Here is a typical set of stage directions that you might find at the beginning of an act:

Curtain opens on comfortable living room. Large sofa stands center; small tables either end. An overstuffed wing chair sits front right, with a matching chair front left. Rear is lined with bookcases and occasional tables and lamps. Rear backdrop shows view out large window, overlooking a small pond. Sound of clock ticking. Enter CONSTANCE, right wing.

In this set, a sofa is standing center stage, with an overstuffed chair at center left and another at center right. Bookcases are at the rear of the stage. A backdrop pictures what is situated outside the house. The character named Constance comes onstage from the right wing, which means that she will enter from the audience's left.

The Audience

The third component of drama is the audience. As a general rule, all drama is intended to be performed in front of an audience—those people who are listening to the plot.

Originally, drama was intended to be performed live, with real people performing the roles in front of a real audience who was present. The early dramas of medieval England were performed in the public street, not inside buildings with a large stage and lighting. By the time of Shakespeare, permanent theater buildings had been constructed, and the audience sat on benches or stood on the floor in front of the stage and watched the play.

We still use this convention today, as there are countless playhouses that perform drama on a stage in front of a live audience. But the advent of electronic communications such as film and television expanded the definition of an audience to include people who are not actually present during the performance. We might refer to these people as the *viewing audience* or the *listening audience* or the *Internet audience*—those people who will watch the performance on film at a later date, or who will be watching it live from a long distance over the internet or on television.

This element of the audience brings up a final distinction between reading drama and seeing it performed. When we read the written script of a play, for example, we can understand what the dialogue means, and we can appreciate some of the humor or tragedy of the plot, but we cannot experience the reactions of other people as they watch the drama with us.

This is an intangible but vital element of drama. Stage plays, for example, are often intended to build upon an audience's reaction. A comedy such as *The Importance of Being Earnest* delivers one humorous line after another, but what makes the comedy really come to life is hearing the laughter of the entire audience building up to a crescendo as the characters throw out their wit.

▶ Types of Drama

There are many different types (or genres) of drama, just as there are many genres of poetry and fiction. But for purposes of the GED, we will concentrate on the two major, overriding genres within drama: tragedy and comedy. (Other, more modern genres such as realism and theater of the absurd still generally fit within the category of tragedy or comedy.)

The Hero's Fortunes

Before we begin, however, let us review briefly the overall plot structure of drama that we have discussed previously. You will remember that a *plot* generally consists of some form of conflict, and that there is some complication of that conflict, followed by a climax and a resolution.

The conflict, as we have discussed, is generally between a protagonist and an antagonist. The climax is the point in the play where some great decision is made or some great action is taken; the protagonist might finally decide to do something decisive about the antagonist's troublemaking, or the antagonist will finally gain the upper hand over the protagonist. At this point in the plot, we say that the protagonist's fortunes shift in one way or another. The resolution then finally resolves the conflict once and for all. Generally, the fortunes of the protagonist are the opposite of what they were when the story began.

This concept of fortune refers to a character's circumstances, whether good or bad—whether the character is lucky or unlucky. It is a very important element in drama, because the characters' fortunes are central to most plot structures.

The Greeks and the medieval British playwrights and poets personified the concept of fortune, depicting Fortune as a woman who stood next to a spinning wheel or mill wheel. Men and women were riding on that wheel, like an ancient version of a Ferris wheel, and Lady Fortune stood by, spinning the wheel whatever way she saw fit. This was the subject of much art and poetry, as well as drama, during the Middle Ages and beyond; and the phrase *Wheel of Fortune* has been kept alive in a modern television show.

The personification of Lady Fortune included the concept that she was fickle; she would show favor to a person one moment, then suddenly throw him into disfavor. The person who was pictured on the top of Fortune's wheel was experiencing comfort and success and good luck—but he or she needed to keep in mind that Lady Fortune might spin that wheel at any moment, plunging the person from success into failure and despair. The reverse was true, of course, for the poor sap who found himself at the bottom of the wheel of Fortune.

Tragedy

A short definition of *tragedy* is that the plot deals with serious issues, and ends badly for the protagonist.

More specifically, a tragedy generally begins with the protagonist at the top of Fortune's wheel. Life is going well, and the protagonist is enjoying good luck and fortune. The protagonist of classic tragedies was frequently a person with some power and influence—often royalty, such as a prince or king.

We quickly discover, however, that the protagonist has an adversary—the antagonist—who is in some form of conflict with him. This is frequently another character, such as another nobleman or a person of lower class, who is jealous of the protagonist's good fortune. Sometimes the antagonist might be an abstract concept—perhaps even Fortune herself. This is the case, for example, in the Greek tragedy *Oedipus Rex*, where the protagonist (Oedipus) is struggling to avoid fulfilling an ancient prophecy of his own downfall.

The climax is the point where the protagonist and the antagonist reach some sort of decisive action. The antagonist might finally gain control over the protagonist, or the protagonist might finally make some fatal mistake. One common theme in drama is that of *hubris*, which refers to mankind's inherent pride. In this case, the protagonist's climax comes when he or she falls into the fatal error of pride.

The climax of a tragedy generally entails something bad for the protagonist. This is the point at which Fortune's wheel takes a sudden spin, and the protagonist finds himself spinning down from good fortune to a bad ending.

The resolution of a tragedy generally is that the protagonist has fallen from his or her high position—whether that position involves power or wealth or just a good reputation. So a tragedy involves the protagonist's fall from happiness into misery.

Tragedies also tend to be more serious in their tone. This does not mean that there is no humor in a tragedy. Many great tragedies include a character or two whose role is to bring comic relief, to relieve the tension of the serious drama by interjecting some element of laughter. But the overall tone and atmosphere of a tragedy is serious.

The subject matter of tragedies also tends to be deep and significant. Tragedies deal with big issues in life, such as pride, betrayal, the dangers of war or politics, and so forth.

Finally, the protagonist of a tragedy is frequently a person of some high moral character or high social position. Many tragedies involve kings and queens, people who are seen as being above the common man. This permits the playwright to demonstrate that everyone is subject to the whims of Fortune—even the great and powerful and wealthy cannot prevent Lady Fortune from spinning her wheel and toppling them down.

Comedy

At the opposite end of drama is the genre of comedy. The short definition for comedy is that the plot deals with common, everyday issues and ends well for the protagonist.

By *common and everyday issues*, we mean simply the sorts of things that the common man might experience in life, such as love, marriage, prosperity, dealings with neighbors, pursuing a career, and so forth. But comedies can also deal with those negative things that everyone is subject to: divorce, infidelity, disagreements with neighbors, losing a job, and so forth. The subject matter may actually be something negative in a comedy, but it is the sort of thing that just about anybody might go through.

A comedy generally begins with the protagonist at the bottom of Fortune's wheel, rather than at the top. Life is not exactly a bed of roses; the protagonist would like to improve his or her position in the world in some way. Shakespeare's comedy *The Tempest* begins with a group of people being shipwrecked on a deserted island. Oscar Wilde's *The Importance of Being Earnest*, which we looked at earlier, begins with two young men who happen to be very wealthy and comfortable—certainly at the top of Fortune's wheel in that respect—but who are in love with two women whom they cannot marry. Their issue is not their wealth or prestige, but the fact that, for one reason or another, they are not permitted to marry their sweethearts.

This is the element of conflict, or opposition, in comedy. Note that both comedy and tragedy include the element of conflict. The protagonist in both genres is faced with some situation or force or person that is opposing him or her.

The key difference between comedy and tragedy is the outcome of that conflict. In comedy, the protagonist eventually overcomes the opposition and wins the conflict. Therefore, the climax in a comedy entails the protagonist gaining the upper hand over the antagonist—the opposite of tragedy.

Here again we see Lady Fortune spin her wheel, but this time the protagonist moves upward on the wheel, from misfortune to fortune, from bad to good. The resolution in a comedy is the happy ending, the point where all details of the conflict are resolved and the protagonist is restored to good fortune. In *The Importance of Being Earnest*, the two young men make some startling discoveries about their true identities, and in the process find that they are now free to marry the women whom they love.

Comedies tend to be more humorous and frivolous in their tone. This does not mean that a comedy contains no unhappiness or danger; many great comedies include some elements of great risk for the protagonist. But overall, the tone is generally comic, humorous, with characters and dialogue that keep the audience laughing.

Finally, the protagonist of a comedy is frequently someone of common birth rather than someone of nobility and power. Comedy is the genre of the common man, stories about people who are not of great privilege or unusually high moral character. Comedies tend to be written in a more conversational, everyday style of speech, whereas tragedies often involve great speeches with very formal and impressive style.

▶ Some Common Dramatic Terms

It is worthwhile to understand a few bits of terminology that are frequently used in drama. Understanding these concepts will help you to understand drama when you encounter it on the GED.

Tragic Flaw

The protagonist in a tragedy frequently has a tragic flaw, which is some element of his or her character that threatens his own well-being. This character flaw may even be the very force that brings about the protagonist's downfall in a tragedy. Hamlet, for example, is brought down by his inability to make a decision. Othello, another Shakespearean tragic hero, is brought down by jealousy.

The emphasis here is not so much on the character's flaw, but on its tragic consequences. Characters in comedies may also have similar flaws in their characters, but those flaws do not bring about the protagonist's destruction. This is what makes a character flaw a tragic flaw: The protagonist's own weakness somehow brings about his downfall.

READING DRAMA

Catharsis

Catharsis is a Greek word meaning *to purge*. The concept in drama is that a good story allows the audience to purge themselves of all their unpleasant emotions, to get it out of their system if you will, leaving them feeling calm and contented.

A tragedy offers catharsis by permitting the audience to grieve over the protagonist's downfall, and to feel the fear and tension as they see that downfall approaching. They can, in a sense, project their own fears of life's uncertainties onto the protagonist, allowing him to take their place on Fortune's shifting wheel. Thus, when the audience leaves the drama, they feel purged and less fearful, less stressed.

Comedy accomplishes the same thing from the opposite direction. It enables the audience to get their minds off their own problems by laughing at the silly antics and witty dialogue of the actors on stage. By laughing at someone else, they can leave the theater feeling purged and ready to face real life once again.

The Antihero

Many modern dramas feature a protagonist who is a variation on the classic protagonist. In classic drama, the audience usually identified in some way with the protagonist, even if the protagonist happened to be a king or prince or some person far removed from the typical audience member. They may have not had much in common, but the audience still basically liked the protagonist and found themselves rooting for him to some extent.

The antihero, however, is someone who inspires pity rather than respect. He or she is often someone that the audience does not even like, but they find themselves drawn into the story because they can see that the antihero's tragic flaw is going to bring destruction. Arthur Miller's play *Death of a Salesman* features an antihero named Willy Loman who is essentially having a nervous breakdown in the play. He is not a likeable character, but the audience does feel sorry for him.

The classic example of the antihero is Don Quixote, the famous nobleman who tries to joust with windmills. Quixote is an antihero in the sense that the audience can see what he cannot see: that there are no more giants and dragons to slay, no more damsels in distress to be rescued. It is noteworthy that Quixote is actually quite likeable, speaking many humorous lines; yet the audience cannot help pitying his lost hopes of becoming a knight in shining armor.

Foreshadowing

Sometimes a drama will give the audience a hint of something significant that is going to happen later in the story. For example, the hero of a play might be poisoned in the last act. An earlier scene might show the protagonist eating something that tastes strange, and making a joke about poison.

The audience recognizes the hint in foreshadowing, but the character frequently does not. If the audience somehow already knows what is going to happen, then the foreshadowing is also an example of dramatic irony.

▶ Practice Questions

Read the following passages and answer the related questions.

Passage 1

The following extract is from *The Diary of Anne Frank* by Frances Goodrich and Albert Hackett. The play takes place during the early years of World War II, and the characters are Jews who are hiding from the Nazis. The audience is aware that Anne and her family will die in concentration camps.

ANNE: I'm a terrible coward. I'm so disappointed in myself. I think I've conquered my fear . . . I think I'm really grown up . . . and then something happens . . . and I run to you like a baby . . . I love you, Father. I don't love anyone but you.

MR. FRANK: [*reproachfully*] Anneke!

ANNE: It's true. I've been thinking about it for a long time. You're the only one I love.

MR. FRANK: It's fine to hear you tell me that you love me. But I'd be happier if you said you loved your mother as well . . . She needs your help so much . . . your love . . .

ANNE: We have nothing in common. She doesn't understand me. Whenever I try to explain my views on life to her she asks me if I'm constipated.

MR. FRANK: You hurt her very much just now. She's crying. She's in there crying.

ANNE: I can't help it. I only told the truth. I didn't want her here. . . [*Then, with sudden change*] Oh, Pim, I was horrible, wasn't I? And the worst of it is, I can stand off and look at myself doing it and know it's cruel and yet I can't stop doing it. What's the matter with me? Tell me. Don't say it's just a phase. Help me!

MR. FRANK: There is so little that we parents can do to help our children. We can only try to set a good example . . . point the way. The rest you must do yourself. You must build your own character.

ANNE: I'm trying. Really I am. Every night I think back over all of the things I did that day that were wrong . . . like putting the wet mop in Mr. Dussel's bed . . . and this thing now with Mother. I say to myself, that was wrong. I make up my mind, I'm never going to do that again. Never! Of course I may do something worse . . . but at least I'll never do *that* again! . . . I have a nice side, Father . . . a sweeter, nicer side. But I'm scared to show it. I'm afraid that people are going to laugh at me if I'm serious. So the mean Anne comes to the outside and the good Anne stays on the inside, and I keep on trying to switch them around and have the good Anne outside and the bad Anne inside and be what I'd like to be . . . and might be . . . if only . . . only . . .

[*She is asleep. MR. FRANK watches her for a moment and then turns off the light, and starts out. The lights dim out. The curtain falls on the scene. ANNE'S VOICE is heard dimly at first, and then with growing strength.*]

ANNE'S VOICE: . . . The air raids are getting worse. They come over day and night. The noise is terrifying. Pim says it should be music to our ears. The more planes, the sooner will come the end of the war. Mrs. Van Daan pretends to be a fatalist. What will be, will be. But when the planes come over, who is the most frightened? No one else but Petronella! . . . Monday, the ninth of November, nineteen-forty-two. Wonderful news! The Allies have landed in Africa. Pim says that we can look for an early finish to the war. Just for fun he asked each of us what was the first thing we wanted to do when we got out of here. Mrs. Van Daan longs to be home with her own things, her needle-point chairs, the Beckstein piano that her father gave her . . . the best that money could buy. Peter would like to go to a movie. Mr. Dussel wants to get back to his dentist drill. He's afraid that he's losing his touch. For myself, there are so many things . . . to ride a bike again . . . to laugh till my belly aches . . . to have new clothes from the

READING DRAMA

skin out . . . to have a hot tub and fill it to overflowing and wallow in it for hours . . . to be back in school with my friends . . .
[*As the last lines are being said, the curtain rises on the scene. The lights dim as ANNE'S VOICE fades away.*]

1. What is the probable setting of this play?
   a. North Africa, 1988
   b. Europe, 1942
   c. a New York City apartment
   d. the mountains of Tennessee
   e. Mars, 2112

2. Anne's attitude in this passage might be described as
   a. rebellious.
   b. hateful.
   c. confused.
   d. carefree.
   e. respectful.

3. Anne's desires for what she'll do when she gets free reveal her to be
   a. frightened about the future.
   b. angry toward the world.
   c. a bit unusual.
   d. a normal teenaged girl.
   e. highly intellectual.

4. The passages marked ANNE'S VOICE are examples of
   a. dramatic tension.
   b. monologue.
   c. dialogue.
   d. asides.
   e. setting.

5. One character says that *we can look for an early finish to the war*. This might be an example of
   a. dramatic irony.
   b. personification.
   c. stage direction.
   d. antagonist.
   e. protagonist.

Passage 2

The following passage is from *The Way of the World* by William Congreve.

[*Setting: St. James's Park*]
[*Enter MRS. FAINALL and MRS. MARWOOD.*]
MRS. FAINALL: Ay, ay, dear Marwood, if we will be happy, we must find the means in ourselves, and among ourselves. Men are ever in extremes; either doting or averse. While they are lovers, if they have fire and sense, their jealousies are insupportable: and when they cease to love (we ought to think at least) they loathe, they look upon us with horror and distaste, they meet us like the ghosts of what we were, and as from such, fly from us.

MRS. MARWOOD: True, 'tis an unhappy circumstance of life that love should ever die before us, and that the man so often should outlive the lover. But say what you will, 'tis better to be left than never to have been loved. To pass our youth in dull indifference, to refuse the sweets of life because they once must leave us, is as preposterous as to wish to have been born old, because we one day must be old. For my part, my youth may wear and waste, but it shall never rust in my possession.
[. . .]
MRS. MARWOOD: You hate mankind?
MRS. FAINALL: Heartily, *inveterately*.

READING DRAMA

MRS. MAR: Your husband?

MRS. FAIN: Most transcendently; ay, though I say it, meritoriously.

MRS. MAR: Give me your hand upon it.

MRS. FAIN: There.

MRS. MAR: I join with you; what I have said has been to try you.

MRS. FAIN: Is it possible? Dost thou hate those vipers, men?

MRS. MAR: I have done hating 'em, and am now come to despise 'em; the next thing I have to do is eternally to forget 'em.

MRS. FAIN: There spoke the spirit of an Amazon, a Penthesilea.

MRS. MAR: And yet I am thinking sometimes to carry my aversion further.

MRS. FAIN: How?

MRS. MAR: Faith, by marrying; if I could but find one that loved me very well, and would be thoroughly sensible of ill usage, I think I should do myself the violence of undergoing the ceremony.

6. What does Mrs. Fainall mean when she says, *Men are ever in extremes; either doting or averse?*
   a. Men either love a woman or hate her.
   b. Old men tend to be extremists.
   c. Poets can't be depended on.
   d. Women should accept men as they are.
   e. Men are often unhappy about their lot in life.

7. How would Mrs. Marwood probably respond if she were rejected by a lover?
   a. "He was a jerk anyway."
   b. "I'll get even, whatever the cost!"
   c. "I'm finished with romance."
   d. "There are plenty of fish in the sea."
   e. "It's better to have loved and lost than never to have loved at all."

8. What is the most likely meaning of *inveterately* in Mrs. Fainall's second speech?
   a. without a backbone
   b. drunken
   c. hesitating
   d. persistently
   e. unpatriotic

9. Mrs. Marwood intends to punish men in what way?
   a. by avoiding them
   b. by getting married to one
   c. with violence
   d. poison
   e. It is not stated.

10. Where does this scene take place?
    a. New York City
    b. Venice
    c. St. James's Park
    d. Windsor Castle
    e. It is not stated.

Passage 3

The following excerpt is from *The Dinner Party* by Neil Simon.

A private dining room in a first rate restaurant in Paris. The present. At stage right is a dining table, set for six.

Against the wall at stage left is a long serving table with large silver tureens of food with bottles of champagne, a few already open.

In the center of the room is a small sofa for two and a chair on each side of the sofa. Everything in the room, from furniture to the wall decorations are French and softly attractive.

At Rise:

Claude Pichon, early forties, in black tie, stands alone in the room, looks at his watch and sips champagne. He looks a little lost. He looks at the dining table, then crosses to the buffet table, lifts tureen covers, sniffs food, then over to the hors d'oeuvres and samples a few. Turns and looks lost again.

There is a double door almost at rear center stage. Another door, smaller, on the side wall. The large door opens and another man enters, about the same age, in black tie as well. This is Albert Donay.

ALBERT: Hello. Am I in the right place? The Gerard party?

CLAUDE: Yes. Well, I think so. I'm the first one here.

[*Albert comes in, closes the door.*]

ALBERT: I'm Albert Donay.

CLAUDE: Claude Pichon.

[*They shake hands. Albert winces in pain, pulls his hand away and tries to shake off pain.*]

ALBERT: AHHH . . . Ooooh.

CLAUDE: I'm sorry. Did I do that?

ALBERT: No, I did. Hurt my finger putting my tie on.

CLAUDE: Yes, bow ties are a bother. Did you make it yourself?

ALBERT: No, it's my father's. He snapped it while my finger was up. [*Holds his finger to his throat*] This is very nice, isn't it?

CLAUDE: Well, it is La Cassette . . . They say that Josephine lived here once. . . . Napoleon used to visit her secretly through that door. [*He points to the small door.*]

ALBERT: Really? How convenient to have a restaurant in your own home.

CLAUDE: I er, don't think it was a restaurant then.

11. What is the setting of this story?
   a. an old-fashioned living room
   b. a present-day Paris restaurant
   c. the era of Napoleon
   d. a private residence
   e. a luxury yacht

12. If you were in the audience, where would you see a dining table set for six people?
   a. at the center of the stage
   b. to the left of the stage
   c. to the right of the stage
   d. to the rear of the stage
   e. You would not see it.

13. The opening paragraphs of this selection (the text in *italics*) is an example of
   a. metaphor.
   b. dramatic tension.
   c. monologue.
   d. stage directions.
   e. dialogue.

14. *At Rise* in the fourth paragraph of the opening italic text means
   a. when the curtain goes up.
   b. when the audience stands.
   c. at sunrise.
   d. at a high point on the stage.
   e. when the music begins.

15. What is the tone of this drama?
   a. serious
   b. historical
   c. humorous
   d. argumentative
   e. whimsical

16. This play is most likely a
    b. monologue.
    b. melodrama.
    c. tragedy.
    d. comedy.
    e. musical.

Passage 4

Read the following excerpt from Christopher Marlowe's *Doctor Faustus*.

>   *Enter* MEPHISTOPHELES.
>   FAUSTUS: Now tell me what saith Lucifer, thy lord?
>   MEPHISTOPHELES: That I shall wait on Faustus whilst he lives,
>   So he will buy my service with his soul.
>   FAUSTUS: Already Faustus hath hazarded that for thee.
>   MEPHISTOPHELES: But now thou must bequeath it solemnly,
>   And write a deed of gift with thine own blood;
>   For that security craves Lucifer.
>   If thou deny it, I must back to hell.
>   FAUSTUS: Stay, Mephistopheles, and tell me, what good will my soul do thy lord?
>   MEPHISTOPHELES: Enlarge his kingdom.
>   FAUSTUS: Is that the reason why he tempts us thus?
>   MEPHISTOPHELES: Solamen miseris socios habuisse doloris. [Misery loves company.]
>   FAUSTUS: Why, have you any pain that torture others?
>   MEPHISTOPHELES: As great as have the human souls of men.
>   But, tell me, Faustus, shall I have thy soul?
>   And I will be thy slave, and wait on thee,
>   And give thee more than thou hast wit to ask.
>   FAUSTUS: Ay, Mephistopheles, I'll give it thee.
>   MEPHISTOPHELES: Then, Faustus, stab thine arm courageously,
>   And bind thy soul, that at some certain day
>   Great Lucifer may claim it as his own;
>   And then be thou as great as Lucifer.
>   FAUSTUS: [*Stabbing his arm*] Lo, Mephistopheles, for love of thee,
>   Faustus hath cut his arm, and with his proper blood
>   Assures his soul to be great Lucifer's,
>   Chief lord and regent of perpetual night!
>   View here this blood that trickles from mine arm,
>   And let it be *propitious* for my wish.
>   MEPHISTOPHELES: But, Faustus,
>   Write it in manner of a deed of gift.
>   FAUSTUS: [*Writing*] Ay, so I do. But, Mephistopheles,
>   My blood congeals, and I can write no more.
>   MEPHISTOPHELES: I'll fetch thee fire to dissolve it straight.
>   [*Exit.*]
>   FAUSTUS: What might the staying of my blood portend?
>   Is it unwilling I should write this bill?
>   Why streams it not, that I may write afresh?
>   FAUSTUS GIVES TO THEE HIS SOUL: O, there it stayed!
>   Why shouldst thou not? is not thy soul thine own?
>   Then write again, FAUSTUS GIVES TO THEE HIS SOUL.
>   [*Re-enter* MEPHISTOPHELES *with the chafer of fire.*]
>   MEPHISTOPHELES: See, Faustus, here is fire; set it on.

READING DRAMA

FAUSTUS: So, now the blood begins to clear again;
Now will I make an end immediately.
[*Writes.*]
MEPHISTOPHELES: [*Aside*] What will not I do to obtain his soul?
FAUSTUS: Consummatum est; this bill is ended,
And Faustus hath bequeathed his soul to Lucifer.

17. The audience knows that Mephistopheles (a devil) will say anything to get the soul of Faustus—but Faustus is not aware of that. This is an example of
    a. tragedy.
    b. dramatic irony.
    c. metaphor.
    d. heroic couplet.
    b. punch line.

18. Why does Mephistopheles answer Faustus' question by saying that *misery loves company*?
    a. It rhymes.
    b. He is quoting from the Bible.
    c. Faustus doesn't speak Latin, so he won't know what it means.
    d. He is joking with Faustus.
    e. He is implying that Faustus will one day regret selling his soul.

19. The word *propitious* in Faustus's seventh speech probably means
    a. a bad omen.
    b. good luck.
    c. a stage prop.
    d. prosperity.
    e. speedy.

20. The lines beginning with *What might the staying of my blood portend* . . . are an example of
    a. a dialogue.
    b. a monologue.
    c. an interjection.
    d. an aside.
    e. a soliloquy.

21. When Mephistopheles says, *What will not I do to obtain his soul*, this is an example of
    a. a dialogue.
    b. a monologue.
    c. an interjection.
    d. an aside.
    e. a soliloquy.

22. If this play ended with Faustus being taken to hell by Mephistopheles, it would be
    a. a tragedy.
    b. a comedy.
    c. a tragicomedy.
    d. a farce.
    e. none of the above

23. The tone of this passage is
    a. humorous.
    b. serious.
    c. ironic.
    d. gloomy.
    e. violent.

Passage 5

The following excerpt is from *Hamlet* by William Shakespeare.

GUILDENSTERN: My honoured lord!

ROSENCRANTZ: My most dear lord!

HAMLET: My excellent good friends! How dost thou, Guildenstern? Ah, Rosencrantz! Good lads, how do ye both?

ROSENCRANTZ: As the indifferent children of the earth.

GUILDENSTERN: Happy in that we are not over-happy; On fortune's cap we are not the very button.

HAMLET: Nor the soles of her shoe?

ROSENCRANTZ: Neither, my lord.

HAMLET: Then you live about her waist, or in the middle of her favours?

GUILDENSTERN: Faith, her privates we.

HAMLET: In the secret parts of fortune? O, most true; she is a strumpet. What's the news?

ROSENCRANTZ: None, my lord, but that the world's grown honest.

HAMLET: Then is doomsday near; but your news is not true. Let me question more in particular: what have you, my good friends, deserved at the hands of fortune, that she sends you to prison hither?

GUILDENSTERN: Prison, my lord!

HAMLET: Denmark's a prison.

ROSENCRANTZ: Then is the world one.

HAMLET: A goodly one; in which there are many confines, wards, and dungeons, Denmark being one o' the worst.

ROSENCRANTZ: We think not so, my lord.

HAMLET: Why, then 'tis none to you; for there is nothing either good or bad but thinking makes it so: to me it is a prison.

ROSENCRANTZ: Why, then, your ambition makes it one; 'tis too narrow for your mind.

HAMLET: O God, I could be bounded in a nutshell, and count myself a king of infinite space, were it not that I have bad dreams.

GUILDENSTERN: Which dreams, indeed, are ambition; for the very substance of the ambitious is merely the shadow of a dream.

HAMLET: A dream itself is but a shadow.

ROSENCRANTZ: Truly, and I hold ambition of so airy and light a quality that it is but a shadow's shadow.

HAMLET: Then are our beggars bodies, and our monarchs and outstretch'd heroes the beggars' shadows. Shall we to the court? for, by my fay, I cannot reason.

ROSENCRANTZ AND GUILDENSTERN: We'll wait upon you.

HAMLET: No such matter: I will not sort you with the rest of my servants; for, to speak to you like an honest man, I am most dreadfully attended. But, in the beaten way of friendship, what make you at Elsinore?

ROSENCRANTZ: To visit you, my lord; no other occasion.

HAMLET: Beggar that I am, I am even poor in thanks; but I thank you: and sure, dear friends, my thanks are too dear a halfpenny. Were you not sent for? Is it your own inclining? Is it a free visitation? Come, deal justly with me: come, come; nay, speak.

GUILDENSTERN: What should we say, my lord?

HAMLET: Why, anything but to the purpose. You were sent for; and there is a kind of confession in your looks, which your modesties have not craft enough to colour: I know the good king and queen have sent for you.

ROSENCRANTZ: To what end, my lord?

HAMLET: That you must teach me. But let me conjure you, by the rights of our fellowship, by the consonancy of our youth, by the obligation of our ever-preserved love, and by what more dear a better proposer could charge you withal, be even and direct with me, whether you were sent for or no.

ROSENCRANTZ: [*To Guildenstern*] What say you?

HAMLET: [*Aside*] Nay, then, I have an eye of you.—If you love me, hold not off.

GUILDENSTERN: My lord, we were sent for.

HAMLET: I will tell you why; so shall my anticipation prevent your discovery, and your secrecy to the king and queen moult no feather. I have of late,—but wherefore I know not,—lost all my mirth, forgone all custom of exercises; and indeed, it goes so heavily with my disposition that this goodly frame, the earth, seems to me a sterile *promontory*; this most excellent canopy, the air, look you, this brave o'erhanging firmament, this majestical roof fretted with golden fire,—why, it appears no other thing to me than a foul and pestilent congregation of vapours. What a piece of work is man! How noble in reason! how infinite in faculties! in form and moving, how express and admirable! In action how like an angel! in apprehension, how like a god! The beauty of the world! the paragon of animals! And yet, to me, what is this quintessence of dust? Man delights not me; no, nor woman neither, though by your smiling you seem to say so.

24. What do the characters mean when they say *on fortune's cap we are not the very button / Nor the soles of her shoe?*
   a. They are not at the top of fortune, nor at the bottom.
   b. They are fortunate to have clothes.
   c. They feel fortunate from head to toe.
   d. They are feeling very unlucky.
   e. They lost their lucky hat.

25. The tone of these lines is
   a. serious.
   b. lighthearted.
   c. sober.
   d. outraged.
   e. hilarious.

26. What does Hamlet mean when he says *for there is nothing either good or bad but thinking makes it so?*
   a. All of life's problems are in your mind.
   b. There is no such thing as good or bad.
   c. Life's good and bad are all a matter of opinion.
   d. He is not sure whether to laugh or cry.
   e. He is hungry.

27. This passage is an example of
   a. narration.
   b. personification.
   c. monologue.
   d. dialogue.
   e. soliloquy.

28. What does Hamlet mean when he says, *Beggar that I am, I am even poor in thanks*?
   a. He is so poor that he can hardly say thank you.
   b. He is asking them for a loan.
   c. His friends are being ungrateful.
   d. His friends are asking him for money.
   e. He is too selfish for friends.

29. If Hamlet had been a comedy, how might it have ended?
   a. The murder of Hamlet's father would remain unavenged.
   b. Hamlet's friends would have betrayed him.
   c. Hamlet would have been reconciled to his stepfather.
   d. Hamlet would have gone to an insane asylum.
   e. Hamlet would have died from laughing.

30. The word *promontory* in Hamlet's last speech most likely means
   a. a slow dance in which couples walk in circles.
   b. a high ridge of rock surrounded by water.
   c. a feeling that something is going to happen.
   d. a residence for college students.
   e. a change in societal position.

Posttest

You are now familiar with the kinds of questions and answer formats you will see on the official GED. Now take this posttest to identify any areas that you may need to review in more depth before the test day. When you are finished, check the answers on page 172 carefully to assess your results.

To simulate the test conditions, use the time constraints of the official GED Language Arts, Reading Test. Allow 65 minutes to complete all 40 items.

Remember, on the official GED, an unanswered question is counted as incorrect, so make a good guess.

Directions: Read each question carefully and determine the best answer. Record your answers by circling the answer letter choice. You may also use the answer sheet to bubble in your answer.

Note: On the GED, you are not permitted to write in the test booklet. For this posttest, practice by making any notes on a separate piece of paper.

ANSWER SHEET

▶ Posttest Answer Sheet

1. ⓐ ⓑ ⓒ ⓓ ⓔ
2. ⓐ ⓑ ⓒ ⓓ ⓔ
3. ⓐ ⓑ ⓒ ⓓ ⓔ
4. ⓐ ⓑ ⓒ ⓓ ⓔ
5. ⓐ ⓑ ⓒ ⓓ ⓔ
6. ⓐ ⓑ ⓒ ⓓ ⓔ
7. ⓐ ⓑ ⓒ ⓓ ⓔ
8. ⓐ ⓑ ⓒ ⓓ ⓔ
9. ⓐ ⓑ ⓒ ⓓ ⓔ
10. ⓐ ⓑ ⓒ ⓓ ⓔ
11. ⓐ ⓑ ⓒ ⓓ ⓔ
12. ⓐ ⓑ ⓒ ⓓ ⓔ
13. ⓐ ⓑ ⓒ ⓓ ⓔ
14. ⓐ ⓑ ⓒ ⓓ ⓔ
15. ⓐ ⓑ ⓒ ⓓ ⓔ
16. ⓐ ⓑ ⓒ ⓓ ⓔ
17. ⓐ ⓑ ⓒ ⓓ ⓔ
18. ⓐ ⓑ ⓒ ⓓ ⓔ
19. ⓐ ⓑ ⓒ ⓓ ⓔ
20. ⓐ ⓑ ⓒ ⓓ ⓔ
21. ⓐ ⓑ ⓒ ⓓ ⓔ
22. ⓐ ⓑ ⓒ ⓓ ⓔ
23. ⓐ ⓑ ⓒ ⓓ ⓔ
24. ⓐ ⓑ ⓒ ⓓ ⓔ
25. ⓐ ⓑ ⓒ ⓓ ⓔ
26. ⓐ ⓑ ⓒ ⓓ ⓔ
27. ⓐ ⓑ ⓒ ⓓ ⓔ
28. ⓐ ⓑ ⓒ ⓓ ⓔ
29. ⓐ ⓑ ⓒ ⓓ ⓔ
30. ⓐ ⓑ ⓒ ⓓ ⓔ
31. ⓐ ⓑ ⓒ ⓓ ⓔ
32. ⓐ ⓑ ⓒ ⓓ ⓔ
33. ⓐ ⓑ ⓒ ⓓ ⓔ
34. ⓐ ⓑ ⓒ ⓓ ⓔ
35. ⓐ ⓑ ⓒ ⓓ ⓔ
36. ⓐ ⓑ ⓒ ⓓ ⓔ
37. ⓐ ⓑ ⓒ ⓓ ⓔ
38. ⓐ ⓑ ⓒ ⓓ ⓔ
39. ⓐ ⓑ ⓒ ⓓ ⓔ
40. ⓐ ⓑ ⓒ ⓓ ⓔ

Questions 1 to 5 refer to the following excerpt from a poem.

Now came on a new order of the ages
That in the *Latin of our founding sages*
(Is it not written on the dollar bill
We carry in our purse and pocket still?)
God nodded His approval of as good.
So much those heroes knew and understood—
I mean the great four, Washington,
John Adams, Jefferson, and Madison—
So much they knew as *consecrated seers*
They must have seen ahead what now appears:
They would bring empires down about our ears
And by the *example of our Declaration*
Make everybody want to be a nation.
And this is no aristocratic joke
At the expense of negligible folk.
We see how seriously the races swarm
In their attempts at *sovereignty* and form.
They are our wards we think to some extent
For the time being and with their consent,
To teach them how Democracy is meant.
"New order of the ages" did we say?
If it looks none too orderly today,
'Tis a confusion it was ours to start
So in it have to take courageous part.
No one of honest feeling would approve
A ruler who pretended not to love
A turbulence he had the better of.
Everyone knows the glory of the *twain*
Who gave America the aeroplane
To ride the whirlwind and the hurricane.
Some poor fool has been saying in his heart
Glory is out of date in life and art.
Our venture in revolution and outlawry
Has justified itself in freedom's story
Right down to now in glory upon glory.
—From "For John F. Kennedy His Inauguration," by Robert Frost.

1. What is the *Latin of our founding sages* referred to in line 2?
   a. the Constitution
   b. the motto on the dollar bill
   c. the Declaration of Independence
   d. the Magna Carta
   e. the Gettysburg Address

2. What is the *example of our Declaration* referred to in line 12?
   a. the IRS
   b. the U.S. Treasury
   c. the Constitution
   d. the Declaration of Independence
   e. the Gettysburg Address

3. The word *sovereignty* in line 17 most likely means
   a. self-rule.
   b. overdue.
   c. expensive.
   d. shiny.
   e. reprieved.

4. Who is/are the *twain* referred to in line 28?
   a. Mark Twain
   b. Abraham Lincoln
   c. railroad engineers
   d. the Wright brothers
   e. the U.S. Navy

5. The poem's tone is
   a. angry.
   b. unconventional.
   c. humorous.
   d. anti-American.
   e. patriotic.

6. The narrator is probably
   a. a baseball fan.
   b. a Frenchman.
   c. an American citizen.
   d. not well read.
   e. indifferent to politics.

7. Why does the poet refer to Jefferson and others as *consecrated seers*?
   a. to make fun of them
   b. because they were blind
   c. because they are dead
   d. to suggest that they were prophets
   e. to remind us that we should vote

8. *They must have seen ahead what now appears* is an example of
   a. dramatic tension.
   b. iambic pentameter.
   c. double entendre.
   d. monologue.
   e. soliloquy.

Questions 9 to 16 refer to the following passage.

My instructions were to present myself at an office in Broadway, opposite St. James's underground station, which I duly did. As a reader of *Ashenden* I was naturally excited at the prospect of entering the portals of the British Secret Service (or SIS as it was usually called), though I assumed that at this first preliminary encounter I should not be admitted to the actual headquarters, but only to some shadow set-up, or facade, used to try out aspirants before actually taking them on. I may add that everyone I saw and everything that happened seemed to support such an assumption. It was only later that I came to realize I had been in contact, not with a hurriedly improvised dummy, but the real thing.

While I was awaiting my own clearance at the main entrance, I was able to observe the people coming and going. A good proportion of them were in the services, with the Navy preponderating. I only saw one, as I thought, false beard—a luxuriant tangled growth, whose wearer turned out, on closer acquaintance, to be a former trade-unionist and Marxist, allegedly from the boiler-maker's union. He was responsible for providing expert guidance in industrial matters; and his beard, he assured me, was genuine, though he admitted that he had allowed it to *proliferate* since joining SIS, as he had also his use of strong language, and tendency to bang the table to emphasize a point.
—From *The Infernal Grove*,
by Malcolm Muggeridge.

9. The narrator is describing
   a. an interesting trip to London.
   b. how he got lost on the London underground.
   c. his involvement with trade unions.
   d. how he joined the British Secret Service.
   e. the headquarters of the CIA.

10. The author was surprised to discover that
   a. the people he met were Russian spies.
   b. his interviewer was wearing a false beard.
   c. he was really in the headquarters of the SIS.
   d. he was hired on the spot.
   e. he was not late for the interview.

11. The narrator most likely
   a. did undercover espionage.
   b. never rode the subway.
   c. had a beard.
   d. was married.
   e. spent time in Afghanistan.

12. The phrase *a hurriedly improvised dummy* refers to
    a. a Russian spy.
    b. another SIS agent.
    c. President Clinton.
    d. department store decorations.
    e. a fake headquarters building.

13. The former Marxist
    a. refers to the author.
    b. interviewed the author.
    c. was shot in Istanbul.
    d. had a black beard.
    e. had a good sense of humor.

14. The word *proliferate* in this context means
    a. recede.
    b. grow.
    c. pay taxes.
    d. jog.
    e. blustery.

15. This passage is most likely from
    a. a drama.
    b. an autobiography.
    c. a sonnet.
    d. a long time ago.
    e. the newspaper.

16. This is an example of
    a. no narrator.
    b. second-person narrator.
    c. third-person narrator.
    d. third-person omniscient.
    e. first-person narrator.

Questions 17 to 25 refer to the following excerpt.

GEORGE: O.K. . . . O.K., whatever you say. . . . [*They both sit on the couch. He tries to kiss her. She moves away*] Look, we've had a nice evening; let's not spoil it, huh? . . . [*He again turns her head and tries to nuzzle in and she turns away from him, not with distaste but with momentary lack of interest; in a mood to pursue what they were talking about.*]

BENEATHA: I'm *trying* to talk to you.

GEORGE: We always talk.

BENEATHA: Yes—and I love to talk.

GEORGE: [*exasperated; rising*] I know it and I don't mind it sometimes . . . I want you to cut it out, see—the moody stuff, I mean. I don't like it. You're a nice-looking girl . . . all over. That's all you need, honey. Forget the atmosphere—they're going to go for what they see. Be glad for that. Drop the Garbo routine. It doesn't go with you. As for myself, I want a nice—[*groping*]—simple [*thoughtfully*]—sophisticated girl . . . not a poet—O.K.?

[*She rebuffs him again and he starts to leave.*]

BENEATHA: Why are you angry?

GEORGE: Because this is stupid! I don't go out with you to discuss the nature of "quiet desperation" or to hear all about your thoughts—because the world will go on thinking what it thinks regardless—

BENEATHA: Then why read books? Why go to school?

GEORGE: [*with artificial patience; counting on his fingers*] It's simple. You read books—to learn facts—to get grades—to pass the course—to get a degree. That's all—it has nothing to do with thoughts.

[*A long pause*]

BENEATHA: I see. [*A longer pause as she looks at him*] Good night, George.

[*George looks at her a little oddly, and starts to exit. He meets MAMA coming in*]

GEORGE: Oh—hello, Mrs. Younger.

MAMA: Hello, George, how are you feeling?

GEORGE: Fine—fine, how are you?

MAMA: Oh, a little tired. You know them steps can get you after a day's work. You all have a nice time tonight?

GEORGE: Yes—a fine time. Well, good night.

MAMA: Good night. [*He exits. MAMA closes the door behind her.*] Hello, honey. What you sitting like that for?

BENEATHA: I'm just sitting.

MAMA: Didn't you have a nice time?

BENEATHA: No.

MAMA: No? What's the matter?

BENEATHA: Mama, George is a fool—honest. [*She rises*]

MAMA: [*Hustling around unloading the packages that she has entered with. She stops.*] Is he, baby?

BENEATHA: Yes. [*Beneatha makes up TRAVIS' bed as she talks*]

MAMA: You sure?

BENEATHA: Yes.

MAMA: Well—I guess you better not waste your time with no fools.

[*Beneatha looks up at her mother, watching her put groceries in the refrigerator. Finally she gathers up her things and starts into the bedroom. At the door she stops and looks back at her mother*]

BENEATHA: Mama—

MAMA: Yes baby?

BENEATHA: Thank you.

MAMA: For what?

BENEATHA: For understanding me this time.

—From *A Raisin in the Sun*, by Lorraine Hansberry.

17. Why is George NOT interested in talking?
   a. He has a headache.
   b. It's time for him to leave.
   c. He's angry with his mother.
   d. He wants to be romantic.
   e. He actually *does* want to talk.

18. Beneatha wants to talk
   a. about their relationship.
   b. about the future.
   c. because she's angry.
   d. because she loves to talk.
   e. about the weather.

19. George wants a girl who
   a. reminds him of Greta Garbo.
   b. is poetic.
   c. dances well.
   d. cooks like his mom.
   e. is not moody.

20. Why does Beneatha say that George is a fool?
   a. He doesn't share her love of talking.
   b. He isn't well educated.
   c. He is too short for her.
   d. She is angry that he left.
   e. It is not stated.

21. Beneatha feels that Mama has understood her because
   a. she offers Beneatha some deep wisdom.
   b. Beneatha loves Mama.
   c. she has been willing to listen and talk.
   d. Mama keeps the house clean.
   e. she has not been understanding in the past.

22. Mama's opinion of George
    a. is very low.
    b. is very high.
    c. is to avoid him at all costs.
    d. is that Beneatha should marry him.
    e. is not stated.

23. This passage is an example of
    a. monologue.
    b. dialogue.
    c. biography.
    d. fable.
    e. haiku.

24. While Beneatha is talking, Mama is
    a. mopping the floor.
    b. putting on makeup.
    c. ignoring her.
    d. unloading packages.
    e. about 5 feet tall.

25. Beneatha and George will probably
    a. never speak again.
    b. make up again.
    c. become professional musicians.
    d. never forgive Mama.
    e. always be fighting.

Questions 26 to 32 refer to the following passage from *Huckleberry Finn*, where Huck is disguised as a girl.

I had got so uneasy I couldn't set still. I had to do something with my hands; so I took up a needle off of the table and went to threading it. My hands shook, and I was making a bad job of it. When the woman stopped talking I looked up, and she was looking at me pretty curious and smiling a little. . . .

The woman kept looking at me pretty curious, and I didn't feel a bit comfortable. Pretty soon she says,

"What did you say your name was, honey?"

"M—Mary Williams."

Somehow it didn't seem to me that I said it was Mary before, so I didn't look up—seemed to me I said it was Sarah; so I felt sort of cornered, and was afeared maybe I was looking it, too. I wished the woman would say something more; the longer she set still the uneasier I was. But now she says:

"Honey, I thought you said it was Sarah when you first come in?"

"Oh, yes'm, I did. Sarah Mary Williams. Sarah's my first name. Some calls me Sarah, some calls me Mary."

"Oh, that's the way of it?"

"Yes'm."

I was feeling better then, but I wished I was out of there, anyway. I couldn't look up yet.

Well, the woman fell to talking about how hard times was, and how poor they had to live, and how the rats was as free as if they owned the place, and so forth and so on, and then I got easy again. She was right about the rats. You'd see one stick his nose out of a hole in the corner every little while. She said she had to have things handy to throw at them when she was alone, or they wouldn't give her no peace. She showed me a bar of lead twisted up into a knot, and said she was a good shot with it generly, but she'd wrenched her arm a day or two ago, and didn't know whether she could throw true now. But she watched for a chance, and directly banged away at a rat; but she missed him wide, and said "Ouch!" it hurt her arm so. Then she told me to try for the next one. I wanted to be getting away before the old man got back, but of course I didn't let on. I got the thing, and the first rat that showed his nose I let drive, and if he'd a stayed where he was he'd a been a tolerable sick rat. She said that was first-rate, and she reckoned I would hive the next one. She went and got the lump of lead and fetched it back, and brought along a hank of yarn which she wanted me to help her with. I held up my two hands and she put the hank over them, and went on talking about her and her husband's matters. But she broke off to say:

"Keep your eye on the rats. You better have the lead in your lap, handy."

So she dropped the lump into my lap just at that moment, and I clapped my legs together on it and she went on talking. But only about a minute. Then she took off the hank and looked me straight in the face, and very pleasant, and says:

"Come, now, what's your real name?"

"Wh—what, mum?"

"What's your real name? Is it Bill, or Tom, or Bob?—or what is it?"

I reckon I shook like a leaf, and I didn't know hardly what to do. But I says:

"Please to don't poke fun at a poor girl like me, mum. If I'm in the way here, I'll—"

"No, you won't. Set down and stay where you are. I ain't going to hurt you, and I ain't going to tell on you, nuther. . . . What's your real name, now?"

"George Peters, mum."

"Well, try to remember it, George. Don't forget and tell me it's Elexander before you go, and then get out by saying it's George Elexander when I catch you. And don't go about women in that old calico. You do a girl tolerable poor, but you might fool men, maybe. Bless you, child, when you set out to thread a needle don't hold the thread still and fetch the needle up to it; hold the needle still and poke the thread at it; that's the way a woman most always does, but a man always does t'other way. And when you throw at a rat or anything, hitch yourself up a tiptoe and fetch your hand up over your head as awkward as you can, and miss your rat about six or seven foot. Throw stiff-armed from the shoulder, like there was a pivot there for it to turn on, like a girl; not from the wrist and elbow, with your arm out to one side, like a boy. And, mind you, when a girl tries to catch anything in her lap she throws her knees apart; she don't clap them together, the way you did when you catched the lump of lead. Why, I spotted you for a boy when you was threading the needle; and I contrived the other things just to make certain . . ."

—From *Huckleberry Finn*, by Mark Twain.

26. The real name of the *little girl* in the bonnet is
  a. Huckleberry Finn.
  b. Sarah Williams.
  c. Mary Williams.
  d. Sarah Mary Williams.
  e. George Peters.

27. Huck tried to thread a needle because
  a. he was going to help the woman with her sewing.
  b. he wanted to learn how to sew.
  c. the woman had asked him to.
  d. he was trying to hide how nervous he was.
  e. No reason is given.

28. How did the woman become suspicious that Huck was NOT a girl?
   a. Huck's accent didn't sound right.
   b. Huck didn't look like a girl.
   c. She had peeked under the bonnet.
   d. She was a keen observer of details.
   e. It was just a lucky guess.

29. What does the woman understand that Huck does NOT understand?
   a. that little girls don't dress the way he thinks
   b. that the difference between the sexes is more than clothing
   c. that you can't deceive a woman
   d. that he can't escape his past, no matter where he runs
   e. nothing; they are completely equal

30. Who is narrating this passage?
   a. Mark Twain
   b. Tom Sawyer
   c. Samuel Clemens
   d. Becky Thatcher
   e. Huckleberry Finn

31. The narrator's diction shows that he
   a. is dressed like a girl.
   b. is uneducated.
   c. doesn't like the woman.
   d. is confused.
   e. can't make up his mind.

32. According to this passage, a male will probably
   a. move a needle toward the thread.
   b. move the thread toward the needle.
   c. catch lead with his right hand.
   d. throw things very stiffly.
   e. kill rats better than females.

Questions 33 to 36 refer to the following passage.

The film *Amadeus* presents a masterful treatment of the most important element of dramatic plot. Indeed, conflict is more than present—it abounds nearly to distraction!

On the surface, we find the most pertinent conflict in the tension between Mozart and Salieri. Here we find Salieri's understandable frustration at Mozart's meteoric rise to fame and success. Yet we also discover that Salieri struggles with the very gift itself which Mozart takes for granted: the ability to create music of such sublime beauty and versatility. Salieri would do anything to have such a gift—and yet he finds that very gift wasted on a "moral dwarf" who doesn't appreciate it at all.

As we go below the surface, however, we begin to discover that there are many layers of tension. Mozart may not worry about the jealousy of Salieri—indeed, he is quite unaware of it, which proves his undoing—but he has some issues of his own to deal with. His father's constant demands and unattainable standards of perfection provide Mozart with enough conflict to fuel a drama in its own right. But then we must add in the tension that he experiences with his wife, who wants nothing more than to keep him alive and healthy long enough to raise his son.

Below this we find more tensions. Mozart, it turns out, has some jealousies of his own—such as the favor of Emperor Joseph. Chief among these jealousies, it turns out, is Mozart's insistence upon doing what he wants. He couches this demand, of course, in terms of protecting his art and obeying his creative muse, but the real truth becomes apparent as the film progresses: Mozart wants to do what

Mozart wants to do. This particular conflict comes to a head when the Emperor forbids him to produce an opera about Figaro, yet Mozart goes right ahead and does so nonetheless.

33. The purpose of this passage is to
   a. explain the life of Mozart.
   b. address areas of conflict in *Amadeus*.
   c. discover who really killed Mozart.
   d. summarize the plot of *Amadeus*.
   e. persuade readers to watch *Amadeus*.

34. Which of the following areas of conflict is NOT present in *Amadeus*?
   a. Salieri is jealous of Mozart's gifts.
   b. Mozart is jealous of Salieri's position.
   c. Mozart's wife is jealous of Mozart's family time.
   d. Emperor Joseph is resisting Mozart's plans.
   e. Mozart wants to have things his own way.

35. The last paragraph is intended to
   a. spoil the plot of the movie.
   b. make the reader wonder who Mozart really was.
   c. analyze the moral character of Mozart.
   d. cast doubt on Salieri's role in Mozart's career.
   e. show that Emperor Joseph was wrong.

36. Conflict is an important element in
   a. plot structure.
   b. dramatic tension.
   c. the life of Mozart.
   d. the life of Salieri.
   e. the life of Emperor Joseph.

Questions 37 to 40 refer to the following contract.

Contractor's Obligations
The Contractor promises and agrees with the Owner as follows:

   1. Contractor shall provide all materials necessary to complete said construction in the most timely manner, in accordance with all relevant building codes and industrial standards.

   2. Contractor shall follow all blueprints, architectural renderings, and other pertinent documents as provided by Owner to the best of his or her abilities. Any deviation from said documents shall be approved and authorized by Owner prior to Contractor beginning work.

   3. Owner shall vacate premises at least twenty-four (24) hours prior to commencement of construction, and the premises shall remain vacated for at least twenty-four (24) hours after construction has been completed. Contractor shall permit Owner access to goods stored on premises during construction, with the stipulation that Owner shall provide notice at least twenty-four (24) hours in advance, and Owner shall remain on premises no longer than necessary to retrieve or store goods.

Risk of Loss
Owner assumes all risk of destruction, loss, or damage to the property due to fire, vandalism, or act of God before, during, and after construction. Contractor assumes all risk of destruction, loss, or damage to his or her own equipment before, during, and after construction. This equipment includes but is not limited to all construction tools, motor

vehicles, personal equipment, and moveable goods used by him or her and/or his or her employees. Contractor further assumes all responsibility for any harm or injury to his or her employees before, during, and after construction.

Firm and Fixed Pricing

Contractor agrees that the price stated in paragraph 6, subsection 3, shall be firm and fixed, and that he or she shall neither increase nor decrease the final cost of all aspects of construction detailed in paragraph 5, subsections 1 through 12.

37. According to the contract, who will be responsible if a construction worker is injured on the job?
   a. the worker
   b. Contractor
   c. Owner
   d. both
   e. not specified

38. What will happen if the price of lumber doubles in the coming months?
   a. The price of the job will remain the same.
   b. The price of the job will increase.
   c. Contractor will renegotiate with Owner.
   d. The job will be put on hold.
   e. It is not specified.

39. When can Owner move back to the premises of this contract?
   a. once the building inspector has given the OK
   b. after Contractor has completed the work
   c. 24 hours after construction is completed
   d. 36 hours after Contractor has closed
   e. not specified

40. How long does Contractor have to complete this work?
   a. 24 hours
   b. 48 hours
   c. six months from starting
   d. It is negotiable with Owner.
   e. It is not specified.

GED Language Arts, Reading Answers and Explanations

▶ Pretest Answers and Scoring Review

1. **c.** This passage is a humorous exchange of opinions between Larry and his mother. Larry wants to invite a lot of friends to visit them in a house that is too small, but he seems oblivious to the fact that his request is inconsiderate.
2. **d.** The conflict is humorous, but it still exists—caused by Larry's demands that his mother host a number of his friends, which his mother thinks is very unreasonable.
3. **b.** No matter how much we want to—even if we have all the *good will in the world*—we cannot fit 13 people into the villa.
4. **c.** The narrator is in the third person, meaning that he is not a character in the story.
5. **b.** You can infer that Larry is self-centered by the fact that he does not recognize the absurdity of his suggestions. His focus is on his own plans, not on how those plans will affect others.
6. **a.** Thoreau is saying that he moved into the woods in order to live *more simply*, hoping to avoid the unnecessary distractions of life in a civilized society.
7. **e.** Thoreau may have done these other things, but the point that he is making in his essay is that we can get the most out of life if we live as simply as possible.
8. **c.** The word *founder* in this context means to sink, as a ship that has hit rocks and is about to sink *to the bottom*, as Thoreau states.
9. **b.** Thoreau is trying to convince the reader that his lifestyle is the best, the most pure. This is obviously open to debate; many readers would not agree that it's best to live alone in the woods. Therefore, the author is trying to persuade.
10. **b.** This is an excerpt from an essay entitled "Walden," by Henry David Thoreau.
11. **d.** The sunrise is being described, which the poet lets us know by informing us that he is picturing dawn. The sunrise is described as slitting the darkness *from ear to ear*, implying that it goes across the whole horizon.

GED LANGUAGE ARTS, READING ANSWERS AND EXPLANATIONS

12. e. The *blue snake* is also described as the *barge-road*, a road that is used by barges. Barges travel on rivers, and the poet is describing a frozen river.

13. a. The word *solstice* refers to the shortest day of the year, which occurs in the middle of winter. The poet is saying that it is six weeks past that, so the days should be getting longer.

14. d. There is no rhyme scheme in this poem, nor do the lines *scan* to any particular meter. It is written in free verse.

15. b. This poem is drawing word images, describing a frozen river in the winter months. It is an example of imagistic poetry.

16. c. The characters' attitude toward marriage is very flippant; they are joking together about their own previous marriage, as well as the marriages that each is in at present.

17. b. This couple used to be married to each other, and have since married others. Now they discover that they miss one another. Absence makes the heart grow fonder.

18. e. Each of the characters had been convinced in the past that the other was being unfaithful. Both confess to thinking that the other was cheating.

19. a. Underneath all the humor, there is a strong sense that this couple is doomed to be unhappy no matter whom they marry.

20. a. This play is very humorous, and deals with everyday subjects (such as marriage) with ordinary people. It is probably a comedy, therefore, and will end happily.

21. b. The couple are not wealthy. We are told in the first sentence that Jim needed a new overcoat and gloves. We are not told any of the other details, but we can infer that they are ordinary working-class people.

22. c. Della is eagerly excited to see her husband, and she wriggles off the table in order to run to him.

23. d. Jim is struggling to make sense out of what he is seeing. His wife has suddenly cut her hair very short, but he has bought her special decorations (combs) to wear in her hair.

24. e. Della starts to cry because she realizes that Jim bought her the very thing that she wanted—despite the fact that the combs were very expensive. She is also overwhelmed with the thought that now her hair is too short to wear them.

25. c. The word *ardent* means *passionate, burning with love*.

26. d. It is easy to picture Della and Jim being very generous with their friends, because they have been so generous and unselfish with one another.

27. b. Jim has sold his watch to buy Della's combs.

28. d. Jim has sold his watch to buy combs for Della's hair, but Della has cut off her hair to buy a chain for Jim's watch. This is an example of irony, where a character's expectations turn out to be the opposite of what happens.

29. a. The narrator is trying to persuade a woman to become intimate with him. He is using the fact that their bloods have already commingled inside the flea, so they should not hesitate to sleep together.

30. c. The poem is divided into three *stanzas*, or groups of verses.

31. a. The flea has sucked blood from the narrator and from the woman, plus it is a living creature in its own right—therefore, there are "three lives in one flea."

GED LANGUAGE ARTS, READING ANSWERS AND EXPLANATIONS

32. **e.** The *living walls of jet* refers to the flea itself. Jet refers to the flea's black color. The couple's blood is commingled inside the flea's body.
33. **b.** The first two lines rhyme, then the next two lines rhyme, and so forth—making a rhyme scheme of *a, a, b, b, c, c, d, d, d*.
34. **b.** The narrator is not taking the idea of love very seriously. He is using distorted logic to persuade the woman to be intimate with him, but it is mostly just a word game.
35. **e.** The woman has killed the flea by squishing it with her nail. The poet refers to the fact that she has *purpled* her nail—meaning that she has gotten the flea's blood on her fingernail.
36. **b.** This memo does spend some time on statistics, but the overall purpose is to ensure that the job site is a safe place to work—free from bullying by labor unions.
37. **d.** *Coercion* means forcing someone to cooperate, bullying a person into submission.
38. **e.** Employee turnover rates have increased over the past several years, and the trend is higher each year.
39. **b.** The passage states specifically that union agitation has been a large factor in employees leaving the company. None of the other issues is addressed in the passage.
40. **a.** There is nothing particularly humorous in this passage, but the writer also does not sound angry or confrontational. The overall tone is very businesslike and professional.

Pretest for Review

QUESTION	SUBJECT TESTED	SECTION TO STUDY
1	Tone	Chapter 3
2	Conflict	Chapter 3
3	Context	Chapter 2
4	Narrator	Chapter 3
5	Inference	Chapter 2
6	Main idea	Chapter 2
7	Main idea	Chapter 2
8	Vocabulary in context	Chapter 2
9	Persuasive writing	Chapters 2 and 4
10	Types of nonfiction	Chapter 4
11	Types of poetry	Chapter 5
12	Poetic language	Chapter 5
13	Vocabulary in context	Chapter 2
14	Meter and rhyme scheme	Chapter 5
15	Imagistic poetry	Chapter 5
16	Tone	Chapters 2 and 3
17	Theme	Chapter 3
18	Inferences	Chapter 2
19	Inferences	Chapter 2
20	Comedy and Tragedy	Chapter 6
21	Making inferences	Chapter 2
22	Characters	Chapter 6
23	Vocabulary in context	Chapter 2
24	Symbolism	Chapter 3

GED LANGUAGE ARTS, READING ANSWERS AND EXPLANATIONS

QUESTION	SUBJECT TESTED	SECTION TO STUDY
25	Vocabulary in context	Chapter 2
26	Making inferences	Chapter 2
27	Reading for context	Chapter 2
28	Irony	Chapters 3 and 5
29	Theme	Chapter 2
30	Stanza	Chapter 5
31	Poetry	Chapter 5
32	Symbolism	Chapter 3
33	Rhyme scheme	Chapter 5
34	Tone	Chapter 3
35	Poetry	Chapter 5
36	Main idea	Chapter 2
37	Vocabulary in context	Chapter 2
38	Reading nonfiction	Chapter 4
39	Reading nonfiction	Chapter 4
40	Tone	Chapter 3

▶ Chapter 2: Reading Comprehension Strategies

Practice 1
1. **c.** The topic sentence in the paragraph is the first sentence, *Reading is an important part of life.* It introduces the topic, which is reading. Notice that some of the other options, such as **d**, are actually statements that need to be proven—and therefore, they cannot be the topic.

2. **d.** This concept is suggested by the thesis statement in the paragraph, which is the second sentence: *Critical reading, however, is a demanding process.*

Practice 2
3. **a.** This is a thesis, a statement that needs to be proven, and the passage makes the thesis statement in the last sentence.
4. **b.** The topic of the paragraph is the Fourth Amendment. You could argue that choice **a** is correct as well, but the topic of the passage is actually not the Constitution as a whole but merely one aspect of it: the Fourth Amendment, which deals with search and seizure.

Practice 3
5. **e.** This thesis statement is given in the final sentence of the paragraph.
6. **e.** The topic of this paragraph is mathematics. Choices **c** and **d** are certainly addressed in the passage, but notice that they are both statements that would need to be proven—and therefore, they cannot be topic statements.

Practice 4
7. **b.** There are many numbers given in this passage, and it would be easy to pick the wrong one if you merely skimmed your eye along looking for numerals. The question is designed to test whether you are paying attention to what you're reading, and also to test whether you can go back through the passage and find specific details. In this case, the fourth sentence tells you that *more than 2,400 varieties* of potato are grown in the

GED LANGUAGE ARTS, READING ANSWERS AND EXPLANATIONS

Andes Mountains. Remember also to look for those signal words that we discussed earlier:

for example
for instance
in particular
in addition
furthermore
some
others
specifically

Practice 5

8. **b.** *Abraham Lincoln was the greatest president of the United States* is an opinion. The other statements are all provable facts, but this one statement is an opinion; there might be someone who would disagree that Abe Lincoln was the greatest president in the history of the United States. On the other hand, you can easily verify whether Lincoln was the sixteenth president by doing a little research. It's a fact; it's not open to debate.

Practice 6

9. **a.** This sentence tells you that some cities have decided to outlaw burning wood in a home fireplace; this is a strict fact, which can be proven true. The statement in choice **d** might at first appear to be a statement of fact, but notice that it addresses the motives of the colonists who participated in the Boston Tea Party. What actually motivated the Boston Tea Party is not a strict matter of fact, because people might have joined the rebellion with many different motives. Only choice **a** can be considered a strict statement of fact versus opinion.

Practice 7

10. **F.** This is a statement of fact that makes no value judgment or debatable assertions.
11. **F.** This is probably a statement of fact, although it's a good example of so-called facts that are actually debatable.
12. **O.** This is an opinion because what determines *safer* or *less safe* is clearly open to debate.
13. **O.** This is an opinion: One person's good investment is another person's money waster.
14. **F.** This statement can easily be tested and proven true.

Practice 8

Following are some possible opinion statements that could be written from the facts.

15. The movie *Crash* deserved to win the Best Picture award in 2006.
16. Summer is the most pleasant of the four seasons.
17. Deciduous trees lose their leaves in winter, so evergreens are a better choice for landscaping.
18. Coffee is brewed from beans, so instant coffee is not natural.
19. Daylight Saving time actually costs more than it saves.

Practice 9

20. **d.** It can be inferred that there is a problem with the security at the garage. There is nothing to suggest that the garage has been busy lately, so choice **a** is not supported by the passage. Choice **b** is far too sweeping a conclusion to draw, suggesting that all parking garage security officers are slackers; the passage does not

GED LANGUAGE ARTS, READING ANSWERS AND EXPLANATIONS

deal with parking garages in general, only with one garage in particular.

One of the fundamental rules in drawing inferences is that the passage must support what you infer. The passage does not make any sweeping statements about parking garages in general, nor does it address the question of whether the identification card system is working. The main idea of the passage is that there is a problem within this particular garage, and the writer is focusing on the garage's security officers in particular. Therefore, we can conclude that the writer is implying that the security guards aren't doing their jobs, even though he does not directly make that statement.

Practice 10

21. b. There is no evidence given in the report that Smith had been drinking, so choice **a** is not supportable. It is, of course, entirely possible that the witnesses lied, but the passage itself makes no mention of that possibility, so choice **c** is not correct. The only statement that can be supported by the passage is that Smith fell asleep while driving down Main Street.

Practice 11

22. d. Notice the words and phrases that the writer has used to describe Coach Lerner: *drill sergeant, marches, barks orders, troops on a battlefield,* and so forth. The writer is deliberately using expressions that make the reader think of being in the Army and undergoing basic training. There is nothing in the passage to suggest that Coach Lerner's techniques are either good or bad, so choices **a** and **b** cannot be supported. The author does not say whether he is new to the team or an old hand, so answer **c** cannot be supported.

Practice 12

23. e. Choice **b** might be tempting, and in fact the author might actually want you to believe that Bush doesn't care about poor people, but the passage does not address poor people or how Bush deals with them, so it cannot be supported.

Notice, however, the words that the writer has used. The president *visited his family's large estate*, which is actually a *huge compound*. The writer could just as easily have described it as *the old family homestead*, but those words would have brought a very different picture into the reader's mind. Pay attention to how a writer describes a thing or person or event, and ask yourself what other words could have been used to describe it. These clues will help you quickly understand what a writer is implying, and you can then safely infer related conclusions.

Practice 13

24. a. The passage supports the statement that Aunt Polly whacked Jim with her slipper. None of the other statements has any support in the passage. You can find this answer by asking yourself why the author is telling you this.

Notice the last sentence in the passage: *. . . he was flying down the street with his pail and a tingling rear.* Why does Twain tell you that Jim had a tingling rear? Then the author adds another fact that, at first glance, may seem irrelevant: He tells us in the last sentence that Aunt Polly had *a slipper in her*

GED LANGUAGE ARTS, READING ANSWERS AND EXPLANATIONS

hand and triumph in her eye. Why does he mention triumph? And why does Aunt Polly have a slipper in her hand instead of on her foot?

When you encounter something in literature that seems odd or out of place, ask yourself why the author included that information. Your answers will help you understand what the author is implying, and what information you can infer.

Practice 14

25. **Cause:** We hired three salespeople.
    Effect: Sales have doubled.
26. **Cause:** I met you.
    Effect: I've been happy.
27. **Cause:** Jim *didn't* buy gas.
    Effect: His car stalled.
28. **Cause:** Tom skipped breakfast.
    Effect: He got hungry at noon.
29. **Cause:** Jane started a diet.
    Effect: She lost 35 pounds.

Practice 15

30. **a.** The author tells you that the character was suffering from *lonesomeness*, and that she decided to go to the movies to stop feeling lonely.
31. **c.** The author hints at the effect of the movie by saying that *there . . . she succumbed to some message in the movie.* This message, the author tells us, is one of the *most destructive ideas in the history of human thought.* The author is letting us know that the movie was the cause of some dangerous idea that the character believed, so the dangerous idea is the effect that the movie had on the character.

Practice 16

32. **a.** *Ostracized* means *shunned* or *avoided by others.* The context tells you that Megan's friends *had never shunned her before,* so you know that *ostracized* has something to do with being shunned or excluded.
33. **d.** *Obdurately* means *stubbornly.* The context tells you that Zachary keeps on applying for the managerial position, even though he is unqualified—and this suggests that he is stubborn.
34. **d.** *Ambiguous* means *unclear* or *having more than one meaning.* The context tells you that the person read the memo *four or five times,* but still could not understand it; it was unclear.
35. **d.** *Incredulous* means *disbelieving.* The context tells you that Bob is timid, and that people reacted strongly when they heard that he had taken up skydiving. The only choice that makes sense in this context is **d.**
36. **b.** *Plausible* means *believable* or *likely to happen.* The context tells you that the police looked elsewhere for the criminal, which suggests that they found his explanation believable.

Chapter 3: Reading Fiction

Passage 1

1. **c.** Zeus created Pandora in order to send sorrow and suffering to humanity.
2. **a.** The expression *opening Pandora's box* refers to doing something that will create more trouble than good. If you bring up an embarrassing or controversial topic in conversation, you might be said to be opening Pandora's box.
3. **c.** This is a classical Greek myth that addresses the origins of human suffering.

GED LANGUAGE ARTS, READING ANSWERS AND EXPLANATIONS

4. **d.** Note that the narrator, the person telling the story, is not a character within the story. The reader is not addressed directly as *you*, so it is not second-person or direct address.

Passage 2

5. **a.** The topic of this passage is ignorance, and the main idea is that we're all like blind men in some areas.

6. **d.** At the beginning of the story, the narrator states that the blind men were walking out of town in order to beg for money.

7. **e.** This passage is not an allegory, because the characters within the story (the king, the servants, and so on) are realistic people, not two-dimensional representations of human character traits.

8. **b.** The story uses a third-person narrator. The narrator is not a character within the story, nor does he refer to himself as *I*.

Passage 3

9. **b.** The fox was very thirsty, and did want the grapes, but no matter how hard he tried they were beyond his reach.

10. **c.** Aesop is teaching that we should not speak badly of things that we cannot do. Even today, this attitude is often referred to as a *sour-grapes attitude*.

11. **a.** The topic of the fable is disappointment. Other elements, such as wild animals and thirst, are used in the parable, but they are used to develop the topic—they are not the topic itself.

12. **e.** The setting of this story is an orchard. Another element of the setting is that it was a *hot summer's day*—all of which is stated in the first sentence.

Passage 4

13. **b.** The narrator is suggesting that all Americans should become slaves to the government—personified here as Uncle Sam. The writer himself, however, is not actually suggesting this; he is using irony to make his point: If taxes get any higher, Americans will become slaves to the government.

14. **b.** The author provides clues to the reader that the narrator is not really saying what the author believes. One such clue, for example, is the statement that *wearing the ball and chain*—traditional symbols of slavery—will bring Americans *true joy*. This is a very subtle clue, and it requires that we be careful readers.

15. **a.** This passage is an example of irony. The narrator is saying the exact opposite of what the author really believes. Notice, however, that the author expects the reader to discover this fact—he does not come out and openly state his true opinions.

16. **c.** The tone of this passage is sarcastic. Remember that sarcasm is a form of irony: saying the opposite of what we really mean.

Passage 5

17. **e.** The tone of this passage is factual. The author is attempting to describe some event, and is including the opinions and observations of those present. Notice, however, that even though the tone is factual, the content of the passage may still be very opinionated.

18. **b.** The author makes her opinion of Robinson obvious in this passage—without ever coming out and stating that she thinks he is guilty. Her choices of wording and sentence structure convey a tone of suspicion and doubt.

GED LANGUAGE ARTS, READING ANSWERS AND EXPLANATIONS

19. **a.** The setting of this passage is a store in an unspecified town. The event that is described—James Robinson entering a store to ask for directions—is taking place within the store itself, even though the testimonies of witnesses and others might have been given later.

20. **b.** Notice the choices of words and phrases that the writer has used in this passage: Robinson, *of course, claims* while witnesses *have pointed out*. The writer is being subtle, but she is still hinting at her own opinion by choosing words and phrases suggesting that Robinson is lying, and therefore, guilty.

Passage 6

21. **d.** The tree symbolizes both the attractiveness of knowledge and the fact that gaining knowledge is hard work.

22. **e.** A simile compares two or more objects, using the word *like* or *as*.

23. **b.** The passage makes it clear that the real treasure to be gained from the tree is the fruit—which requires that a person take some risk and do some work to gain it.

Passage 7

24. **d.** The tone of this passage is humorous. The author is describing coyotes in a way that will amuse a reader, rather than trying to inform us of scientific facts.

25. **e.** The author is not literally suggesting that fleas can ride bicycles, or coyotes can outrun lightning; he is deliberately exaggerating the coyote's speed in order to be funny.

26. **a.** The author is being humorous. This is another example of an author using a narrator to say something outrageous, depending upon the reader to recognize that the author himself isn't really suggesting that fleas can ride bicycles.

Passage 8

27. **c.** This is a metaphor. Remember that a simile uses *like* or *as* to compare things, while a metaphor does not actually compare the objects—it says that one object *is* another object. In this case, the metaphor tells us that the woman's eyes *were* green gems.

28. **d.** The reference is an example of personification. The writer is discussing the abstract concept of the passage of time, but he is treating time as if it were a living human being with hands and cruelty and so forth.

29. **b.** The woman has lost her beauty over time, and in her past she has also lost love—either the ability to love, or a person that she loved—or both.

30. **e.** The author is implying someone that she loved has died. We know this because the image of the *grim reaper* is another example of personification, in which death is represented as a living creature that walks around with a huge scythe to reap the souls of men and women.

▶ Chapter 4: Reading Nonfiction

Passage 1

1. **b.** A *score* is 20 years, so *four score and seven* would equal 87 years.

2. **d.** In the second paragraph, Lincoln says *We have come to dedicate a portion of that field, as a final resting place for those who here gave their lives. . . .* The *final resting place* would be a cemetery.

3. **b.** The word *hallow* means to make something holy or sacred.
4. **a.** Lincoln has come to dedicate a piece of the battlefield for a cemetery, but he suggests that it is already holy ground because of the men who were willing to give their lives for their country.
5. **e.** The *unfinished work* is ensuring the future of the United States. Lincoln stresses this in the last sentence, saying that those men who gave their lives should not have died in vain.
6. **c.** The *last full measure of devotion* is giving one's life for one's country. Lincoln is praising those men who fought for the unity of America, even to the point of losing their lives.

Passage 2

7. **d.** The main idea of this passage is that employees must dress professionally. The other answers might be implied in the passage, but the main idea is that appearance matters in the office.
8. **b.** A *mandate* is a command, and is the root of the word *mandatory*.
9. **c.** Running shoes might be considered appropriate attire when an employee has back problems. Note that the memo permits sneakers and running shoes *when required by medical or health issues*.
10. **b.** T-shirts are not directly addressed in the memo, but similar clothing is addressed—such as bluejeans and shorts. One can safely infer, therefore, that T-shirts are unacceptable if shorts are unacceptable.
11. **e.** The memo does address casual days, but does not specify when they are or how often they occur.
12. **b.** The tone of the memo is informative. There is no anger or confrontation in the writer's tone—but there is no humor, either. The document is simply informing employees of the rules.

Passage 3

13. **b.** The central issue is streets that don't allow buses. The controversy is seen from two sides: those who like the special restrictions, and those who don't. The common element, however, is the streets themselves.
14. **a.** The central thesis of Martin Fillman's argument is that the restricted streets prevent buses from bringing tourists to businesses in town.
15. **e.** Melanie Greenhouse mentions three or four reasons why she doesn't like the buses, but there is no central thought that draws them together.
16. **e.** The article tells us that the Commission did not make any decision, but not why. Nor is there enough information for the reader to make any inferences on such a question.

Passage 4

17. **c.** You can recognize it as a biography since it is about a person's life, but the person telling the story is also the subject, so it is an autobiography.
18. **e.** When the *yesterdays* outnumber the *tomorrows*, a person has already lived more than half of his or her lifetime.
19. **a.** Tripe is actually the stomach lining of a cow, but you don't need to know that to determine from the context what the word means as used here. The author makes it clear that he considers the shallow philosophy to be of little value.

GED LANGUAGE ARTS, READING ANSWERS AND EXPLANATIONS

20. b. The central thesis of the passage is that we sometimes deceive ourselves when we resolve overnight to live differently tomorrow.

21. d. The author is reflecting on the fact that he has lived a half century, and is considering how that time has gone by both quickly and slowly.

Passage 5

22. d. Churchill repeats *never give in* to emphasize his point. Churchill's word choice shows the reader that he sincerely means what he says—he is not willing to compromise.

23. a. It means that other nations thought that Britain would collapse. A sponge might be used to erase chalk from a chalkboard, or *slate*, which would imply that Britain was *erased*. Churchill says that those other nations are wrong.

24. e. *Our country stood in the gap* means that British soldiers were willing to risk their lives to save their country. To *stand in the gap* is a military metaphor. An enemy might knock down a section of the nation's defenses, but the soldiers have jumped into that gap to prevent the enemy from entering.

25. c. The tone of this passage is inspirational. Churchill is trying to encourage his listeners to keep on fighting against the Germans.

26. b. The thesis of this passage is that Britain will win if they don't give up. This is the reason that Churchill's word choice is important to notice, such as his repetition of *never, never, never*.

Passage 6

27. e. The excerpt is an example of critical review. The author is writing about the movie *Lawrence of Arabia*, and is addressing some of the themes in that film.

28. b. The central theme of *Lawrence of Arabia* is that man's pride will bring about his destruction. The author speaks about the pride of Lawrence, explaining how the film shows Lawrence's rise and fall.

29. b. *Hubris* is *pride*. The author defines it indirectly in the article by saying that *hubris* is *the pride of a man*.

30. a. You could infer that the author admires the film *Lawrence of Arabia*. The author's tone is very enthusiastic about the movie, even referring to it as *a high-water mark in the annals of filmmaking*.

▶ Chapter 5: Reading Poetry

Passage 1

1. b. Line 2 of stanza 1 states that Death *kindly stopped* for the speaker. Choice **a** is incorrect because *indifferent* would suggest that Death did not acknowledge the speaker. Choices **c** and **d** are incorrect because the poem does not relate that the character, Death, is either an immortal god or a demon.

2. c. This choice fits the kindness of Death, as stated by the speaker, as well as the fact that Death *knew no haste*. Also it includes the idea that the speaker *put away . . . labour and leisure, too, for his civility*. This supports the image of Death as gentle, timeless, and *leaving of life's cares behind*.

GED LANGUAGE ARTS, READING ANSWERS AND EXPLANATIONS

3. **b.** The meaning of the word can be deduced from the context of the line. Because he is driving slowly, *Death knows no haste*. This is a matter of opposites. None of the other choices are the opposite of *slowly*.

4. **c.** The *swelling of the ground . . . the roof scarcely visible . . . [the cornice] but a mound*. All of these are descriptive of a grave with its gravestone.

5. **a.** Death is a pleasant companion; the speaker only describes him in positive, gentle terms.

Passage 2

6. **b.** The eagle *watches from his mountain walls* and falls *like a thunderbolt*. Saying that the eagle *watches* and then falls *like a thunderbolt* implies alertness and then striking, respectively. The most logical choice is that the eagle is hunting.

7. **b.** The word *azure* means blue and is often used to describe the sky. Neither a forest nor cliffs are azure (choices **a** and **c**), and the poem does not specifically mention either a grassy field or nature (choices **d** and **e**).

8. **a.** It is the wrinkled sea that *crawls*.

9. **c.** The first line repeats the letter *c*: *He **c**lasps the **c**rag with **c**rooked hands*. Alliteration is a repetition of a consonant sound in one or more lines of a poem.

10. **e.** The last line tells us that the eagle falls *like a thunderbolt*. A *simile* compares two or more things by using *like* or *as*.

Passage 3

11. **a.** Those who do not love their homeland will not be honored after they have died. Notice that the poem opens by suggesting that a person must have a *soul so dead* if he or she does not love home.

12. **c.** The word *pelf* means *wealth* or *riches*. You can determine this meaning from the context because Scott has been listing various forms of riches and honor; and in the same line of the poem, he mentions *titles* and *power*.

13. **e.** Those who do not love their homeland will die twice in the sense that first they will die physically, and then their memory will die with them—they will be forgotten. Scott does not mention any specific form of death; his focus is merely on the fact that such people do not contribute anything to society and will, therefore, be forgotten by future generations.

14. **b.** Scott probably loved his homeland, since his poem is condemning people who don't. He was, in fact, from Great Britain, but this is not mentioned in the poem.

15. **c.** The word *concentred* is a poetic form of *centered* or *focused*, and Scott is suggesting that such people are self-centered and selfish. This can be determined by the context, which drives home the idea that unpatriotic individuals are selfish, focused entirely upon riches and power and honor—rather than on the nation, which makes those things possible.

Passage 4

16. **b.** This is a sonnet, a poem that follows a very specific format. Sonnets have 14 lines; most are written in iambic pentameter and follow a specific rhyme scheme.

17. **a.** Shakespeare is suggesting that it would be inadequate to compare his love to summertime, because the summer does not last long, whereas his love is eternal. The phrase *summer's lease* refers to the fact that the seasons

GED LANGUAGE ARTS, READING ANSWERS AND EXPLANATIONS

are only temporary. The *short date* that he refers to means that the season is short, not that it is almost summertime.

18. **d.** The context speaks of the *eye of heaven* as shining, and also of being *too hot*. These things apply to the sun, not to the moon or to birds. The *gold complexion* also suggests the sun, not the eye of a god looking down.

19. **e.** The poet is speaking to someone he loves, and he is trying to express the idea that his love will last forever.

20. **d.** Shakespeare is saying that, even though his lover will one day die, the poem itself will live forever. This means that, in some way, his lover will live forever, as well.

Passage 5

21. **a.** The poem describes a group of soldiers, called the Light Brigade, who are charging into certain death because they were commanded to do so. They are charging into the face of cannons, and they suspect that someone *blundered* (gave the wrong command)—but they are obeying just the same.

22. **c.** A *blunder* is a mistake, something that someone did accidentally. In this poem, the blunder appears to be that a superior officer gave the Light Brigade a bad command. The soldiers have no chance of surviving.

23. **d.** The soldiers know that someone has issued a foolish order, but they also know that a soldier obeys his superior officers. *Theirs not to reason why* means that it is not a soldier's duty to question the orders that he is given; his duty is to obey those orders—even when it is clear that the order means certain death.

24. **b.** The phrases *jaws of death* and *mouth of hell* are examples of personification because the author is taking the abstract concept of death and treating it as though it were a living person—a person who has a mouth and jaws. The image then becomes quite powerful, as the reader can picture death actually biting and eating its victims.

25. **b.** The author is honoring the brave men who charged against the enemy's cannons, even though they knew that they would not likely survive the charge. The poem does depict the horrors of war, but that is not its central focus. Tennyson is concerned mostly with the brave obedience of the Light Brigade.

Passage 6

26. **a.** The speaker is saying that he owes a debt to those who made the road, but an even greater debt because they have stopped using it and left him to walk on it in peace.

27. **c.** The rhyme scheme is *a, b, a, b, c, c*.

28. **b.** The word *proxy* means *on behalf of* someone else. If you vote by proxy, for example, you are allowing someone else to cast your vote on your behalf. The speaker in the poem is saying that a fox or mouse will make footprints in the snow on his behalf when he can't be there.

29. **c.** Most of this poem is written in iambic trimeter. The iambic meter is one unstressed syllable followed by one stressed syllable, and there are three feet per line—making it trimeter. Pentameter, on the other hand, is five feet per line.

30. **a.** This is an imagistic poem, one that tries to help the reader to visualize something by describing it in words. Frost is trying to paint a picture in the reader's mind of the autumn road that he's walking on, and even what that road will be like when covered with snow and walked by mice and foxes.

GED LANGUAGE ARTS, READING ANSWERS AND EXPLANATIONS

▶ Chapter 6: Reading Drama

Passage 1

1. **b.** This drama takes place in a small hide-away in Amsterdam during World War II. The last bit of dialogue states the date as *November, nineteen-forty-two*.

2. **c.** Anne has just awakened from a nightmare, as she and her family are hiding from the Nazis. Her words might sound rebellious or even hateful on the surface, but the tone of the passage gradually reveals that she is just confused and unsure of the future.

3. **d.** Anne lists things that she and her family are looking forward to doing when they can come out of hiding. She includes riding her bike, taking a hot bath, seeing friends at school—the sort of things that most girls her age (13) would be longing for.

4. **b.** The passages marked *ANNE'S VOICE* are examples of monologue, where the character of Anne is speaking directly to the audience and sharing her thoughts and insights. Other characters in the play would not be listening in on these lines.

5. **a.** The characters are hoping that the war will soon be over and they can come out of hiding, but the audience knows that it will be several years yet before World War II ends. The audience also knows that only one character in the play will survive the Nazi concentration camps—but the characters don't know these things.

Passage 2

6. **a.** Mrs. Fainall is saying that men go from one extreme to the other: They either love a woman by doting on her (paying her extreme attention), or hate her. To be averse to something is to dislike it intensely.

7. **e.** She would probably express the age-old view that it is better to have loved and lost than never to have loved at all. She states something very similar near the beginning of the passage: *'tis better to be left than never to have been loved.*

8. **d.** The word *inveterately* means *firmly, with determination*. An inveterate sports fan, for example, is passionate about sports, and will do nearly anything to watch or participate.

9. **b.** Mrs. Marwood states that she wants to *carry [her] aversion further* by getting married to a man.

10. **c.** This scene is set in St. James's Park in London. The stage directions at the beginning of the passage state this.

Passage 3

11. **b.** The scene opens with stage directions that specifically state the setting: *A private dining room in a first rate restaurant in Paris. The present.*

12. **b.** This question is a bit tricky, because you have to first read the stage directions which state that the dining table is at *stage right*—then you must remember that stage right is actually on the audience's left.

13. **d.** The scene opens with some specific stage directions that tell the actors and the director where the furniture is located, what the room looks like, where each actor is to stand, and what each is doing as the curtain goes up.
14. **a.** The stage direction *At rise* is telling the actors what they must do when the curtain goes up at the beginning of the play.
15. **c.** The dialogue in this play is intended to be funny, as the characters banter back and forth about relatively silly topics.
16. **d.** You can guess that this play is probably a comedy because the characters are ordinary people, discussing unimportant things—the sort of things that anybody might discuss, as opposed to deep, philosophical issues. Also, the tone is humorous and light, not heavy and serious.

Passage 4

17. **b.** Dramatic irony occurs when the audience knows something that a character does not know. Faustus is aware that he is selling his soul to the devil. What he does not know is that Mephistopheles is willing to say anything to get his soul—but that he will not fulfill his promises. The audience knows this, but Faustus does not.
18. **e.** Mephistopheles is actually quite forthright with Faustus, letting him know that he will one day regret what he's doing, yet Faustus persistently ignores the warnings. Also, Mephistopheles knows that Faustus understands Latin, and he is subtly flattering him by turning the common proverb *misery loves company* into Latin.
19. **b.** The word *propitious* means *lucky, promising something good*. Faustus is saying that he hopes to have good luck flowing his way, even as the blood is flowing from his arm. Marlowe, however, is deliberately hinting that bad things are going to come.
20. **b.** Faustus is alone on stage, and he is addressing the audience, so he is speaking a monologue. A soliloquy (**e**) would be much longer.
21. **d.** This time, Mephistopheles is speaking to the audience in an undertone, which only the audience can hear. This is known as an *aside*. (You'll notice that Marlowe even includes that as a stage direction.)
22. **a.** It would be a tragedy if the protagonist were brought down. A comedy might end with Faustus defeating the devil and gaining something good in the process.
23. **b.** Faustus is deciding whether or not to sell his soul to the devil. There is humor in the play, as is often the case with tragedies, but the overall tone is quite serious.

Passage 5

24. **a.** Rosencrantz and Guildenstern are saying that life is going as well as can be expected. If they were on *fortune's cap*, life would be too good, and they could expect a fall; while being on *the soles of her shoe* would mean that life was awful.
25. **b.** Hamlet has just met up with two friends that he has not seen in a long time. They are enjoying some friendly banter as they ask one another how life has been since they have last met.

GED LANGUAGE ARTS, READING ANSWERS AND EXPLANATIONS

26. **c.** Denmark seems like a beautiful city to Hamlet's friends, but in Hamlet's opinion, it is nothing but a prison. He feels trapped there because he knows that his father was murdered, but he can't bring himself to do anything about it.

27. **d.** This passage is *dialogue*, where three characters are on stage speaking to one another.

28. **a.** Hamlet is feeling very melancholy or depressed, and he knows that he should be grateful to his friends—but he's having a difficult time expressing any gratitude.

29. **c.** A comedy ends with the protagonist's fortunes being better than they were when the drama began. In fact, Hamlet was a prince and his fortunes were very good at the beginning of the play—there was really little that could happen other than tragedy.

30. **b.** A *promontory* is a high ridge of rock that juts into water. Hamlet is saying that he knows the world to be beautiful, but he is so depressed that the whole world seems sterile and hard and barren, like a bare piece of rock.

▶ Posttest Answers and Scoring Review

1. **b.** Frost is referring to the Latin motto *E pluribus unum*, which is found on the dollar bill. The Latin phrase means *out of one, many*.

2. **d.** The Declaration referred to is the Declaration of Independence. Frost is addressing a number of American documents that summarize elements of American history.

3. **a.** The word *sovereignty* means *self-rule*. A sovereign nation is independent from other nations. The poet makes this clear in the context of the poem, which is discussing American's independence.

4. **d.** Frost is referring to the Wright brothers as the *twain* who invented the airplane. The word *twain* means *two*.

5. **e.** This poem was written on the occasion of President Kennedy's inauguration. Frost is recounting some of the nation's history, urging the new president to continue that tradition.

6. **c.** The narrator makes it clear that he is enthusiastic about America's history, but he also lets us know that he supports the election of the new president. This permits us to infer that he is an American citizen.

7. **d.** The phrase *consecrated seers* suggests that Jefferson and Madison were prophets, and that they were looking forward to the sort of things that the poet envisions in America's future.

8. **b.** This line is an example of iambic pentameter: five feet, each with one unstressed syllable followed by one stressed syllable.

9. **d.** The narrator is describing his first visit to the headquarters of the British Secret Service, and how he became a spy.

10. **c.** The author thought that the building where he was interviewed was a fake, not the genuine headquarters for the British Secret Service. He tells us that he was surprised when he discovered that it was the real thing.

11. **a.** The narrator is telling us how he became involved with the British Secret Service. We can safely infer, therefore, that he did espionage work. He may have been in Afghanistan, but we are not told that in this passage.

GED LANGUAGE ARTS, READING ANSWERS AND EXPLANATIONS

12. **e.** The *improvised dummy* would be a false representation of the real headquarters building, put together in a big hurry to mislead job applicants.

13. **d.** The former Marxist is the man who the narrator thinks is wearing a false beard. The beard, however, turns out to be real, as the author later discovers.

14. **b.** The word *proliferate* means *to spread and grow richly*. In this context, the word refers to the man's black beard—which he had allowed to grow and expand.

15. **b.** This is a selection from an autobiography. You can tell because it is a story about someone's life, and the person telling the story is the subject as well.

16. **e.** The selection is told in the first person. The narrator is a character within the story, and refers to himself directly as *I* and *me*.

17. **d.** George is trying to nuzzle with Beneatha on the couch, but she just wants to talk. This frustrates George, who eventually does become angry—but before he was angry he just wanted to be romantic.

18. **d.** The one thing that Beneatha and George seem to agree on is that she loves to talk. What she wants to talk *about* is not stated; in fact, it is possible that any topic will do.

19. **e.** George states that he wants to be with a woman who is not moody. He does mention Garbo and poetry—but in a negative light, as qualities that he is not interested in.

20. **a.** Beneatha becomes angry when George does not share her view of talking and reading and education. She thinks that she is more sophisticated than George, but in reality, she just loves to talk and he doesn't.

21. **c.** Mama actually offers no wisdom, other than the most obvious advice. Beneatha, however, feels that Mama has been understanding simply because Mama has listened to her talking.

22. **e.** Mama does tell Beneatha that she should avoid fools, but she does not actually say that George is a fool. In fact, she makes no assessment of George at all; she just lets Beneatha do the talking.

23. **b.** This is a passage of dialogue: two or more characters talking together.

24. **d.** Mama is unloading packages that she carried with her on stage. We know this from the stage directions that are given in her lines.

25. **b.** The nature of the disagreement in this scene is not very serious in the long run, and it is probable that Beneatha and George will make it up later.

26. **a.** The person dressed up like a little girl is actually Huck Finn. He tells the woman that his name is Sarah Williams, then Sarah Mary Williams to cover the first lie—then lies a third time by claiming that his name is George Peters.

27. **d.** Huck tells us that he was so nervous that he couldn't sit still. He wanted to do something with his hands, so he tried to thread a needle.

28. **d.** The woman first detected that Huck was not a girl when he threaded the needle. From then on she was paying attention to little details that made her more certain—details she spells out in the passage.

29. **b.** The woman understands that there are deep differences between the sexes, differences far more significant that simple clothing. She shows Huck that boys act like boys without even knowing it—even when they try not to.

GED LANGUAGE ARTS, READING ANSWERS AND EXPLANATIONS

30. e. The story is told in the first person by Huckleberry Finn himself.

31. b. Huck's language shows that he has not been educated. His grammar and sentence structure are not formal, and his use of slang suggests that he has not gone to school.

32. a. The woman tells Huck that women will thread a needle by moving the thread toward the needle, while men do it the other way around. According to her observations, a male will move the needle toward the thread.

33. b. The review is addressing the areas of conflict that are dealt with in the film *Amadeus*. This is stated indirectly in the first two sentences.

34. b. Each of the tensions listed is dealt with in the review, except for number 2. According to the article, Mozart is not jealous of anything to do with Salieri; it is the other way around.

35. c. The last paragraph takes a scrutinizing look at the character of Mozart—specifically his tendency in the film to demand his own way. It does not draw any conclusions, however—such as who was at fault.

36. a. Conflict is an essential element in plot structure. There needs to be some form of conflict between the protagonist and someone else—usually the antagonist—for there to be a plot.

37. b. The answer can be found in the last sentence of the Risk of Loss section. The Contractor is stated as the party responsible for worker safety.

38. a. The answer can be found in the section called Firm and Fixed Pricing. The Contractor has agreed that the price will not increase or decrease, regardless of external conditions—such as the price of lumber.

39. c. The answer can be found in item number 3 of the section on Contractor's Obligations. That paragraph states that the Owner must vacate the premises 24 hours prior to construction, and cannot return until at least 24 hours after completion.

40. e. This detail is not specified in this passage. There is no reference to any time frame for construction, only time frames for when the Owner can use the premises.

GED LANGUAGE ARTS, READING ANSWERS AND EXPLANATIONS

Posttest for Review

QUESTION	SUBJECT TESTED	SECTION TO STUDY
1	Reading from context	Chapter 2
2	Reading from context	Chapter 2
3	Vocabulary in context	Chapter 2
4	Reading poetry	Chapter 5
5	Tone	Chapter 3
6	Making inferences	Chapter 2
7	Word choice	Chapter 2
8	Meter	Chapter 5
9	Main idea	Chapter 2
10	Reading nonfiction	Chapter 4
11	Making inferences	Chapter 2
12	Vocabulary in context	Chapter 2
13	Facts and details	Chapter 2
14	Vocabulary in context	Chapter 2
15	Autobiography	Chapter 4
16	Narrator	Chapter 3
17	Drama, plot	Chapter 6
18	Dialogue	Chapter 6
19	Dialogue	Chapter 6
20	Dialogue	Chapter 6
21	Drama, characters	Chapter 6
22	Making inferences	Chapter 2
23	Dialogue	Chapter 6
24	Stage directions	Chapter 6
25	Making inferences	Chapter 2
26	Identifying details	Chapter 2
27	Characterization	Chapter 3
28	Making inferences	Chapter 2
29	Compare and contrast	Chapter 2
30	Narrator	Chapter 3
31	Identifying details	Chapter 2
32	Identifying details	Chapter 2
33	Main idea	Chapter 2
34	Making inferences	Chapter 2
35	Identifying details	Chapter 2
36	Conflict	Chapters 3 and 6
37	Business documents	Chapter 4
38	Making inferences, business documents	Chapter 4
39	Business documents	Chapter 4
40	Business documents	Chapter 4

Appendix: Prefixes, Suffixes, and Word Roots

▶ Prefixes

The following table lists the most common English language prefixes, their meanings, and several examples of words with each prefix.

PREFIX	MEANING	EXAMPLES
a-, an-	not, without	atypical, anarchy, amorphous
ab-, abs-	from, away, off	abnormal, abduct, abscond
ante-	prior to, in front of, before	antedate, antecedent, antebellum
ant-, anti-	opposite, opposing, against	antidote, antagonist, antipathy
bi-	two, twice	bisect, bilateral, bicameral
circum-	around, about, on all sides	circumference, circumnavigage, circumspect
co-, com-, con-	with, together, jointly cooperate	coexist, community, consensus
contra-	against, contrary, contrasting	contradict, contraindication
counter-	contrary, opposite or opposing; complementary	counterclockwise, countermeasure, counterpart
de-	do the opposite or reverse of; remove from, reduce	deactivate, dethrone, detract
dis-	away from, apart, reversal, not	disperse, dismiss, disinterested
du-, duo-	two	duo, duet, duality
ex-	out, out of, away from	expel, exclaim, exorbitant
in-, il-, im-, ir-	in, into, within	induct, impart, inculcate, illuminate, irradiate

PREFIXES, SUFFIXES, AND WORD ROOTS

PREFIX	MEANING	EXAMPLES
in-, il-, im-, ir-	not	invariable, incessant, illicit, inept, impervious, irreverent
inter-	between, among, within	intervene, interact, intermittent
intra-	within, during	intramural, intravenous
intro-	in, into, within	introvert, introduction
mal-	bad, abnormal, evil, wrong	malfunction, malpractice, malign
mis-	bad, wrong, ill; opposite; lack of	misspell, miscreant, misanthrope
mono-	one, single, alone	monologue, monogamy, monocle
multi-	many, multiple	multiple, multimillionaire, multifarious
neo-	new, recent, a new form of	neologism, neonatal, neophyte
non-	not	nonconformist, nonentity, nonchalant
over-	exceeding, surpassing, excessive	overabundance, overstimulate
poly-	many, much	polyester, polytechnic, polyglot
post-	after, subsequent, later (than), behind	postpone, postpartum, postoperative
pre-	before	precaution, precede, presage
pro-	earlier, before, prior to; in front of; for, supporting, in behalf of; forward, projecting	proceed, proclivity, profess
pseudo-	false, fake	pseudonym, pseudoscience
re-	back, again	recall, reconcile, rescind
semi-	half, partly, incomplete	semiannual, semiconscious
sub-	under, beneath, below	subconscious, subdue, subjugate
super-	above, over, exceeding	superhero, superficial, supercilious
trans-	across, beyond, through	transmit, translate, translucent
tri-	three, thrice	triangle, tricycle, triumvirate
un-	not	unable, uninterested, unorthodox
uni-	one	unite, uniform, unilateral

PREFIXES, SUFFIXES, AND WORD ROOTS

▶ Suffixes

The following table lists the most common English language suffixes, their meanings, and several examples of words with each suffix.

Noun Endings

SUFFIX	MEANING	EXAMPLES
-age	action or process; house or place of; state, rank	drainage, orphanage, marriage
-al	action or process	rehearsal, disposal, reversal
-an, -ian	of or relating to; a person specializing in	guardian, pediatrician, historian, American
-ance, -ence	action or process; state of	adolescence, benevolence, renaissance
-ancy, -ency	quality or state	agency, vacancy, latency
-ant, -ent	one that performs, promotes, or causes an action; being in a specified state or condition	disinfectant, dissident, miscreant
-ary	thing belonging to or connected with	adversary, dignitary, library
-cide	killer, killing	suicide, pesticide, homicide
-cy	action or practice; state or quality of	democracy, legitimacy, supremacy
-er, -or	one that is, does, or performs	builder, foreigner, sensor
-ion, -sion, -tion	act or process; state or condition	attraction, persecution, denunciation, evasion, contagion
-ism	act, practice, or process; state or doctrine of	criticism, anachronism, imperialism
-ist	one who (performs, makes, produces, believes, etc.)	anarchist, feminist, imperialist
-ity	quality, state, or degree	clarity, amity, veracity
-ment	action or process; result, object, means, or agent of an action or process	entertainment, embankment, amazement
-ness	state, condition, quality, or degree	happiness, readiness, goodness
-ology	doctrine, theory, or science; oral or written expression	biology, theology, eulogy
-or	condition, activity	candor, valor, succor
-sis	process or action	diagnosis, dialysis, metamorphosis
-ure	act or process; office or function	exposure, legislature, censure
-y	state, condition, quality; activity or place of business	laundry, empathy, anarchy

PREFIXES, SUFFIXES, AND WORD ROOTS

Adjective Endings

SUFFIX	MEANING	EXAMPLES
-able, -ible	capable or worthy of; tending or liable to	flammable, culpable, inscrutable, invisible
-al, -ial, -ical	having the quality of; of, relating to, or characterized by	educational, peripheral, ephemeral, menial, hysterical
-an, -ian	one who is or does; related to, characteristic of	human, American, agrarian
-ant, -ent	performing (a specific action) or being (in a specified condition)	important, incessant, preeminent
-ful	full of; having the qualities of; tending or liable to	helpful, peaceful, wistful
-ic	pertaining or relating to; having the quality of	fantastic, chronic, archaic
-ile	tending to or capable of	fragile, futile, servile
-ish	having the quality of	Swedish, bookish, squeamish
-ive	performing or tending toward (an action); having the nature of	sensitive, cooperative, pensive
-less	without, lacking; unable to act or be acted on (in a specified way)	endless, fearless, listless
-ose, -ous	full of, having the qualities of, relating to	adventurous, glorious, egregious, bellicose
-y	characterized by, full of; tending or inclined to	sleepy, cursory, desultory

Verb Endings

SUFFIX	MEANING	EXAMPLES
-ate	to make, to cause to be or become	violate, tolerate, exacerbate, emanate
-en	to cause to be or have; to come to be or have	quicken, lengthen, frighten
-fy	to make, form into	beautify, electrify, rectify
-ize	to cause to be or become; to bring about	colonize, plagiarize, synchronize

PREFIXES, SUFFIXES, AND WORD ROOTS

▶ Word Roots

The following table lists the most common word roots, their meanings, and several examples of words with those roots.

There are more than 150 roots here, but don't be intimidated by the length of this list. Break it down into manageable chunks of 10 to 20 roots, and memorize them section by section. Remember that you use words with these roots every day.

ROOT	MEANING	EXAMPLES
ac, acr	sharp, bitter	acid, acute, acrimonious
act, ag	to do, to drive, to force, to lead	agent, enact, agitate
ad, al	to, toward, near	adjacent, adhere, allure
al, ali, alter	other, another	alternative, alias, alien
am	love	amiable, amity, enamor
amb	to go, to walk	ambulatory, preamble, ambush
amb, amph	both, more than one, around	ambiguous, ambivalent, amphitheater
anim	life, mind, soul, spirit	unanimous, animosity, equanimity
anni, annu, enni	year	annual, anniversary, perennial
anthro, andr	man, human	anthropology, android, misanthrope
apo	away	apology, apocalypse, apotheosis
apt, ept	skill, fitness, ability	adapt, adept, inept
arch, arche, archi, archy	chief, principal, ruler, beginning	hierarchy, monarch, anarchy, archetype
auto	self	automatic, autonomy, automaton
be	to be, to have a certain quality	befriend, bemoan, belittle
bel, bell	war	rebel, belligerent, antebellum
ben, bon	good	benefit, benevolent, bonus
cad, cid	to fall, to happen by chance	accident, coincidence, cascade
cant, cent, chant	to sing	chant, enchant, recant, accent
cap, capit, cip, cipit	head, headlong	capital, principal, capitulate, precipitous
cap, cip, cept	to take, to get	capture, intercept, emancipate
card, cord, cour	heart	encourage, cardiac, discord
carn	flesh	carnivore, reincarnation, carnage
cast, chast	cut	caste, chastise, castigate
ced, ceed, cess	to go, to yield, to stop	exceed, concede, incessant

181

PREFIXES, SUFFIXES, AND WORD ROOTS

ROOT	MEANING	EXAMPLES
centr	center	central, concentric, eccentric
cern, cert, cret, crim, crit	to separate, to judge, to distinguish, to decide	ascertain, critique, discern, discretion, incriminate
chron	time	chronic, chronology, synchronize
cis	to cut	scissors, precise, incisive
cla, clo, clu	shut, close	closet, enclose, preclude, enclave
claim, clam	to shout, to cry out	exclaim, proclaim, clamor
cli, clin	to lean toward, bend	decline, recline, proclivity
cour, cur	running, a course	recur, incursion, cursory, discourse
cracy, crat	to govern	democracy, autocracy, bureaucrat
cre, cres, cret	to grow	creation, increase, increment, crescent, accretion
cred	to believe, to trust	incredible, credit, incredulous
cryp	hidden	crypt, cryptic, cryptography
cub, cumb	to lie down	succumb, incubate, incumbent
culp	blame	culprit, culpable, exculpate
dac, doc	to teach	doctor, indoctrinate, docile
dem	people	democracy, epidemic, pandemic
di, dia	apart, through	dialogue, diatribe, dichotomy
dic, dict, dit	to say, to tell, to use words	predict, dictionary, indict, indicate, indite
dign	worth	dignity, indignant
dog, dox	opinion	dogma, orthodox, paradox
dol	suffer, pain	condolence, indolence, dolorous
don, dot, dow	to give	donate, endow, anecdote
dub	doubt	dubious, indubitable, dubiety
duc, duct	to lead	conduct, induct, conducive
dur	hard	endure, durable, obdurate
dys	faulty, abnormal	dysfunctional, dystopia, dyslexia
epi	among, upon	epidemic, epigram, epigraph
equ	equal, even	equation, equanimity, equivocate
err	to wander	error, erratic
esce	becoming	adolescent, coalesce, acquiesce
eu	good, well	euphoria, eulogy, euthanasia

PREFIXES, SUFFIXES, AND WORD ROOTS

ROOT	MEANING	EXAMPLES
fab, fam	speak	fable, famous, affable
fac, fic, fig, fait, feit, fy	to do, to make	fiction, factory, figment, surfeit, clarify
fer	to bring, to carry, to bear	offer, transfer, proliferate
ferv	to boil, to bubble	fervor, fervid, effervescent
fid	faith, trust	confide, fidelity, infidel
fin	end	final, finite, affinity
flag, flam	to burn	flammable, inflammatory, flagrant
flect, flex	to bend	deflect, reflect, flexible
flu, fluc, flux	to flow	fluid, fluctuation, superfluous, influx
fore	before	foresight, forestall, forebear
fort	chance	fortune, fortunate, fortuitous
fra, frac, frag, fring	to break	fracture, fraction, infringe, fragile
fus	to pour	confuse, infusion, diffuse
gen	birth, creation, race, kind	generous, genetics, homogenous
gn, gno	to know	ignore, recognize, incognito
grad, gres	to step	progress, aggressive, digress, gradual
grat	pleasing	grateful, gratitude, ingratiate
her, hes	to stick	cohere, adherent, inherent, hesitate
(h)etero	different, other	heterosexual, heterogeneous, heterodox
(h)om	same	homogeneous, homonym, anomaly
hyper	over, excessive	hyperactive, hyperextend, hyperbole
id	one's own	idiom, idiosyncrasy, ideology
ject	to throw, to throw down	eject, dejected, conjecture
join, junct, juxt	to meet, to join	joint, junction, juxtapose
jur	to swear	jury, perjury, abjure
lect, leg	to select, to choose	election, select, eclectic, legislate
lev	lift, light, rise	elevator, lever, alleviate
loc, log, loqu	word, speech	dialogue, eloquent, loquacious, elocution
luc, lum, lus	light	illustrate, lucid, luminous
lud, lus	to play	illusion, elude, allude
lav, lug, lut, luv	to wash	lavatory, dilute, deluge, alluvial
mag, maj, max	big	magnify, major, maximum

PREFIXES, SUFFIXES, AND WORD ROOTS

ROOT	MEANING	EXAMPLES
man	hand	manual, manufacture, manifest
min	small	minute, diminish, minutiae
min	to project, to hang over	prominent, imminent, preeminent
mis, mit	to send	transmit, remit, intermittent
mon, monit	to warn	monitor, admonish, remonstrate
morph	shape	amorphous, metamorphosis, anthropomorphic
mor, mort	death	immortal, morbid, moratorium
mut	change	mutate, immutable, permutation
nam, nom, noun, known, nym	rule, order	economy, taxonomy, autonomy
nat, nas, nai	to be born	native, nascent, renaissance
nec, nic, noc, nox	harm, death	innocent, noxious, innocuous, necrosis, pernicious
nom, nym, noun, known	name	nominate, homonym, nominal, pronoun, renown
nounc, nunc	to announce	pronounce, denounce, annunciation
nov, neo, nou	new	novice, novel, neophyte
ob, oc, of, op	toward, to, against, completely, over	object, obstruct, obsequious, occupy, oppose, offend
omni	all	omnipresent, omnipotent, omniscient
pac, peas	peace	pacify, appease, pacifier
pan	all, everyone	panorama, pandemic, panacea
par	equal	disparate, parity
para	next to, beside	parallel, paragon, paradox
pas, pat, path	feeling, suffering, disease	passionate, antipathy, apathetic
pau, po, pov, pu	few, little, poor	poverty, pauper, impoverish, puerile
ped	child, education	pediatrician, encyclopedia, pedantic
ped, pod	foot	pedestrian, expedite, podiatry
pen, pun	to pay, to compensate	penalty, punishment, penance
pend, pens	to hang, to weigh, to pay	depend, compensate, pensive
per	completely, wrong	perplex, permeate, pervade, perversion
peri	around	perimeter, peripheral, peripatetic

PREFIXES, SUFFIXES, AND WORD ROOTS

ROOT	MEANING	EXAMPLES
pet, pit	to go, to seek, to strive	compete, petition, impetuous
phil	love	philosophy, philanthropy, bibliophile
phon, phone	sound	telephone, homophone, cacophony
plac	to please	placid, placebo, complacent
ple	to fill	complete, deplete, plethora
plex, plic, ply	to fold, to twist, to tangle, to bend	complex, comply, implicit
pon, pos, pound	to put, to place	expose, component, juxtapose, impound
port	to carry	import, portable, importune
prehend, pris, prise	to take, to get, to seize	surprise, apprehend, reprisal
pro	much, for, a lot	proliferate, profuse, proselytize
prob	to prove, to test	probe, probation, reprobate
pug	to fight	repugnant, pugnacious, impugn
punc, pung, poign	to point, to prick	point, puncture, punctilious, pungent, poignant
que, quis	to seek	inquisitive, conquest, query
qui	quiet	quiet, tranquil, acquiesce
rid, ris	to laugh	riddle, ridiculous, derision
rog	to ask	interrogate, surrogate, abrogate
sacr, sanct, secr	sacred	sacred, sacrament, sanction, consecrate
sal, sil, sault, sult	to leap, to jump	assault, insolent, desultory
sci	to know	conscious, science, omniscient
scribe, scrip	to write	scribble, circumscribe, prescription
se	apart	separate, segregate, seditious
sec, sequ	to follow	consecutive, sequel, obsequious
sed, sess, sid	to sit, to be still, to plan, to plot	subside, assiduous, dissident, sedentary, session
sens, sent	to feel, to be aware	sense, sentiment, dissent
sol	to loosen, to free	dissolve, resolution, dissolution
spec, spic, spit	to look, to see	perspective, speculation, circumspect, conspicuous, despite
sta, sti	to stand, to be in place	static, obstinate, steadfast
sua	smooth	suave, persuade, dissuade
tac, tic	to be silent	tacit, reticent, taciturn

PREFIXES, SUFFIXES, AND WORD ROOTS

ROOT	MEANING	EXAMPLES
tain, ten, tent, tin	to hold	detain, sustain, tenacious, detention, continue
tend, tens, tent, tenu	to stretch, to thin	extend, tenson, tenuous, intent
the, theo	god	atheist, theology, apotheosis
tract	to drag, to pull, to draw	attract, detract, tractable
us, ut	to use	abuse, utility, usurp
ven, vent	to come, to move toward	convene, venture, intervene